MW01278282

Critique of Western Philosophy and Social Theory

Critique of Western Philosophy and Social Theory

David Sprintzen

First published in 2009 by PALGRAVE MACMILLAN® in the United States - a division of St. Martin's Press LLC, 175 Fifth Avenue, New York, NY 10010.

Where this book is distributed in the UK, Europe and the rest of the world, this is by Palgrave Macmillan, a division of Macmillan Publishers Limited, registered in England, company number 785998, of Houndmills, Basingstoke, Hampshire RG21 6XS.

Palgrave Macmillan is the global academic imprint of the above companies and has companies and representatives throughout the world.

Palgrave® and Macmillan® are registered trademarks in the United States, the United Kingdom, Europe and other countries.

ISBN: 978-0-230-62120-6

Library of Congress Cataloging-in-Publication Data

Sprintzen, David.
    Critique of Western philosophy and social theory / David Sprintzen.
        p. cm.
    ISBN 978-0-230-62120-6 (alk. paper)
    1. Social sciences—Philosophy. 2.   Philosophy and science.
3.   Metaphysics. I.   Title.
    H61.S795 2010
    190—dc22

                                                        2009016955

A catalogue record of the book is available from the British Library.

Design by Macmillan Publishing Solutions.

First edition: December 2009

10 9 8 7 6 5 4 3 2 1

Printed in the United States of America.

For
Alice and Daniel

with affection, appreciation, love, and respect

We are not victims of the world we see, we are victims of the way we see the world!

(From a speech by U.S. Representative Dennis Kucinich)

Contents

Acknowledgments

Our work emerges out of personal and social networks, owing more to the sustaining contributions of others than we are often aware. I have certainly been energized and sustained by those numerous communities of friends, colleagues, and coworkers in which I have been immersed in my personal, professional, and community activities. It would obviously be impossible for me to express adequate appreciation to all those who have played an important role in the development of the views expressed in this work, but there are clearly some whose contribution has been so profound that I would feel remiss were I not to personally acknowledge it. That is particularly true in a work such as this, which seeks to bring together the results of philosophical speculation with experiences drawn from years of community organizing.

First, it is to those individuals who have taken the time and effort to read all or part of this manuscript at different stages in its development and to provide me with invaluable feedback that I wish to express my sincere appreciation: Alex Bardosh, Barbara Haber, Jeffrey Isaac, Rolf Martin, Sheldon Stern, Larry Steckman, and Eric Walther. Then there are the friends and colleagues of our informal discussion group who heard and provided important critical comments on several chapters: Alex and Linda Bardosh, Aytac and Jim Edwards, Carol and Larry Kaplan, and Arnold and Ruth Silverman. And I have been sustained and nurtured, energized and enlightened, by a lifetime of personal friendship and philosophical dialogue with Jim Edwards, John McDermott, and Ronald Santoni. Their relationships are among my most precious treasures.

My philosophical reflection has been given an experiential depth and practical sophistication from years of community organizing that was not at all anticipated by my academic training. The experiences gained by building the Long Island Progressive Coalition, along with its local offshoot, Jobs with Justice on Long Island, and its statewide affiliate, Citizen Action of New York, have been truly educative. So many people have been involved in this process that it would be impossible to name even a representative sample of them. But a few have been so central to the creation of these organizations that I want to explicitly express my appreciation to them. First, there was the late Michael Harrington, a remarkable scholar, activist, and caring individual, whose political vision was an inspiration to me. In the early years of the Progressive Coalition, the contributions of Marge Harrison and Marc Silver were particularly vital, as have been the years of leadership provided by Richard Kirsch and Karen Scharff in building Citizen Action. But none have been more vital to my community work than the recent directors of the Progressive Coalition, Judy Pannullo and Lisa Tyson. They, more than anyone, have built the Progressive Coalition into the effective organization that it has become. I have been blessed by their friendship, sustained by their commitment and dedication, and informed by their insight and practice. My appreciation to them is deep and abiding.

I owe a special expression of appreciation to my administrative assistant, Abbey Bilinsky, who has been so important in getting and keeping my office in order and in making possible the final organization of this manuscript. And I am particularly grateful to Herbert Richardson, whom I have never met, but who took the time to provide me with his wise counsel on the manner in which I could best present my work to a publisher.

A special thanks is in order to my coreligionists at the Ethical Humanist Society of Long Island who not only provide a sustaining moral community but also exemplify a continuing commitment to the preservation and enhancement of human dignity and to the promotion of a more caring world.

And none of this would have been possible for me without a lifetime of affectionate support provided by my son, Daniel, and my wife, Alice. She, an artist and craftsperson of remarkable originality, with a creative and playful imagination that continually surprises me with new ways of looking at the world, has also designed the cover of this book.

Part I

Rethinking the World

I

A World in Crisis

There can *be* no difference anywhere that doesn't make a difference elsewhere—no difference in abstract truth that doesn't express itself in a difference in concrete fact and in conduct consequent upon that fact, imposed on somebody, somehow, somewhere, and somewhen. [1]

The Challenge

"The eternal silence of these infinite spaces frightens me," wrote Pascal, commenting insightfully on the pervasive human need to domesticate the world. We need to see it as a place that speaks our language, and in which we can feel at home. From earliest childhood, we "humanize" animals, and "spiritualize" the natural world. Whether benign or malignant, spirits are at work in the world. From Santa Claus for children to God for adults, we need to believe that good behavior will be rewarded, evil punished, and all will be right in the end, if only we follow the "true path."

But the facts are against us. Located on a minor planet in an average solar system on a peripheral arm of an average galaxy among billions of galaxies stretching off into a practical infinity of space and reaching back some 13.7 billion years to a so far inexplicable "Big Bang," the scientific understanding of our conditions of existence render our traditional (religious) creation stories as little more than children's fairy tales. [2] They show no understanding of the processes at work in nature, nor any ability to honestly address the challenges confronting humans, sequestered as we are on this innocuous planet far from the "center" of anything.

I suspect it was facts like these, along with his understanding of the ways humans intentionally, even if often unconsciously, deceive themselves, that led Freud to pessimistically observe that "what the common man understands by his religion . . . is so patently infantile, so foreign to reality, that to anyone with a friendly attitude to humanity it is painful to think that the great majority of mortals will never be able to rise above this view of life. It is still more humiliating to discover how large a number of people living today, who cannot but see that this religion is not tenable, nevertheless try to defend it piece by piece in a series of pitiful rearguard actions."[3]

Of course, uncertainty reigns at the extremities, and we cannot definitively prove the negative. We cannot prove the nonexistence of a God or gods, or of the transmigration of souls or reincarnation, nor the absence of eternal life, or the ultimate purposelessness of the universe. The current inability of science to adequately address the genesis of the Big Bang, the nature of Dark Energy and Dark Matter, as well as the detailed specifics of each stage of species transformation in the evolutionary process leaves large gaps for minds desperate for transcendent purpose to fill. But such theories are for the most part either essentially vacuous, internally incoherent, or without any rational bearing on the world revealed by science, when, that is, they are not in direct conflict with it. No doubt, self-conscious creatures are understandably agonized by the tragic nature of the human condition, indelibly marked as it is by uncertainty, vulnerability, finitude, and purposelessness. Thus, compassion is in order, along with humility about the theoretical and practical claims that can rationally be made. Failing that, we are liable to contribute to aggravating rather than ameliorating our shared condition. But ignorance and mythic illusions are likely to do as much damage as ideological certainty, and when one feeds the other, given current levels of technological development, the entire biosphere is threatened. We are a species now capable of producing on a global scale the kind of complete collapse of civilization that has been so well documented for the Easter Islanders, among many others.[4]

When thinking of our contemporary situation, I am reminded of the airline pilot who sought to provide his passengers with a progress report. "There was good and bad news," he said. "The good news is that we're cruising at 600 miles per hour at 34,000 feet, encountering only normal and expected pockets of resistance, and making good time. The bad news is that we're lost."

As civilized humans, we used to know—or thought we knew—where we were, why we were here, and where we were going. To answer precisely these questions for us was the main point of religion: answers to which seem to constitute a vital human need. But the traditional answers are no longer adequate. Not only are there many competing religious stories to choose from, but the advances of modern science and technology have also raised serious questions about the adequacy of each of them, thus generating serious doubts about the intellectual assurance that any can offer. Increasingly, the more intellectually astute among us are subtly driven to inquire about who and where we are and where, if anywhere, we are going? And the vast majority have at least an inkling of the problem and experience a troubling, if often inarticulate, sense of unease.

A dawning sense has thus emerged on the horizon of contemporary consciousness that we are not here for any particular reason and are not going anywhere! This seems to be the obvious and unsettling reality revealed by modern science. Human beings have never before possessed such knowledge and power to direct their collective destiny. Yet, never in recorded history have we been so uncertain about our direction and purpose. There is certainly no shortage of prophets—of salvation or doom—some privately inspired, hawking their wares in pamphlets on street corners, others armed with divine revelation, sustained by centuries of tradition, promoting their message through sophisticated media outlets to millions of followers. But few are those—and hardly convincing—whose prescriptions—and proscriptions—are consistent with the experimentally warranted truths of modern science. Rather, we are confronted with mythic stories promising salvation to the devout, while often threatening or actively promoting damnation for the reprobate. However diverse the messages, and often incredible, most seem to claim insight into the Truth—joined with the promise of assured salvation for followers of the True Path.

Religions across the world have built up, on, and around these mythic stories, giving personal meaning, institutional sustenance, and salvific promise to our lives. They have provided us with the dramatic sense of being on a cosmic journey, a divinely ordained providential mission that grounds moral values and social institutions, orients our individual and collective lives, gives direction to human undertakings, and offers the vision and holds out the promise of eternal felicity.

No doubt, these mythic stories speak to a deep—might we say, ontological—craving of the human being for a world of assured meaning and purpose within which cosmic frame each of us can feel fundamentally "at home"—that we belong and that all will be well in the end. We have relied on these traditional stories—and the religions that give them institutional weight—to provide our lives with the meanings that sustain and energize our efforts. And no doubt, we will continue to do so—regardless of the "evidence"—for years to come. For, in the words of the Judeo-Christian Bible, we "do not live by bread alone." We are self-conscious animals, and have to make sense of our world. Not only must we make sense of our world but we also need it to be a world that calls us to significant action. It must invite our involvement and hold out the promise of fulfillment.

We need to know *that* successful action is possible, *what its path is,* and that *support* is available if we proceed properly—even if that is at the expense of other human beings. This ontological need to dramatize our existence is the experiential foundation of the mythic in human life and culture. Myths are stories that dramatize the meaning of human existence for each culture, providing the taken-for-granted lived metaphysic of a people. They thus provide the vitalizing cosmic frame and energizing interpretive structure within which the life story of each individual unfolds.

Not only do our myths dramatically structure our beliefs, framing the horizon of our actions and feelings, but they also determine the very sense and purpose of our lives: our hopes and fears, expectations and regrets, anxieties and satisfactions; in sum, our very sense of self—who we are and how we feel about our self and our world. We are story-telling creatures. We are enchanted by stories. We are continually making them up, whether fictitious or real, about ourselves and others. The very meaning of our life tends to find expression in our own story or set of stories, which locates us in a wider cultural context, providing coherence and direction to our personal endeavors. Myths and religions are basically the publicly authorized cosmic frame within which individual life has traditionally found its existential roots, and from which it has been able to be cultivated and to grow.

These cosmic stories cannot be viewed, however, as only that—stories, made up for their "literary" amusement. They have been, and must be, taken quite seriously by their believers, if they are to perform their emotionally vitalizing and metaphysically sustaining function. For who can believe what they know to be untrue and still feel good about himself or herself? That is so odd, if not impossible, that it is practically a contradiction in terms to say that we believe what we know to be false. Belief practically means, by definition, thinking that something is true. We live with and through our beliefs, which we must take for true.

And there's the rub. For these same mythic stories and religious traditions gave birth—initially and primarily in the West—to a technical and scientific revolution that, in transforming the daily lives of individuals, has increasingly undermined the intellectual coherence, personal credibility, and practical relevance of those very traditions. Increasingly, the practical world of the everyday operates independently of, if not at odds with, the mythic frame of traditional religions. More and more, individuals find themselves living in two incompatible worlds, "earning a living" in a world dominated by the institutions and thought patterns of modern science, business, and technology, while interpreting and celebrating our life in the ceremonial world of traditional moral and religious observance. No doubt, we try to "make a go" of it—seeking to make these worlds cohere, with much personal and social energy expended in seeking to convince ourselves of the success of that effort—in fact, of demonstrating that there isn't even a problem. But, however much this effort appears to succeed on the conscious level, the fault line is too profound, the tension too pervasive, the foundation too uncertain, to be so easily patched up. Rather, the disintegrative effects of modernity are eating away at the roots of the traditions, evacuating them of their meaning while those traditions impose modes of thought that make a mockery of intellectual inquiry and place awesome technological means at the disposal of increasingly incoherent and profoundly dangerous belief systems and institutional practices that threaten the very foundations of civilized life.

No doubt, this mythopoetic "quest for certainty" and psychological reassurance to which traditional religions appeal takes hold at a deeper level of our being and is far more compelling than any need for factual truth and rational confirmation. Yet, the pervasive structure of our daily lives is increasingly determined by social institutions and technological instruments whose very existence would be inconceivable without that very science whose factual claims are so psychologically and religiously scandalous. Modern civilization is thus confronted with an increasingly agonizing contradiction: between the science (and technology) upon which its survival and development depends and the mythology and religion without which humans seem to feel totally lost.

One "solution" to this profound ontological crisis has been the proliferation of both "secular" and "new age" substitutes for traditional religions. From the French Revolution's efforts to institute a "Republic of Virtue," through the rise and fall of Communism, Fascism, Nazism, and scientism, on the one hand, to the multiform proliferation of spiritualist cults, on the other, the "cure" has often been worse than the "disease." But a "dis-ease" it truly is. There is no need here to dwell upon the disasters occasioned by these messianic secular efforts to create a "New Man," by bringing "heaven to earth," through technology, or to create a "Master Race" by "purifying" humanity of the "scum of the earth," other than noting their testimony to the extent to which humans will go to satisfy their craving for a Definitive Solution and Salvific Resolution to the human condition. Our challenge is both to understand the ontological roots of these "demonic" strategies and to develop well-founded and constructive theoretical, social, cultural, and personal alternatives.

Modern World in Crisis

The "existential" drama at the heart of modernity is the recent result of a truly cataclysmic transformation in our institutions and modes of belief that at least rivals in scope and significance, if it does not surpass, the transformation occasioned by the "Scientific Revolution" of the sixteenth and seventeenth centuries. It was that revolution in the Western world that led to the transformation of an agriculturally based and theologically centered medieval world into the scientifically based commercial and industrial civilization of the modern nation state. Originally initiated in western Europe, this transformation has increasingly become global, first spreading essentially east and south across Europe and west across the Atlantic Ocean, and then incorporating Asia, Africa, and Oceania. By the end of the twentieth century, only a relatively few remote regions remained significantly unaffected by the pervasive influence of an ever-expanding Euro-centered civilization.

Consider only the most obvious. Throughout most of the modern era—from roughly 1600 to 1900—it seemed to all that Copernicus had radically expanded the Western view of the universe, while Newton had given its definitive laws of motion. Only the details had to be worked out.[5] The Copernican-Newtonian universe had finally placed the Sun at the center of the solar system, with the Earth as but one of the nine planets revolving in elliptical orbits around it. This solar system in effect shattered the medieval cosmos, dethroning humanity's home from its purported Christiano-cosmic centrality. Not only was the Earth effectively dethroned, but the very meaning of heaven was also radically transformed. No longer the abode of the angels hovering overhead among the celestial spheres, the stars were despiritualized and removed millions, if not billions, of miles away.

The scope of that transformation can be suggested just by listing some of the major "events" that took place from roughly 1450 to 1650: the "discovery" of the "New World," Guttenberg's invention of moveable type, the emergence of capitalism and the nation state, the Protestant Reformation and the destruction of a unitary Western Christendom, the Muslim conquest of Constantinople, and the Scientific Revolution. These transformations effectively put an end to feudalism. They transformed a way of life that had characterized the West since the end of the Roman Empire, that is, for 1,000 years, setting us on the path to "modernity." It will be instructive to review these transformations later on, but now we wish simply to note them in order to suggest the scope of the transformations currently underway. It is often easier to appreciate the significance of an event in the past, than to take in what is currently so close that it tends to pass unseen.

As with the emergence of modernity, all our major institutions, practices, and belief systems are now undergoing fundamental transformation. We are participant-observers to the apparent end of the following essential structures of the modern Western world, each of which will be addressed in some detail in the chapters that follow:

- classical science with its Copernican solar system and Newtonian mechanical causality;
- an Earth-centered cosmos;
- traditional monotheistic religions and biblical "history";
- the purposeful, even providential, unfolding of cosmic development and human history;
- the nation state and what was left of economic autonomy;
- the dominance of the "free" market;
- the ability to treat nature as essentially raw material and a substitutable factor of production;
- relatively insular and ethnically homogeneous societies;
- the doctrine of individualism and the social contract;
- "liberal" democracy and local self-government;
- the mind-body duality and the autonomous self;
- relatively fixed and apparently biologically determined gender and even species identities.

Traditional certainties are under attack across the board. As the commercial and industrial revolutions and the Protestant Reformation undermined the feudal order in the West in the sixteenth and seventeenth centuries, so the globalization of information, communication, production, and investment have undermined traditional national and local sovereignty in the late twentieth century. Similarly, breakthroughs in the natural sciences continue to fuel technological transformations that vastly expand the scope of these revolutionary political changes, while forcing radical revisions in our conceptions of the nature of time and space, of matter and energy, and of society, self, consciousness, and life.

Few can still doubt—even if they do not yet appreciate—the comprehensive and global scope of this "Second Scientific Revolution." It is one of the central theses of this work that we are currently in the midst of a global cultural and metaphysical transformation at least equal in scope to that which began to transform the planetary culture four centuries ago. Our fundamental modes of thought and action, institutional structure, personal identity, economic development, and relation to nature, all require radical revision if human life on this planet (and beyond) is to survive and prosper. We are thus confronted with a world whose structures of meaning and corresponding institutional foundations are being undermined, thus presaging a revolutionary transformation the import of which, however unclear at present, cannot fail to be radical and comprehensive. My task in this work will be both to critically evaluate the contours of that transformation and then to outline the structures of an alternative metaphysic and sketch a frame for the social and institutional order it suggests.

Metaphysical Problems and Methodological Concerns

Let me be clear, however. My primary concern in this work is essentially metaphysical, not social or political. By that, I mean an effort to understand "how" we think and "what" we believe to be real: the basic dramatic story line of our lived world. I propose to explore the basic structures of our thought and of the reality that it seeks to express. It is these structures that crucially determine what we experience as real, as possible, and as worth doing. How we make sense of the world depends in large part on what we are "looking for." And what we are looking for is largely determined by what we have been taught, or brought up, to expect to find. It is here that the "existential" and "philosophical" significance of traditional myth and religion is to be found. For our education, both formal and informal, trains us to "see" the world in a certain way—to unselfconsciously interpret events in accordance with pervasive patterns of thought—those generative "paradigms" and prevailing "conceptual matrices," in the suggestive words of Thomas Kuhn—that provide a culture with its distinctive structure of meanings and the conceptual ground plan for its interpretation of the world. In effect, they structure the mental space within which private aspiration and public debate take place—determining the range of options considered and the scale of values in terms of which priorities are established.

I might then rephrase a central thesis of this work as the claim that our traditional and taken-for-granted paradigms have failed. By a paradigm I mean a representative model graphically suggesting that set of perceptual and conceptual lenses *through which* we look at and interpret what is real. It is the patterned way we make sense of what is "out there." Things happen. Events regularly take place that impact upon us, directly or indirectly. We must adjust, compensate, and re-act. But first, and certainly if we are to respond effectively, we must interpret, make sense of, *what* has happened, and *why* it has occurred. Perceiving is not just having our senses stimulated with nerve impulses flowing, our brain processing, and our muscles reacting. It is *interpreting, making sense of*—which also involves, however minimally, *explaining*. We have to have some theory of causality—why what happened happened—if we are to respond in an ordered and hopefully successful manner.

All of this presupposes a *way* of seeing and thinking. A conceptual framework that tells us what *kind of things* there are and *how* they are likely to behave. Usually this pattern can be expressed in a rather simple model (or paradigm), often using what is most familiar to provide an interpretive pattern for that which is less so. For example, we now tend to use computers to model the way the brain works, as years ago, when automobiles were first invented, they tended to be viewed as "horseless carriages." (On the other hand, the ancient Hebrews tended to view their successes and failures in terms of the actions of their God.) Thus, our paradigms guide us in perceiving and interpreting the world. They structure our thinking about the real, what it is and how it acts. They provide the "metaphysical" mapping of ordinary experience. At the most basic level, metaphysics is simply the study of root or fundamental paradigms, their structure, and possibilities for and resistances to change.[6]

Our personal experience is both nurtured and weighed down by the history of our culture. The meaning of events is essentially determined by the objective patterns of cultural interpretations. The ruling powers predominate, no doubt. But they too are essentially reproducing a set of values and beliefs by which they have been nurtured—usually with little self-consciousness about its strengths and weaknesses.[7]

It is as if we were looking at the world through conceptual lenses of whose contours we were essentially unaware. As rose-colored glasses initially produce a rosy world to which one ultimately adapts, so a subject-predicate grammar structures a metaphysics of substantive things, which act and interact, to which we have become totally acclimated. Such a world allows for clear designation of self and nonself. It draws clear boundaries, thus placing the person in front of a horizon of fixed things over which he or she may better exercise effective control. It facilitates practical activities by separating the self from things, and inviting their impartial and utilitarian organization. It clearly has survival value in the "struggle for existence."

It is important not only to appreciate the limitations and inadequacies of the prevailing metaphysics, but also to understand how it may subtly lead us to view things in a false, misleading, and often destructive fashion. For metaphysics constitutes the essentially taken-for-granted interpretive frame within which people, places, actions, things, events, and structures obtain meaning. It is what I have elsewhere called the mindscape through which we view, frame, and interpret the world.[8] The existent only becomes a meaningful world for us to the extent to which it is interpreted within the conceptual frame provided by our personal and cultural mindscape. Thus, we see what we see, as we see it, at least in large part because our particular mindscape unselfconsciously predisposes us to see it that way. (That is not, of course, to suggest that we are totally free to "see it" any way we want. The force of brute fact, the recalcitrance of the existent, as well as the inertia of cultural patterns and historical interpretations, certainly have their say. But there is a remarkable range for the "creative imagination" of individuals and cultures, to which both experience and anthropology well attest.)

Let me briefly underscore the practical and potentially liberatory significance of these initial remarks. Human action presupposes beliefs and
desires. In order to act, one must believe some—in fact, many—things,
and one must have some more or less clearly defined preferences.⁹ We
must *want* something. Hence, *how* we act is framed by *what* we believe and
want. And these are mutually interrelated. It makes no sense to want what
you believe is not possible to obtain, nor to act in order to bring about
that which you are convinced is unobtainable. Even more, the existence
and functioning of social institutions presuppose beliefs about human
nature, desires, motives, capacities, and possibilities. Thus, it is conceivable
that some institutions exist only because of systematic misunderstandings
about human nature and possibilities, or because of theoretical misinter-
pretations of natural or social processes, whether willful or inadvertent.¹⁰
To the extent, therefore, that our "mindscape" systematically "deforms"
natural or social experience, we may be said to be its "prisoners," in need
of liberatory conceptual therapy.

The preceding remarks are provided as a brief explanation and example
of the meaning and significance of the metaphysical, about which more will
be explained later. They are offered in order to better situate the inquiry
here being undertaken. For I am most concerned to explore those fault
lines in our culturally embedded worldview that will crucially determine
the emerging new world order. Only then can I suggest a possible alternative metaphysical paradigm and use that revised framework to reframe
discussions of our personal, social, and cultural problems. Finally, I will
offer some practical suggestions for the reconstruction of meaningful
community life in the world thus reconfigured.

To be more precise, Chapter 2 will provide a comprehensive but brief
overview of the existential challenge confronting the modern world.
Chapter 3 will outline key fault lines in modernity's dominant scientific
metaphysic. Chapter 4 will both provide a detailed critical analysis of the
materialist reductionism that lies coiled at the heart of that scientific world
view and offer the outlines of an alternative (naturalistic and nonreduc-
tionist) metaphysic. It is hoped that this perspective will provide both a
more sound framework for scientific research programs and a more intellectually coherent and existentially fruitful grounding for new and vitalizing cultural stories. That will complete the historical and metaphysical
overview that constitutes Part I. Part II will then address the theoretical
and practical implications of this metaphysical reframing. Chapter 5 will
build on the metaphysic of emergent fields developed in the previous
chapter to reframe our understanding of the world of culture, society, and
the individual. Chapter 6 will locate that social world within the frame
of an ecologically reconfigured evolutionary world of global economics.

Chapter 7 will apply these ideas to an analysis of modern Western civilization, focusing on a critique of Western individualism. Chapter 8 will provide the outlines for a case study of American culture. And Chapter 9 will seek to sketch the contours of a program for the reconstitution of cultural life within the dramatic frame of a scientifically defensible mythology consistent with this "New World Order." This will require rerooting the human drama within an evolutionary and ecocommunal framework that articulates and sustains a celebratory and quasi-cyclical conception of a nondirectional history.

No doubt, this is a highly ambitious undertaking. And I have a quite modest sense of my capacity to adequately address the issues raised. But I will offer analyses and suggestions that may stimulate and guide others to take this effort further. I believe such a common endeavor to reconstitute a transformed world view is necessary if we are to provide a dramatically sustaining vision within which to inscribe the scientific, cultural, and metaphysical challenges by which civilization is now confronted. For we are both the producers and products of the world that is coming to an end. What is yet to be determined, however, is the nature of that end, and of the new world to which it is giving birth. Not believing in any divinely ordained providence, which the nightmarish history of the twentieth century should certainly have dispelled for those not already disabused by both the results and the procedures of modern science, nor in the "Enlightenment's" secular faith in "progress," we must recognize the inherent uncertainty of historical change. The dying world does not presage a new and better one. Civilizations and cultures die as well as grow.[11] The results await human action—though they are often more than not the unintended consequences of what we are trying to accomplish. Hence, the emerging world remains to be constructed—though not out of whole cloth. Rather our possibilities and prospects are deeply grained by the world of the present, by both its material and theoretical structures. To understand that world in its strengths and weaknesses holds the key to framing our common future.

2

Living in a World Without God: An Overview

The eternal silence of these infinite spaces frightens me

(Blaise Pascal, Les Pensées)

The Madman in the Market Place

Friedrich Nietzsche tells the story of a madman

who lit a lantern in the bright morning hours, ran to the market place, and cried incessantly, "I seek God!" As many of those who do not believe in God were standing around just then, he provoked much laughter. Why, did he get lost? said one. Did he lose his way, said another? . . . Thus they yelled and laughed. The madman jumped into their midst and pierced them with his glances.

"Whither is God," he cried. "I shall tell you. *We have killed him* . . . But how have we done this? . . . What did we do when we unchained this earth from its sun? Whither is it moving now? . . . Are we not straying as through an infinite nothing? . . . God is dead. . . . And we have killed him . . . Who will wipe this blood off us? . . . What festivals of atonement, . . . shall we have to invent? . . . There has never been a greater deed; and whoever will be born after us—for the sake of this deed he will be part of a higher history than all history hitherto."

Here the madman fell silent and looked again at his listeners; and they too were silent. . . . At last he threw his lantern on the ground, and it broke and went out. "I come too early," he said then; "my time has not come yet. This tremendous event . . . has not yet reached the ears of man . . . deeds require time, . . . before they can be seen and heard. This deed is still more distant . . . than the most distant stars—*and yet they have done it themselves.*"

> It has been related further that on the same day the madman entered diverse churches and there sang his *requiem aeternam deo.* Led out, . . . he is said to have replied, . . . "What are these churches now if they are not the tombs and sepulchers of God?"[1]

Prophetically perhaps, after lapsing into total madness, Nietzsche died in 1900, thus appropriately inaugurating the contemporary era. The causes of his insanity are uncertain, but his insight into the vast dislocations that our increasingly uncertain religiosity must inevitably bring remains his undying legacy.

For those who express fervent attachments to those "sepulchers of God," it becomes ever more urgent to reflect upon the meaning of our contemporary convulsions and, amidst the potential dangers of nuclear annihilation and nationalistic and religious fanaticism, to seek to find our bearings amid the cacophony of conflicting ideologies, each of which claims, more shrilly than the next, exclusive insight into the meaning of our common condition.

What does it mean to live in a world in which belief in the traditional God is under severe and competing challenges, and in which individuals and peoples must forge the meaning of their destiny without the aid of assured transcendent significance? Even more, to confront a world that is more and more subject to the technological transformations consequent upon a scientific naturalism that raises serious questions about the meaning of life and the possibilities of human freedom. And what are the possibilities for, and conditions of, a creative and sustaining response to these challenges? It is as a contribution to those reflections and in order to share some tentative conclusions that might serve as parameters for a constructive response that this work is dedicated. But let me first briefly explore the problem we face.

Our Contemporary Problem

Underlying the diffident contentiousness of our society reside profound challenges to modern religious belief. It seems as if all of us want, in fact, deeply need, to believe that life has a meaning and a purpose that transcends our personal existence. For those born and bred within the cultural frame provided by Judeo-Christian or Islamic civilization, that need has long been satisfied by belief in the existence of a divine being who is the source of Creation and the guarantor of its purposefulness. But those belief systems that have given expression to a cosmic faith and a transcendent purpose for civilization are made increasingly implausible by the developments of the modern world—and most clearly by the achievements of natural science.

One need go no further than the opening lines of Genesis to see that the biblical conception of the universe and of the creation of the human species are at odds with the widely accepted truths of scientific research. Even the so-called "creationists" understand that!

But if the scientific and technological developments of modernity are increasingly incompatible with the established dogmas of the religious tradition, what then happens to the values and beliefs upon which we have come to rely? Must they not also be discarded? And if so, where are we to look for replacements? Can we even be sure that there *are* any replacements?

Once again, Friedrich Nietzsche takes us right to the heart of the matter:

> The greatest recent event—that "God is dead," that the belief in the Christian God has ceased to be believable—is even now [in the 1880s] beginning to cast its first shadows over Europe . . . [this] event itself is much too great, too distant, too far from the comprehension of the many even for the tidings of it to be thought of as having *arrived* yet, not to speak of the notion that many people might know what has really happened here, and what must collapse now that this belief has been undermined—all that was built upon it, leaned on it, grew into it; for example, our whole European morality.²

This crisis of belief inevitably becomes a crisis of purpose and values. As human beings, we not only need to believe in something, but we also need a direction, a purpose, and a set of values deriving from that purpose, by which to live and to meaningfully organize our relations with others. We need them, but no longer have them—at least not with the kind of assurance needed to give sustaining direction to our lives. We proclaim the values with which we have been brought up—and often defend them with a shrillness directly proportional to their increasing uncertainty. But how confident of them are we really? And how do we square these beliefs with the rest of our activities? How much of our professions of fervent devotion are really attempts to convince ourselves?

How else are we to make sense of the prevalence of religious fundamentalism in so much of the world—among Jews, Muslims, Hindus, and Christians. When you think about the incongruity of Christian or Muslim fundamentalists employing the most up-to-date communications technology to propagate a doctrine that rejects the scientific truths that make that technology possible, you can only marvel at the capacity of the human mind for self-deception—as well as the extent to which human beings will go in their desperate need to believe.

Though these beliefs may often themselves be innocuous enough, their widespread propagation produces habits of mind that ill suit their believers for intelligently confronting the complex problems of modern civilization. When they are joined with modern technology under the control of powerful political organizations, their capacity to wreak havoc becomes truly awesome. When some religious perspectives invite adherents to describe the world as a confrontation between God and Satan, where the urge, or the temptation, is strong to seek to purge that world of "the evil one," it is hardly sufficient simply to be understanding. And since the control of sophisticated weapons of mass destruction can fall into the hands of those who contemplate their use in order to fulfill biblical prophecy or in pursuit of a "divine mission," we know that our civilization is in very deep trouble.[3]

I have thus far described the challenge posed by both science and modern civilization to traditional beliefs and values. It is almost impossible to overstress the depth and significance of this confrontation—however much many in all parties may wish to hide the fact. But even more rarely appreciated is the degree to which, for example, the procedures of modern science are at variance with the attitudes, practices, and modes of thinking encouraged by traditional religion.

Science demands hypothetical theories whose truth is tested by posing questions to reality in the form of experiments, whose results are objectively determinable. Religions, on the other hand, tend to propound revealed dogmas, think by way of analogy and story, read events as allegories of pre-existent truths, and have no procedure by which beliefs can be falsified.

When a scientific view is challenged, it can be brought to test, with a rational faith that in the long run events may occasion its modification or rejection. When a religious belief is challenged, the more likely result is ideological combat, often issuing in holy war. How else is one to mediate between competing claims to revealed and absolute Truth?

That is, of course, the point. Traditional religion offers the hope of guaranteed answers, of assured and salvific Truth. It tells you what to believe and how to act. It is psychologically reassuring in its self-confident certainties. Science, on the other hand, creates doubt, and only offers probabilities and relative truths. It must remain tentative and open-minded on matters of value and public policy. However helpful it may be in offering us assistance in practical and technical matters, it hardly speaks with assurance to the human need for meaning and purpose. And it cannot promise success, or offer a reassuring vision of our future. It is hardly consoling.

How then can it speak to the depths of our anxieties? Deep down, we all know that the world is frightening, death is inevitable, and nothing is assured. We deeply need to belong, to feel a part of something that transcends and sustains us, giving purpose to our efforts. I am reminded of Martin Luther's poignant observation that "there must be a God, otherwise everyone would be alone."

Of course, the aloneness to which he referred is not personal but cosmic. The loneliness to which Albert Camus was referring when he described the human situation as absurd. What he meant is simple, and well sums up the significance of our discussion of science. He observed that human beings need to feel that their life has transcendent significance, but that the world revealed by modern science preexisted the emergence of our species, will outlast us, and seems to go its own way in total disregard of our desires or interests. In short, the world is not made to our measure, and offers no reliable evidence of transcending divine purposefulness.

As self-conscious beings then, we are somewhat like cosmic aliens, aware of our temporal origins and of our impending death, but finding no purpose for our being here other than that which we, either individually or collectively, can give to ourselves. No wonder our fascination with the possibility of finding life on other planets, solar systems, or galaxies. At least then we would not be quite so totally alone!

As science, industry, and technology proceed and our civilization becomes increasingly dependent upon them, is it really any wonder that we see such tendencies toward the continual rebirth of religious fundamentalism? It is as if there was an instinctive and unconscious reaction against the challenge felt to that which is most holy. The more science advances, the more profound the fundamentalist urge and need to insist upon the Truth of traditional belief. They seem wedded to each other.

The Roots of the Crisis

Having been born and raised entirely within this modern scientific era, it is often difficult to adequately appreciate what was lost in that seminal Western transition to modernity. Let me therefore share with you Joseph Campbell's description of the beliefs of the average intelligent medieval person. (Campbell was a professor at Sarah Lawrence College and an expert on cross-cultural mythologies.)

> The more seriously considered medieval concept ... was that ... the earth was not flat, but a solid stationary sphere in the center of a kind of Chinese box of seven transparent revolving spheres, in each of which there was a ... planet: the moon, Mercury, Venus, and the sun, Mars, Jupiter, and Saturn, the same after which our days of the week are named. The sounding tones of these seven ... made a music, the "music of the spheres," to which the notes of our diatonic scale correspond. There was also a metal associated with each: silver, mercury, copper, iron, tin, and lead ... the soul descending from heaven to be born on earth picked up, as it came down, the qualities of those metals.

Music and the arts were to put us in mind of those harmonies, ... The seven branches of learning were accordingly associated with those spheres: grammar, logic, ... rhetoric, ... arithmetic, music, geometry, and astronomy ... The crystalline spheres themselves ... were not ... of inert matter, but living spiritual powers ... beyond all there was that luminous celestial realm where God ... sat on his triune throne; so that when the soul, at death, returning to its maker, passed again through the seven spheres, it left off at each the accordant quality and arrived unclothed for the judgment. The emperor and the pope ... governed ... according to the laws and will of God, ... there was a perfect accord between the structure of the universe, the canons of the social order, and the good of the individual. ... The Christian Empire was an earthly reflex of the order of the heavens, hieratically organized, with vestments, thrones, and procedures of its stately courts inspired by celestial imagery, the bells of its cathedral spires and harmonies of its priestly choirs echoing in earthly tones the unearthly angelic hosts.[4]

How far we are from there! What has happened is that a series of radical shocks have dislodged us from our cosmic home. No longer do we feel we belong in the world in the way in which our medieval ancestors—to say nothing of "primitive humans"—had felt they belonged. The rise of modern science is but one of those shocks; the Protestant Reformation, the Europeans' "discovery" of the "New World," the emergence of capitalism, and the accompanying industrial revolution are others.

Consider how the conception of the world in which we live has been radically transformed. Compare the simple clarity of Dante's description of the known world with Einstein's notion that the Universe is finite and unbounded, or Hubble's discovery of an expanding universe. Consider further the implications of that famous equation $e = mc^2$, in which matter and energy are equated. The crucial point for us here is that to equate them is to suggest that they are convertible, that is to say they are the same thing in different forms. No longer is matter basically that simple stuff we hold in our hands. Neither simply graspable nor divinely ordained, we cannot even be sure of what it is made.

Protestantism, for its part, essentially cut individuals loose from the church hierarchy, and thus from their social roots and cosmic home, to fend for themselves. Its emphasis upon the individual's direct confrontation with God subtly served to increase awareness of our uniqueness, singleness, and, ultimately, cosmic aloneness. That aloneness was then mitigated by an unquestioning faith in the divine ordination of the world. Remove the cosmic grounding of that faith and the burden of Protestant individualism is hardly bearable.

I have spoken of the emergence of modern science, and I have hinted at the transformations occasioned by the industrial revolution. But in the West, these forces took shape within the contours of a social order defined by capitalism. A few words on the consequences of that mode of modernization are now in order.

Capitalism is a social and economic structure in which commodities are produced for sale in a more-or-less competitive free market in order to make a profit. At the center of this system is the proverbial "market," an "unseen hand" that regulates economic activities.

Consider some preconditions of market relations. Capital and labor must be free to move wherever the profit is greater. This free mobility of capital and labor must inevitably result in the systematic destruction of settled community life, as jobs follow investments and communities are left to fend for themselves. Meanwhile, nature is treated as but a collection of raw materials for production and a repository for waste. With an unprecedented drive for growth and development, this free enterprise system has literally "created a world after its own image," radically transforming the conditions of life of people across the planet.

At the same time, value has become price. Not only are goods judged by what they cost, but increasingly so are people. Do we not ask of a person what he or she is worth? Does this not involve a radical transformation in both our conception of value and of that person whom we used to believe was "made in the image of God?"

When the market determines the value of things, what then happens to the meaning of place? Our attitude toward community should tell us something about what has happened to the traditional sense of the sacredness of "our place"; not only "our place" but also our place in a world that has a place, and a place for us in that world. In conjunction with modern science, capitalism has radically dislocated our sense of having a meaningful place. Even house and land are "on the market" and have a price.

And finally, where time is money, life is but a schedule. Where commodities become central, work is but a job, and daily life but a series of relatively meaningless tasks aspiring to leisure, vacation, or retirement. Where then is service and vocation? In this desacralized world, we even market religion. How then is our life to have meaning? But does it even matter?

The Demands of Human Nature

Why need this be so unsettling, one might ask? Certainly we have made great strides in improving the material quality of our lives. Who would want to return to the life of the Middle Ages—with its, at best, subsistence agriculture, before plumbing, anesthesia, and public health? Since there can be no question of returning to a past that was far from idyllic, can we not accommodate to modernity and simply "pay the necessary price?" But to what purpose?

Here again Neitzsche is helpful. "When one gives up the Christian faith, one pulls the right to Christian morality out from under one's feet . . . Christian morality is a command; its origin is transcendent; it is beyond all criticism, all right to criticism; it has truth only if God is the truth—it stands and falls with faith in God."[5] Without their divine origins, the Ten Commandments—or the Suras of the *Koran*—are simply contestable orders. By what right do they claim our adherence?

Beyond the moral quagmire of modernity, however, there is a deeper spiritual issue. As the Bible perceptively observed, human beings do not live by bread alone. More than any other animal, we need to make sense of our life. Ernest Becker, that much neglected, though I think quite brilliant, thinker—who had the fortune, or misfortune, to receive the Pulitzer Prize two months after his death in 1974—pinpointed our central existential problem. While biologically rooted in nature, our self-consciousness draws us partially out of it, opening up a unique field of opportunities, possibilities, and anxieties.

We share with all herd-animal life, observed Becker, "the utter anxiety of our finitude, our lifelong urge to drown our feelings of helplessness and inadequacy in some self-transcending source of sure power."[6] This sense of the herd animal, that is, of a being that needs to be rooted in and with others, is, however, radically transformed in the human situation because of our unique capacity as self-conscious beings. That unique self-consciousness, in which we are both the subject and object of our own awareness, makes it impossible for us simply to be a part of nature. Instinct and habit are no longer sufficient. We need to understand, to make sense of our life.

Have you ever considered how truly remarkable is that simple human capacity to ask oneself "what shall I do?" Could anything be more ordinary? More universally taken for granted? Yet consider how the capacity to ask that question radically transforms the being of the animal that asks it. At the same moment, I am both the subject asking the question and the object being asked about. I stand outside of myself, and view myself as an object in the world among others—an object in space and time, with a unique history and destiny. Note how easily the "what shall I do?" becomes "what shall become of me" or "what shall I make of myself," as well as "how did I get here?" No wonder human beings seem to be the only beings for whom death is experienced as an existential problem. Is it any wonder that ethnologists long considered evidence of the burying of the dead as a sign of the presence of *Homo sapiens*?[7]

Here resides the existential root of religion—in that conjoint experience of wonder at being and fear of death to which self-consciousness opens us up. Hence also the pervasive universality of religious belief and practice. For all humans must ask themselves where do I come from—one of the first questions children ask—and where am I going?

The religious hunger of the human being is certainly one of our most universal traits. There is probably no society in the world where some form of religious belief and practice does not exist. You can almost say that to talk about the human being is to talk about a religious being. In this increasingly secularized world, we must confront quite specifically the meaning and significance of that religiosity.

It is not unusual for sophisticated thinkers to have recognized both the existential importance of religion and its scientific dubiousness. I need only mention the names of Sigmund Freud, Karl Marx, David Hume, and Jean-Paul Sartre, among others. Freud's *The Future of an Illusion* is, after all, a book about religion. And Marx's comment about religion being the opiate of the people is quite well-known. What is probably not so well-known is the context within which Marx uttered that phrase—a context that well suggests the existential pathos that generates religious belief.

Marx wrote:

Religion is . . . man's self-consciousness and self-awareness so long as he has not found himself or has lost himself again. . . . It is the *fantastic realization* of the human being inasmuch as the *human being* possesses no true reality. The struggle against religion is, therefore, indirectly a struggle against *that world* whose spiritual *aroma* is religion.

Religious suffering is at the same time an *expression* of real suffering and a *protest* against real suffering. Religion is the sigh of the oppressed creature, the sentiment of a heartless world, and the soul of soulless conditions. It is the *opium* of the people.

The abolition of religion as the *illusory* happiness of men, is a demand for their *real* happiness. The call to abandon their illusions about their condition is a *call to abandon a condition which requires illusions.* The criticism of religion is, therefore, *the embryonic criticism of this vale of tears* of which religion is the *halo.*[8]

Marx is offering a humanistic manifesto, however limited by its primary focus upon social, economic, and political realities. He is giving voice to an optimism about the possibilities of human beings to collectively address the frightening burdens faced by finite and self-conscious beings who know they are fated to die.

Whether, for example, you approach this problem as did Marx, or from a psychoanalytic perspective with Freud, or give an existential and philosophical interpretation with Heidegger, Sartre, or Camus, you cannot avoid recognizing the depth of the human need to be meaningfully supported in the burdens of human living, and the profound desire to have confidence in some sustaining support.

If we must feel that our life "makes sense" in order to live it with confidence and hope, then nothing will be felt to be more fundamentally threatening than challenges to our sense of life's meaning. They will be neither taken lightly nor easily dismissed. However rational and well-meaning may be those who are seen to raise the challenge, those challenged are likely to experience a deep, perhaps unconscious, temptation to view the source of the threat as demonic. Why else would one threaten to rob me of the meaning of my life? Such is quite likely to be at least part of the unconscious response.

The widespread reemergence or revitalization of fundamentalism, however peripheral intellectually, is thus central to the comprehension of the modern world. For it is responding to a real and legitimate threat. However caricatured the analysis of its adherents, they have given vivid expression to that universal human temptation to personalize our existential disquiet through demonization. Their dramatization of our latent but emerging collective paranoia takes us to the heart of the problems of modernity with which we must come to terms.

"The eternal silence of these infinite spaces frightens me," commented Pascal at the onset of the modern world. The vastness and impersonality of modernity is truly frightening. Søren Kierkegaard, the brilliant nineteenth century Danish existential theologian, well understood that it is dread in the face of nothingness that lies coiled like a serpent at the root of this experience. But the "evil one" personalizes that nothingness and gives our experience more familiar contours. Then, at least, we are confronted with an objective and comprehensible enemy against which we can marshal our incipient despair into an invigorating holy war. Instead of demoralizing depression, we now encounter a renewed invitation to participate in a struggle that not only gives meaning to our life, but even offers the opportunity of contributing to our salvation. What could be more uplifting?

It is precisely the unconscious fear of the dread generated by the intimation that our existence may be devoid of divine purpose that seems to be at the existential center of much of our contemporary turmoil. To escape from that dread, many have cloaked their lives with illusions to which they are prepared to sacrifice most, if not all, of the human race. It seems so difficult for us to accept being simply "cosmic aliens." Nietzsche's madman predicted this turmoil. Most of us recognize and sense subliminally what we have yet to grasp conceptually. Certainly no coherent and adequate response has been formed. But this is not for lack of trying. For what are those totalizing sociopolitical movements of Nazism, Fascism, Communism, and "The Republic of Virtue," if not modern attempts at secular messianisms?

Many have said that humans are not capable of facing their condition honestly—that we need illusions. Eugene O'Neill brilliantly suggests as much in *The Iceman Cometh*. Yet such a pessimistic vision runs counter to the enlightenment faith that has sustained the development of Western civilization during recent centuries, however much it may also have fueled those secular messianic projects.

If humanity is to preserve itself—not even to speak of approaching an ideal of its collective self-realization—it will have to find a more adequate way of addressing that existential dread of which we have spoken. That may be the only way of saving us from those all too destructive fanaticisms of religion, nation, class, or tribe. We must find a way to celebrate our life collectively, to give it purpose and meaning, and to generate value, without requiring either divine justification or a demonic antagonist. That is a really profound challenge. Human beings, certainly in the West, have yet to fully take stock of it. How, it must be asked, can that be done? Let me initially and quite briefly suggest some parameters of a constructive response, to a more extensive discussion of which I shall return later.

Parameters of a Constructive Response

Dread expresses a profound human truth: at any moment, and for no reason, disaster may strike, revealing the tenuousness of our existence, and its lack of overriding transcendent significance. To counter that inescapable reality is precisely why God has been needed. The essential message of mainstream religions is that all will be well. They speak to the very depths of our being. They quiet the latent anguish—an anguish that must be acknowledged, respected, and addressed. The question we must ask is can that anguish be addressed without retreating into illusion, and what are the parameters of such a response.

No doubt, I have so far dwelled excessively upon the negative. But I felt that was necessary because there is too often a tendency on the part of many to avoid or downplay the dread. Perhaps that is a consequence of the modern West's enlightenment origins, or due to a "faith in people," or because of a fear, perhaps subliminally, that, without a saving faith in the transcendent, humans cannot really address the terrors of our human condition. Whatever the reason, it is my deepest belief that a truly constructive and sustaining humane vision can only be built into the teeth of that reality. We must confront our animality, contingency, and finitude head on—only then can we find the strength to celebrate our life on this earth.[9]

Becker had said that we need to feel that we are a locus of value in a world of meaning. I would like to amplify that observation by suggesting that we need to feel we are a meaningful center of activity and value in a socially rooted cosmic drama. We need to construct a social order that gives us a sense of place and that sustains a sense of the meaningfulness of our personal effort. Without sustaining communities, we are cut loose; without such soil, we cannot take root and grow. Even more, purpose is either absent or arbitrary, while character is little more than a vagrant weed.

Such communities themselves need a habitat. The ecological movement at its best is not a celebration of primitivism but a recognition that we are beings of the Earth. We need viscerally to feel our earthly rooting. We need to build our human habitat in consonance with a new "ecosense." That means that the Earth can no longer be viewed as "our dominion," nor as simply "natural resources" or "raw materials" in need of development. The quantitative ideal of material growth must give way to a cosmic vision that treasures qualitative development and the aesthetic.

Such are the grounds on which to develop a sustaining humane perspective, in which the human need to belong is fed by a social order whose values merge respect for individuality with the nurturing of community. In their pastoral letter on the U.S. economy, drafted in the 1980s, the U.S. Catholic bishops sensitively described the demoralization that inevitable overtakes individuals who are denied a meaningful place in a sustaining community.[10] To do justice to human dignity requires attitudes, values, and institutions that actively encourage participation, not marginalization.

To address these needs, we must develop vital, nurturing communities whose members share the joys and sorrows of daily life. These must be more than merely associations in search of enlightenment or to provide help for the needy. We need to build into these societies (or churches) that affective and personal dimension often found in very large extended families or "clans," without their attendant provincialism and exclusiveness.

Such communities must thus remain both open to diversity and supportive of the individuality of their members and yet sufficiently cohesive so as to be effective forces for humanization in the wider society. Only by providing both emotional and social sustenance for their members with the opportunity to participate in a common effort with self-transcending human significance can they begin to effectively address the pervasive spiritual hunger of our "postreligious" world.

There is nothing salvific in these initial remarks. They offer, I hope, constructive suggestions for a naturalistic vision with which to so face the anguish of modernity that we can still celebrate the joys of our Earth and feel that our life is truly worth living. It will be the task of the remainder of this work to develop these analyses and give content and specifics to the metaphysical perspective and practical programs thus far sketched. One last ironic note that may help to place our efforts in proper perspective: many in the West have long believed that only religious people can be moral. The former president of the United States Ronald Reagan was being quite true to the popular Judeo-Christian heritage when he said that he couldn't trust the Soviets because they were atheists and morality requires divine sanction. The nuclear predicament has, however, somewhat reversed that traditional perspective. Faced with the collective capacity to destroy ourselves, the only people who can rationally confront this prospect with equanimity are those religious believers with absolute confidence in transcendent guarantees. For they alone can envisage an afterworld to which our present life is but a preface. In a certain sense, giving up that transcendence—and the fanaticism to which it can all too easily give rise—may well be a precondition for really facing the fact that we're all in it together. What we need to do is find a way to collectively celebrate our shared destiny.

3

The End of An Era:
Twilight of The Gods

Interesting philosophy is … usually, … implicitly or explicitly, a contest
between an entrenched vocabulary which has become a nuisance and
a half-formed new vocabulary which vaguely promises great things …
This sort of philosophy does not work piece by piece, analyzing concept
after concept, or testing thesis after thesis. Rather, it works holistically
and pragmatically. It says things like "try thinking of it this way."[1]

The Legacy

The modern Western world is thus ending with the "sound and fury"
that so often accompanies the death throes of a civilization. But this
death is not altogether tragic, for it encloses within itself the seeds of a new
world struggling to be born. The outlines, if not the detailed contours, of
that emerging "new world order" are not hard to see, however lacking in
specifics. They are most often the underside of that world whose death
and transfiguration we have been experiencing throughout the long and
often painful century that, mercifully for so many, sadly for a few, has now
come to an end.

We may, for the sake of convenience, date the emergence of modernity from the burning at the stake of Giordano Bruno—the herald
of the infinite universe—in 1600. From then to the murder of
Archduke Francis Ferdinand at Sarajevo in 1914—whose death sig-
naled the end of that relatively progressive Enlightenment era of
industrial development and imperial expansion—humanity witnessed
the worldwide expansion of an initially European Christian civilization, itself transformed by the Scientific Revolution and capitalistic
industrialization.

Much can be said of the significance of modern Western civilization, not the least of which is that it was not always so civilized. This point was underscored by Mohandas K. Gandhi, who, when asked what he thought of Western civilization, replied that it would be a good idea. His response suggests both the increasingly worldwide scope of what was primarily the provincial history of Western Europe and the dubious nature of its moral contribution. Whether by conquest or trade, European civilization has increasingly impacted, and then transformed, the entire globe, creating, in the prophetic words of Karl Marx, "a world after its own image." But, of course, not simply, entirely, or without counteraction—as the impacted cultures have responded in both imitation and resistance to the forces of Western "modernization," itself always a highly questionable legacy.

It is not for us here to pass judgment on that legacy—however important and appropriate such judgment inevitably may be. Rather, we need first to understand its structure and consequences: to delineate the contours of that world that has been legated to us so that we may better confront both its strengths and weaknesses—diagnosing its failures and piercing the armor of its conventionality for the fault lines of an emerging new world order.

The Prevailing Metaphysics

Every culture has a more or less coherent way of making sense of the world for its members. We can obtain an insight into that world by locating its fundamental or pervasive paradigms. These "models," "root metaphors," or basic stories reveal the existential structure of the world, determining what is real for its people: what forces or powers are thought to be at work, how they operate, and how people may interact with them in order to facilitate the realization of their goals and purposes. In short, they structure the culture's field of meaning, charting the fault lines for its inquiry and action. To address the most fundamental challenges facing our civilization requires, therefore, engaging those root metaphors or paradigms that structure our "mindscape." For it is those basic paradigms that I believe have failed. Let us first take a look at the basic paradigms of the two competing systems that undergird the Western world, the scientific and the religious—both of which presuppose a quasi-Aristotelian object metaphysic, to a brief consideration of which I will turn shortly. Then I will review some of the problems that are their legacy, suggesting the need for, and significance of, an alternative metaphysical framework, to the development of which I will turn in the chapter that follows.

The Scientific Approach

By the scientific, I refer to that conception of the natural world that essentially emerged in the sixteenth and seventeenth centuries, finding its crowning and "definitive" formulation in Sir Isaac Newton's *Principia Mathematica*. For Newton and his progeny, as has been said, nature is essentially the mechanical, and later electrical, motion of objects in space and time. Objects are the organized compounding of elementary particles (or corpuscles) in accordance with mechanical laws. Events are the potentially predictable results of the mechanical interaction of such objects. Thus, complex objects are made up out of, and in principle are reducible to, their atomic elements. The somewhat simplified model that captures this metaphysic views space as three-dimensional, flat, and Euclidean, with the interactions among objects being akin to those among billiard balls. Such is Newtonian mechanics, which models a "clockwork" universe that is materialistic, atomistic, mechanistic, deterministic, and in principle entirely predictable. In such a "matter-of-fact" world, however, as increasingly became clear, there is no rational place for free and purposeful behavior, values, spirituality, God, and immortality.[2] In the famous words of the French Newtonian, the Marquis de La Place, as the story goes, when asked by Napoleon about the lack of any mention of God in his view of the world, he replied, "I have no need of that hypothesis."

Fundamental to this way of thinking is the view that the world is made up of *things* that *act*. That is the metaphysical assumption of ordinary Western experience and consciousness. It is so pervasive that it is essentially taken for granted. It defines (and constrains) our imagination and is embodied in the grammar of Western civilization. We think in subject-predicate language. It has been well said that our grammar is a practical embodiment of the Aristotelian metaphysics or perhaps better, that that metaphysics was a reflective expression, elaboration, and justification of that grammar.

Such a world is made up of things, or people, that act and are acted upon. The medieval formalization of this system was expressed by the famous Tree of Porphyry, in which all Being was divided into ten categories: Substance and the nine "Accidents" or Properties. These are: quantity, quality, relation, time, place, position, action, habit, and passion. We need not detain ourselves here with a detailed discussion of these properties of being, other than to note that each refers to a different way in which a substantive thing—the metaphysical equivalent of a grammatical noun—might act or be acted upon, modified, qualified, or located.

It should be no surprise, therefore, that so much of modern Western philosophy from the time of Descartes has been devoted to the problem of "substance." What is the world fundamentally made of? In what way can we get access to that basic "Real?" To grossly oversimplify, these two questions divided rationalists from empiricists in epistemology, and idealists from materialists in metaphysics. The materialists argued—in opposition to the then prevailing idealist or religious perspective—that the basic substance was matter, and they tended to be empiricists in their belief that access to the Real came only through the senses. Hence, knowledge depended upon experience, and Truth could only be approximated by inductive inference. Idealists, on the other hand, tended to see Form, Structure, Essence, Spirit, or Soul as the basic Reality to which access was best had—and absolute Truth indubitably obtainable—by way of Intuition, Revelation, Appeal to Authority, or Rational analysis.

This schematization, though of course vastly oversimplified and super-ficial, is essentially correct and is only offered to underscore the perva-sive centrality of the subject-object metaphysics that set the essentially unexamined context within which these discussions took place. The same can be said for the emerging new world of the natural sciences in the six-teenth and seventeenth centuries. Physics begins in the tension between a materialist empiricism that looks to experience and tries to understand the movement of matter and an essentially Platonic mathematical ide-alism—itself suggestively emerging from within that religious world-view—that pursues the logic of numbers. While the latter often sustains an astrological or numerological mysticism of quasi-Pythagorean bent, the former often tends toward exotic experimentation merging with alchemy and witchcraft. These influences were, however, hardly distinct—often finding expression in one and the same person, who might draw from any and all of these sources.[3]

Slowly two distinct emphases took hold, often in productive yet never fully resolved tension with each other. These tended to echo the above-mentioned philosophical conflict. The mathematical description of natural processes tended to provide the logic of the operations of mate-rial reality, itself increasingly understood, in Democritean fashion, as the operation of atoms in the void. Thus, *things* were ultimately reducible to atoms—themselves not further divisible—that operated in accord with the mechanical laws of gravitational attraction.[4] These were completely describable in mathematical terms, for, said Galileo, mathematics is "the language of nature."

But note, this is but a more detailed and sophisticated expression of the Aristotelian metaphysics of substance, in which substance has been reduced to possessing only the qualities that can be quantitatively addressed, while it is those very numbers that describe the behavior of the atomic substances. But, though it is from the work of our senses that we obtain contact or confirmation of the existent, it is never really clear how that sense contact can reveal, confirm, or connect with the Reality whose Truth is the object of mathematical demonstration.

Problems with the Newtonian World

This emerging "Newtonian" world functioned like a well-built mechanical clock, hence the expression "clockwork universe." Its operation was completely determined by the laws of mechanics, its only real qualities being those that belong to matter in motion. In such a world, some rightly asked, where is the place for God, spirit, consciousness, mind, choice, freedom, or value? The obvious answer had to be: they have none. They are simply the result of "inadequate ideas," in Spinoza's apt phrase. They are the product of our subjective fantasy or imagination, the completely predictable consequence of the effect of material interactions on the complex mechanisms that we are. The qualities we experience, whether sensual or evaluative, are but subjective illusions created by the objective workings of material nature, the only real qualities of which are those that can be completely described by mathematical physics.

There were, of course, some obvious problems with this materialistic reductionism, most centrally, what is the status of that scientific mind that is the active subject undertaking the mathematical inquiry and scientific interpretation? No one struggled more mightily with this perplexing question than Descartes, who was reduced to dividing the world into unthinking matter (including automata) and mind, with the latter unceremoniously lodged in the pineal gland where, by an inexplicable power (understood by God), its mental operations, communicated their "motions" to the "animal spirits" that eventually moved our limbs, thus effecting our freedom.

But finding Descartes' solution ludicrous does nothing to undercut the seriousness of a problem with which we are still wrestling—in ways both far more sophisticated and fraught with the most profound consequences for both our conception of the nature of the human and our strategies for practically addressing fundamental human problems. For the problem that Descartes was wrestling with is precisely that of reductionism, the addressing of which is one of the central challenges of this work, to which we will turn in the following chapter.

This tension between the materialistic and idealistic strands of a developing modern science is clearly expressive of a more fundamental and pervasive problem confronting the metaphysics of that emerging world. As science consolidated its hold on our collective imagination—with the precision, comprehensiveness, and coherence of its theoretical perspective, and the effective power and technical mastery of its practical applications—it increasingly coalesced around a materialist interpretation of nature. Mathematics may be the language of Nature, but matter moving in accord with the laws of causal necessity was its substance. Mathematical deductions were identified with causal relations, with future events logically predicted from antecedent conditions—the causal linkages being guaranteed by the laws of materialist determinism. Increasingly, the qualities, properties, and values of the experienced world were viewed as epiphenomena—reduced to being "nothing but" the completely predictable and explainable effects of the interactions of mathematically describable material elements, none of which themselves had any of these properties. But let us first get a somewhat more global understanding of the significance of this issue.

What was that world whose ending defines the experience of the twentieth century? What are its presuppositions and expectations? What are the essentials of its belief system that have outlived their usefulness? As noted above, the modern world is thought to be made up of people and things. In the formative Enlightenment interpretation, the world of things obeyed Newtonian principles, with matter in motion, operating in accord with the deterministic laws of mechanics, and of the conservation of energy and matter.

This world had a fixed structure best exemplified by the orderly coherence of the solar system. Its laws were eternal, atemporal, and ahistorical. Space was infinite and everywhere the same, while time flowed smoothly from past to future. Material things were made from minute indestructible bits, called atoms, concatenated in organized levels of increasing complexity. Physical laws explained and ideally were expected to be able to predict the behavior of material things, in accord with the model of the billiard ball. Complex things were made from simple things according to fixed laws of association.

Thus, if one could but know the initial position of each particle in the system, along with the natural laws of association, one could theoretically explain and predict all subsequent behavior. That also meant that one could explain complicated things with the laws drawn from the simple, since the more complicated were "nothing but" the result of the interactions of the simpler particles. The universe was viewed as a giant clock, set in motion by God at the beginning of time, and running more or less unaided from then on. Some might have felt the need for occasional divine intervention for scientific or spiritual reasons, while others "had no need of that hypothesis."

There were several important scientific problems coiled at the heart of the Newtonian system, none more fundamental than that concerned with the means by which gravity operated. Newton's equations called for instantaneous action at a distance—in fact, across very large distances, such as from the Sun to the Earth, and beyond. To the Cartesians, this smacked of magic and superstition, which they were determined to completely expunge from reality. Similarly, they rejected Democritean-Newtonian atomism, which required the real existence of a void between atoms. Quite sensitive to this problem, Newton sought to make a virtue of necessity. He asserted that he "framed no hypotheses," but that his method was only to present equations describing the observed behavior of objects, without any attempt to explain why they behave as they do. The unsatisfactory nature of this solution, however, was clearly felt by Newton—as attested to by his extensive and fruitless pursuit of astrology and numerology—and many other sensitive and thoughtful inquirers. Nevertheless, his more practical empirical method, popularly developed by John Locke, became the model for scientific inquiry for the following centuries.

One simple way of getting a sense of the cultural importance of this issue is to ask for the place of God and religion in the Newtonian "clockwork universe." As the eighteenth century proceeded, the emerging "rational" answer was that God was the clock maker. He designed and produced the World-clock, which operates automatically in accord with His Laws. Some felt that the "evidence" of miracles, such as those reported in the Bible, showed that God continues to watch over, care for, and occasionally intervene in the World, while others trusted that His divinely designed plan assured that all will be right in the end. Some, like Newton himself, felt that anomalies and irregularities in the System required occasional Divine corrections, while most all felt discomforted by the increasing distance or absence of a personal God. While still more rational or skeptical observers began to publicly air doubts about either God's personal concern for His creatures, His divinely guaranteed benevolence, or even His very existence, the vast majority of people and institutions clung to their traditional religious beliefs out of the most deep and passionate need to believe in the transcendent purposefulness of "creation," regardless of the "evidence."

No wonder that the Newtonian cosmos has been felt by most as essentially unbearable—and yet inescapable. Its power to explain the world, and even more, to produce technology by which our world could be, and was, transformed, could not be denied. Yet who among us can *live* in such a world—cold, impersonal, predetermined, and apparently without purpose. Thus, most have held ever more tightly to their religious traditions—whether as traditional spirituality or more "modernized," personal, idiosyncratic, Romantic, "Orientalist," or "new age"—as their "haven in a heartless world." The experienced need for such a spiritual refuge from the

Newtonian cosmos—not to speak of the business world of market capitalism—is thus quite obvious, however intellectually ambiguous.

This situation was only made worse—far worse—by the publication of Charles Darwin's *The Origin of Species*. With Darwin's description of "natural selection" as the "mechanism" of evolution, the notion of a divine purpose at work in the world was further, perhaps definitively, undercut. Not only is the world cold and mechanical, now it is completely random and purposeless, with animals even feeding off other animals, almost literally a "dog-eat-dog" world. Human beings not only kill to live, but are themselves only the chance products of eons of "descent through modification." They have evolved from "lower" animals such as "apes" due to random variations that were "naturally selected" solely because of their contribution to "differential reproductive success." So much for our vaunted human dignity and self-respect as the center and goal of a purposeful divine creation.

The Religious Perspective

No wonder that deeply felt and quite pervasive need for a "refuge" from this world. That has been a major theme of the religious response, most particularly for Western monotheistic religions—Judaism, Christianity, and Islam—and their modern offshoots. (Oriental religions are another matter, in both their original nature and Western adaptations, to which we will refer later.) What needs to be underscored here is the extent to which they are fundamentally opposed to the Newtonian and Darwinian worlds. Where, for example, this scientific world is seen to be made up of matter that is eternally in motion in accord with mechanical, necessary, and purposeless natural laws, religions see a spiritual world, created by God, ruled by moral values, in which humans are generally free and responsible agents in the service of divine purpose. In such a world, it is not matter but spirit that is ultimately real, and causality is to all intents and purposes an expression of conscious intention.

Thus, side-by-side with the emerging materialist determinism of the scientific worldview, the tradition of Western religion continued to offer a spiritual interpretation of the world that provided a theoretical foundation for concerns about freedom, dignity, purpose, quality, and value. Clearly, the religious interpretation was affected by, and sought to respond to, the increasingly influential scientific perspective. Science, on the other hand, while it needed to be sensitive to religious concerns—at a minimum, so as not to offend sensibilities that might lead authorities to suppress research, or even to punish the researchers, but even more because scientists were humans also, concerned to make sense of their lives—due to its increasing success, became in practice more and more independent of religious perspectives, for it had "no need of that hypothesis."

However the religious perspective might be compromised by science, it continued—and continues—to exercise great power over the popular mind. No doubt, at least in part, because it speaks to a deeply felt, even ontological, human need for purpose and meaning. But also, because it speaks to serious problems with scientific materialism to some of which we have already made reference, while others will be considered in what follows. For example, it provides theoretical and practical underpinning for moral action in the social world. How else are we to make sense of political engagements, or judgments of personal responsibility and institutional legitimacy? Yet, here too, no coherent, integrating approach seems possible between the moral claims of human action and the scientific claims of economic, sociological, and psychological causality. Let's briefly survey these issues.

Atoms in the Social World: The Person, The Soul, and Value

Complementing things in the natural world were people, in the social world, with feelings and beliefs, hopes and aspirations. Like spiritual atoms, such "individuals" have tended increasingly to be viewed as relatively self-enclosed, free, and autonomous centers of being and action. Acting purposefully, motivated by goals, seeking to realize values, and constrained by obligations and responsibilities, they were sources of initiative and creativity, dynamic centers of purposeful action in a social world of stylized ritual, routine, and fixed hierarchies. Unlike the objects of an all-too-predictable nature, they were given to spontaneous choices and often passionate bursts of activity and dedication. Deeply concerned about their own destiny or fate, their focus was always toward the future. Somehow the purpose of life, even of creation, was the salvation of the individual's soul, or at a less grandiose religious level, personal happiness. It was clear that human beings were conscious and even self-conscious. They acted purposefully, for reasons. They had goals that drove them on, often into quite strenuous activity—as much motivated by fear of what might happen to them, as by hope for what they might accomplish or be granted.

But what was never clear was the precise relation between these self-conscious, autonomous, and purposeful beings and the material world of things that surrounded them. Were they things, too? If not, what were they made of? Where did they come from? And how were they able to relate to those things? It always seemed to be a presupposition of this view that the things of the world were little more than potentially useful tools or implements for people's use. It often seemed that that was their only reason for existence. Hadn't the Bible said that God had given man "dominion" over the creatures of the Earth? And didn't capitalism define things as commodities, to be sold in the market in accord with their exchange value, that is, with what people would pay for the right to possess and use them? Even nature came to be seen as "raw materials" and "natural resources." Can we say that Earth so viewed has any other value for the "popular" mind or the business world than its potential usefulness to serve human purposes?

But if everything has a purpose and a use, what useful purpose does the human being have? Is not one of the dangers of modernity precisely the application of this instrumental attitude to other people? Are we not in danger of reducing ourselves simply to useful instruments in the plans of others? Isn't this one of the hidden meanings of the notions that "time is money" or that we identify a person's worth with his or her financial assets, as when we ask, "what is he worth?" Doesn't this reduction of others to instruments in our world by implication tend simultaneously to reduce us to instruments in their world? Doesn't this orientation actually suggest that the value of individuals lies outside of themselves, for example, in the purposes they serve? But whose purposes? And where can value be found if not within human experience?

Yet we often behave as if the world revolves around us—individually or collectively. Isn't it true, as Nietzsche said, that the deep psychological meaning of the doctrine of the immortality of the soul is that the world revolves around me? Is not modern Western individualism but the secularization of that doctrine? Does not individualism treat the ego or "I" as the center of value? Does it not act as if the social order is simply the result of a practical calculation by self-interested individuals that they would be better off living in political society than outside of it, in the proverbial "state of nature?" Here is the origin of the doctrine of the social contract, the premier political theory of modern Western civilization.

Individualism thus raises serious questions about the nature and source of value. Since the individual is the only "intrinsic" value, all else tends to be only "instrumentally" valuable. Others are but objects in my world, to be valued and used as I see fit. But, dialectically, so am I but an instrument in the world of the other. No wonder that individualism tends to produce both a utilitarian ethic and a social contract theory of political organization. Let me explain.

Individualism: Utility and the Social Contract

Individualism is both a metaphysical and a moral theory. The former presents a view of the basic nature of social and human reality, already suggested, thus framing the discussion of ethical and political issues. The latter advocates the moral primacy of the individual person.

Drawing upon the Newtonian paradigm, metaphysical individualism sees reality, both natural and social, as made up of atomistic units. Its social version sees reality as constituted by relatively autonomous, asocial, but self-conscious, rational, and self-interested persons. They engage in a version of cost-benefit analysis that calls for and justifies the establishment of a minimal social and political order whose primary aim is to provide the legal terrain for a formally equitable administration of the rules of individual self-seeking. No one has set this forth more clearly than Thomas Hobbes, to whose basic individualistic metaphysics and "social contract" theory the emendations by Locke, his Enlightenment followers, and their utilitarian progeny thereafter have not offered any fundamental modifications. For all of them, society is essentially the legally organized field within which self-seeking individuals come together to work out their personal destiny and pursue individual satisfaction under the banner of utility. Whatever be the empirical aspirations of utilitarianism to make Lockean theory (or its more generous Jeffersonian version)[5] more scientifically respectable, nothing substantial of its individualism has been discarded.

But this individualism as historically developed has several serious flaws. It never adequately addresses the manner in which these autonomous individuals are formed. How did they come to have the skills and abilities—the capacity for rational insight into the future, the ability to know their desires—to evaluate potential strategies in the light of empirical probabilities in order to develop intelligent courses of action? Even more, how did they develop that set of drives, desires, goals, and aspirations that provide humans with the ends that their utilitarian strategies seek to serve? Are we to assume that the human being is born with all and precisely those inherited capacities that determine its adult nature? Or are we not rather faced with a theory whose primary function is not to explain the world but to provide an ideological justification for established structures of power and wealth?

Beyond these issues of character formation and skill development, how then are we to understand our social nature? Are other people simply material quasi-robotic human instruments to be used by us as best seems fit? Do we not need to share experiences with others? Do we not need to care for, and be cared for by, others? Can we lead an adequate and personally fulfilling life solely by gratifying our egoistic and bodily desires?

Even more, how can individualism account for the very existence of society and language? Must they not have preceded us in existence?

Must we not have been born into a society with established rules, laws, norms, institutions, values, and modes of thought and expression, as embodied in an articulate language, for us to even be able to develop the capacity to self-consciously have and rationally reflect upon and evaluate our desires in the light of established ways of interpreting the natural and social world? How can there even be rational and articulate thought without the prior existence of linguistically structured and culturally established objective meanings that are internalized by the individual in the process of socialization and maturation? Is it only by chance, and incidentally, that we speak the language of—and essentially share the values and see the world as—those who "bring us up?" Are not even the structure and content of our dreams at least in large part determined by the set of cultural meanings within which we come to consciousness? Do we assume that people in medieval or Oriental society had the same dreams as did those in the West at the beginning of the twenty-first century?

How then does the modern individualist justify his or her standard of value? Clearly, each has needs and desires, as do all others. But so do animals. On what grounds does one claim that some of them ought to be respected? By what standards do we choose among our preferences? Or between those of different individuals? Desires, in and of themselves, are clearly not self-justifying. But they can certainly be quite demanding! Do we simply assert them by the force and power of our individual will? Or that of the collectivity with which we have made a tactical alliance? (For what can possibly bind such modern individualists together other than practical self-interest, which itself can—and rationally should—always be reconsidered and revised in the light of changed circumstances?) Is there anything in such a perspective that could justify personal sacrifice for another, or for the group, tribe, or society? Is not the threat of social disintegration an ever-present possibility?

Clearly, such individualism is on very shaky moral ground, to say the least. In fact, it is on no moral ground whatsoever.[6] That fact is almost always acknowledged de facto, however subtly hidden, by the inevitable moral appeal to diverse sources of transcendent justification. In the West, that has usually involved reference to the divine and the revelation of "His" purpose. Clearly, the doctrine of an immortal soul has helped to undergird the theological justification—to which has been added a practical justification with the view that God gave humans "dominion" over the things of this world. An eighteenth-century gloss on that notion was the view that since Nature embodied divine purpose, the human desire for happiness was divinely inspired and constituted a moral justification of the maxim of utility. A companion view of God's providential ordering was the emerging capitalist mythologization of the "free market" in which, as if by "an unseen hand," self-seeking individuals were guided onto the correct path for the provision of human happiness through the promotion of "the wealth of nations." Nineteenth-century utilitarianism (and its companion economic doctrine of marginal utility) only sought to provide greater practical and scientific respectability to this doctrine.

One should note, of course, that this hegemonic doctrine never went completely unchallenged—both from within and without the frame of the establishment. The challenges from without came primarily from workers' movements, mostly under the influence of the many varieties of socialism or anarchism, or from the world of literature and the arts. Both were fueled in part by the emerging "Romantic" reaction to the Enlightenment, with particular emphasis on its either Rousseauian or Hegelian formulations. These sought to develop a vision of a historically developing social and cultural world out of which the individual emerged and within the developing network of which it was to find its home and complete self-realization.

The Hegelian vision, in particular, was one of many—as was Romanticism—that also contributed to the growth of an internal, and to some extent underground, reaction to the hegemony of bourgeois individualism. For some, this took the form of the celebration of the culture of the Volk and its historical expression in the nation state. For others, it took the form of the celebration of "Der Einzelner"—the Single One—and the refusal of the individual to submit to the rules and norms of conventional society.[7] For the more established mainstream religious critics, on the other hand, it expressed itself in a reaffirmation of the traditional values of transcendent religion and ritual observance. Here, in a strange way, it merged with, and reinforced, the Romantic, Rousseauian, and even more, the Kantian emphasis upon the innate force of conscience—Kant's Categorical Imperative—more generally viewed as an objective expression of God's divine order working through human nature. Perhaps, not surprisingly, that conscience—often in conflict with man's "fallen nature"—seemed to demand and authorize precisely the behavior needed to provide social cohesion and moral justification for the bourgeois order.

At the same time, the doctrine of "man's dominion" over the creatures of this world well suited an expanding commercial and industrial order whose mantra was unlimited economic growth fueled by self-seeking individuals mobilizing "private enterprise" without government "interference"—though with appropriate government support (financial, political, and military)—to use The Market for the maximum exploitation of the Earth. In its more unselfconsciously celebratory versions, this unleashing of individual initiative and free enterprise promised unending advancements in human well-being and even the promotion of human perfectibility. But little, if any, attention was ever paid either to the environmental constraints placed by a finite planet on this vision of unending economic growth or to the social, moral, or environmental consequences of unchecked population growth. Rather, nature was—and, to a great extent, still is—treated as essentially "raw material," land being simply one of the factors of production, along with labor and capital. It was just taken for granted that, in Locke's words, whatever one "mixed his labor with" was his, and there was "as much and as good" left over in "Nature's store" for others. Of course, this was hardly true even then, and has long ceased to have any significance for that vast majority who labor for others. What they produce is hardly "theirs." And there are increasingly few opportunities for those other than the owners of large "property" to return to the "common store" for the provision of their needs.

But the more pervasive and fundamental problem is that the economy is, and has always been, but one of the ways in which humans interact with the Earth within which we "live, move, and have our being." The Earth cannot be an unending source of "raw materials," nor an unlimited repository for human and industrial waste. It is the stuff of which we are made—not just materially, but also socially, morally, aesthetically, and spiritually. We cannot continue to act as if the Earth provides an unending supply of raw materials with which to fuel an ever-growing economy demanding increasing consumption and material well-being for an ever-expanding human population. We must address both our material and spiritual roots in the Earth as well as the objective constraints established by the latter's "carrying capacity," however difficult that may be to determine.

Moral Perplexity

Nowhere is the spiritual challenge posed by individualism more apparent than in its efforts to address the meaning of life and the problem of death. The practical everyday meaning of happiness in Western society has been the search for pleasure. This issue bedeviled utilitarianism, with John Stuart Mill striving to moderate and humanize Jeremy Bentham's blatant and crass quantitative egoistic hedonism. Where Bentham sought to elaborate a "felicific calculus" that would scientifically decide policy options by providing a mathematically precise determination of the amount of pleasure that would result from alternative courses of action, Mill sought to replace that calculus with a more classical vision of human happiness that spoke to the "permanent interests of man as a progressive being." But he remained completely unable to provide a coherent foundation for that qualitative moral vision that did not reduce values to quantitative, though more subtle, sensual pleasure.

The drive for pleasure has been well addressed—at least for the privileged—by the consumer orientation of "advanced" capitalism. But it has clearly failed to speak to the individual's "spiritual" needs. It has celebrated the growth of consumption, even advocating the notion of an individual's "entitlement" to whatever would satisfy his or her needs. This "morality" is doctrinally enshrined in the economist's assertion that tastes are subjective, and all are equally worthy of being satisfied. "Objectively," one can only "value" a taste by the willingness of individuals to expend their hard-earned money by paying the market-determined price.

The exclusive preoccupation with "objective" quantitative pleasure at the expense of "subjective" significance seems to leave individuals subtly, yet quite profoundly, unsatisfied. Humans "do not live by bread alone," and an exclusive focus on quantitative pleasure fails to address the human need for meaning and purpose. Rather it seems to lead—among those having advanced beyond the material level of bare subsistence—to an ever-increasing search for more, diverse, exotic, and intense pleasures, with ever-expanding consumption, and the unending pursuit of power and expanded personal recognition, as people seek to fill the qualitative lack with quantitative increase. How else, for example, can we understand the ever more pressured search for ever more opportunities to create artificial scarcities over which we may compete in order to "prove ourselves," augmenting our reputation, and enhancing the dramatic significance of our lives? The proliferation of drug and alcohol use among the more "successful" may be seen as but one expression of this subtle dissatisfaction with daily life, as is the fascination with crime, tragedy, and sports. Drugs are themselves the perfect expression of our being "hooked" on pleasure, an easily available consumption item by which we may provide an immediate "lift" to counter the subtle tendency to depression that is the ever-present consequence of an exclusive focus on immediate gratification. Of course, one inevitably "comes down" from such "highs," leading to the need for renewed stimulation, resulting in the modern version of life's treadmill.

Underlying this potentially depressive cycle are the failure of commitment, the tenuousness of sacrifice, and the haunting reality of death. There is no need to dwell here on these points, other than to draw some obvious conclusions. *To the extent* to which we view ourselves as essentially self-encapsulated individuals—the economist's proverbial "economic man," for example, always looking out for "Number One"—*to that extent* society is *nothing but* the practical instrument of a calculated strategy, of which other people are the present instruments, and The Market the primary vehicle for social cohesion. What then can rationally justify commitment to any institution, cause, or person? On what basis can such an individual sacrifice the one thing in life that is precious, his or her own self, to anything else? What then, other than force or self-interest, can be expected to hold together a society or family? (Other than religious mythology, that is.) Is this not the pathetic reality attested to by that automobile bumper sticker that proudly proclaims, "I'm spending my child's inheritance?" Finally, how can such an individual confront the complete annihilation of self that is death? Does not death pose the most fundamental challenge of all, threatening the very meaning of existence itself, for that individual, the meaning of whose life is summed up by the search for self-affirmation?

Cultural Challenges

Here we encounter the complete secularization and materialization of historic Protestant individualism, without the saving comfort provided by the possibility of transcendent grace. Clearly, there is something quite unsettling about such a vision, a point underscored by both Luther's remark, echoing that of St. Paul, about the necessity of a God for otherwise everyone would be completely alone, and Kierkegaard's assertion, echoing Tertullian, that we believe because it is absurd. So unsettling is this vision, which few seem able to face quite directly, that so many seem to need to assuage their hedonic egoism with an almost reflexive religiosity, while others merge their search for individual salvation with an idealization of romantic love, through which they envision an existence whose significance is transfigured by the saving presence of The Loved Other. Of course, that idealized "love" of the other inevitably confronts the practical logic of egotistic individualism's instrumental use of the other, creating an essentially unresolvable tension within love that Sartre dramatically and somewhat provocatively described as the unstable union of sadism and masochism. Commitment, sacrifice, love, and death all confront modern individualism with apparently insurmountable challenges that place contemporary society on grounds ever more uncertain, confronting an ever more desperate future.

Bentham's felicific calculus thus returns with a vengeance. Another popular 1990s automobile bumper sticker well caught the pathology of this ethic with its assertion that "Whoever dies with the most toys wins." Here the individualistic ethic fuels an economic growth imperative, sustaining a pyramid scheme of global proportions, which nevertheless fails to address either our personal need for sustaining significance or the long-term capacity of the Earth to sustain human activity.

These remarks are not meant in any way to suggest that economic growth does not—and has not—provided quite significant and tangible benefits to large numbers of people. In fact, it has made possible a material standard of living that far exceeds anything of which even the most wealthy of prior eras, including royalty, could have dreamed. That level of material well-being has further allowed and even facilitated a level of intellectual, emotional, and cultural development for vast numbers of people, myself included, that was never before possible. But those advantages have not been equitably or adequately shared within nations or across the planet—and far more significant numbers have seen their communities destroyed, their lives deprived of both traditional and culturally sustaining institutions and meaning, and their material quality of life decline. At the same time, the lives of those who have so palpably benefited materially and, to a significant sense, socially have been increasingly confronted with a moral and cultural challenge for which the current hegemonic ideology does not offer sustaining solace. Meanwhile, the environmental impact of this economic growth has become increasingly evident, as the cumulative effects of a profit-oriented, energy-intensive, fossil fuel–driven economy are beginning to take their toll.

One compensatory strategy to obtain the social integration threatened by the disintegrative dynamic of egoistic hedonism is the maintenance of need. This can be facilitated—far more than by advertising or the sophistication and expansion of consumer products—by permitting or even encouraging the persistent growth of population. This performs a twofold function. It expands the consumer market, fueling the continual economic expansion of production and profits. Meanwhile, growth in the supply of labor provides both the workers required by an expanding economy—only a relatively small percentage of whom are highly skilled and well paid—and a surplus labor supply that continually drives down labor costs, for the radical increase in worker productivity occasioned by technological innovation reduces the relative number of workers needed for advance production systems. Most of the rest struggle to find jobs in relatively low-skilled low-paying retail and service industries where they compete with the growing numbers of underemployed—thus appropriately driving down wages and living standards and keeping people focused on "getting by"—"making both ends meet." While not having the time or luxury to worry very much about the meaning of their lives, such individuals can rather easily accept the doctrine of hedonic individualism as the justification for taking a break from the drudgery of their working days and striving to assuage their sufferings in the sophisticated "bread and circuses" of the modern consumer economy.

At the same time, the dynamic "Free Market" continually transforms social patterns, undermining established institutions, from the family and local community to the nation state. Settled community life is continually upset as the "free mobility" of capital requires the "free mobility" of labor, with investment ever in search of more profitable venues.

The very doctrine of national sovereignty becomes anachronistic as national autonomy cannot withstand the force of market relations. Developments in communications and transportation technology globalize market relations, placing a premium on the size of corporations and the scope of their operations, while providing them with the wealth and power to essentially design the market system to their specifications. It is important to realize that markets are not natural or self-determining phenomena. They are socially constructed, whether intentionally or not, by human activity. For "markets are [nothing but] 'a set of arrangements by which exchange takes place.'" These arrangements, which frame and structure exchange, include "property rights, physical and social infrastructure, the distribution of income and wealth, the myriad regulations that govern economic affairs—all [of which] . . . are products of human decisions. What is more, when we think of markets in terms of these things, it is possible to trace the relationships between particular decisions and their impacts. It becomes relatively easy to recognize not only that markets are constructed but also to see how they are constructed."[8] "To say that we should 'leave things to the market,' is no more nor less than to say that we should leave things to history as it has come to us,"[9] that is, to the historically constituted institutional structure of existing power, wealth, and property.

Even more than with markets, environmental effects cannot be easily confined within the historically created borders of political entities. The environment does not recognize sovereignty, though policy decisions by political as well as economic bodies can significantly affect it. National and international organizations and political institutions must be redefined and, along with markets, reconstructed if we are to seriously address the objective consequences of expanding human economic activity.

Thus, the need for sustaining communities has never been more keenly felt, more spiritually needed, and more under siege. Clearly, the historically developed political expressions of communities—whether in town, village, city, county, state, or national governments—have not been designed, and are not well structured, to address the transformed conditions of a technologically revolutionized and effectively globalized market. Neither are the theories or control mechanisms of this transformed social economy organized to address the problems created by its increasingly imposing challenge to the Earth's carrying capacity. We are confronted, therefore, with two conflicting challenges: the need to develop political institutions on a world scale that can order market relations in a manner consistent with the demands of ecology and human community and the need to reconstitute meaningful social communities within which human beings may find their bearings, nurturing their psychic roots, social location, and personal significance.

These problems are the legates of the modern world order, in either its institutional or conceptual formulations. In some cases, they are the inevitable consequence of its institutional operations and for others, the logical conclusions from its mode of thinking. For still others, they result from a theory and practice that, while not logically consequent from current structures, are determined in large part by the pervasive and controlling power of culturally prevailing paradigms and root metaphors. In short, both the problems encountered by our culture and the prevailing "research programs" and modes of inquiry are determined in large part by the reigning metaphysics. It is thus incumbent upon us, if we wish to theoretically reconfigure and constructively address these problems, to tackle that metaphysic directly, first critically evaluating its foundations and then suggesting a framework for an alternative metaphysic. To that task I will turn in the following chapter.

Let me conclude the present discussion by observing that the pervasive confrontation between the generally reductionist perspective of the natural and social sciences and the spiritual and ethical perspective of religion have not only left us with a divided legacy, but their implicitly antagonistic metaphysical foundations, with each feeling that the truth of its perspective would be compromised by incorporating elements from its "antagonist," have subtly contributed to undermining serious theoretical efforts to find common ground. Each has essentially pursued the elaboration of its own perspective while doing little more than paying the necessary lip service to the other, whose existence, however, neither can avoid acknowledging. At the same time, the growing practical and theoretical ascendancy of the scientific metaphysic has increasingly placed the religious perspective on the defensive. The latter has recognized, even if not usually quite explicitly, and responded often with an increasingly shrill, assertive, and uncompromising fundamentalist reaction. It is almost as if it will compensate for its felt theoretical inadequacy by the very power of its assertion and the outrageousness of its claims. Similarly, where the inadequacy of the religious perspective was acknowledged, the ontological demand for definitive solutions has all-too-often and too easily given rise to secular messianisms whose efforts to impose their particular versions of utopia have often been as, if not more, destructive as the most determined religious fanaticism. No matter how historically significant these "fundamentalist" reactions, however, whether transcendent or secular, it is the increasingly ascendant scientific philosophy whose theoretical limits and conceptual reformulation set the theoretical agenda for the positive reconstitution of humanity's future—to which the religious will have to adapt, if we are to survive into the foreseeable future and prosper on this planet.

4

A Ripple in a Field

Like other things one does not talk about, unclear thinking about what is fundamental can come back to haunt us later on. Its most insidious effect is to lead us out into the desert by inducing us to search on smaller and smaller scales for meaning that is not there.[1]

You think because you understand *one* you must understand *two*, because one and one makes two. But you must also understand *and*.

Ancient Sufi teaching[2]

The Challenge

In the introduction to an otherwise brilliant discussion of the unavoidable natural constraints placed upon the possibilities of unlimited economic growth, Hermann Daly addresses the confrontation of scientific determinism with religious morality. In speaking of a prior meeting at which major scientific figures had sought to marshal the support of religious leaders for a campaign to preserve the Earth from the inevitable ravages of an essentially uncontrolled economic system, he observes:

Sagan, Wilson, and Gould proclaim the cosmology of scientific materialism, which considers the cosmos an absurd accident, and life within it to be no more than another accident ultimately reducible to dead matter in motion. In their view there is no such thing as value in any objective sense or purpose, beyond short-term survival and reproduction, which are purely instinctual and thus ultimately mechanical. Calling for a moral compass in such a world is as absurd as calling for a magnetic compass in a world in which you proclaim that there is no such thing as magnetic north. A sensitive compass needle is worthless if there is no external lure toward which it is pulled. A morally sensitive person in a world in which there is no lure of objective value to pull and persuade this sensitized person toward itself is like the compass needle with no external magnetic force to act on it.

One might reply that objective value does not exist externally, but is an internal affair created by humans (or by God in humans only) and projected or imposed by humans on the external world. This is the solution of dualism, and has been dominant since Descartes. Purpose, mind, and value enter the world discontinuously in human beings; all the rest is mechanism. Such a view, however, is contrary to the evolutionary understanding of kinship of human beings with other forms of life that is affirmed by science. For mind, value, and purpose to be real, they must, in an evolutionary perspective, already be present to some degree in the world out of which humans evolved, or else they must be the object of a special creation. The latter, of course, is not acceptable to science and the theory of evolution. Scientific materialism resolves the dilemma by denying the reality of purpose, mind, and value in human beings as well as in the external world. The subjective feelings that we refer to as purpose or value are mere epiphenomena, ultimately explainable in terms of underlying physical structures and motions.

The main alternative to scientific materialism, one that still takes science seriously, is the process philosophy of Alfred North Whitehead. This view is radically empirical. What we know most concretely and directly, unmediated by the senses or by abstract concepts, is our inner experience of purpose. That should be the starting point, the most well known thing, in terms of which we try to explain less well known things. To begin with highly abstract concepts such as electrons and photons, and to explain the immediate experience of purpose as an "epiphenomenon" incidentally produced by the behavior of these abstractions, is an example of what Whitehead called "the fallacy of misplaced concreteness." I do not wish to pretend that Whiteheadean philosophy is easy, or without problems of its own, but merely to say that for me it strains credulity a lot less than scientific materialism.

Gould himself has noted, "We cannot win this battle to save species and environments without forging an emotional bond between ourselves and nature as well—for we will not fight to save what we do not love." But is it possible to love an accident? Rather, is it possible for an accident to love an accident? For an accident to fight to save another accident? I doubt it, but I do not doubt that it is possible for people who call themselves scientific materialists to fall in love with the world they study and have come to know intimately. God's world is lovable, and scientists often fall in love with it much more deeply than theologians! But should they not confess that love, and ask themselves how it is that they could have fallen in love with something their science tells them is an accident? In their daily life are they particularly fond of random events, or do they find them annoying? There is something fundamentally silly about biologists teaching on Monday, Wednesday, and Friday that everything, including our sense of value and reason, is a mechanical product only of genetic chance and environmental necessity, with no purpose whatsoever, and then on Tuesday and Thursday trying to convince the public that they should love some accidental piece of this meaningless puzzle enough to fight and sacrifice to save it.

The absurdity is highlighted by the scientists' recognition that they have nothing to appeal to in their effort to rouse public support other than religiously based values that they themselves consider unfounded! Are they not temporarily living by the fruit of the tree whose taproot they have just cut? As ... [one religious participant] puts it,

Such thinkers consider any vision of purpose in the universe to be archaic and illusory... . Indeed it *is* rare to find scientists, literati or philosophers publicly claiming that our universe has any point to it or that any transcendent purpose influences its evolution. But can this cosmic pessimism adequately nourish the vigorous environmental activism that many of these same thinkers, now hand in hand with members of the religious community are calling for today?

To call this a "quite ingenuous proposal," as ... [he] does, is to be kind ... It is indeed a paradox that people whose professed beliefs give them no good reason to be environmentalists are usually trying harder to save the environment than are people whose beliefs give them every good reason to be environmentalists! The scientists are implicitly calling for a religious reformation, not just a moral compass that magically functions in an amoral universe—to point the scientists in the direction of public funds to save the environment.

As Alfred North Whitehead observed,

Many a scientist has patiently designed experiments for the purpose of substantiating his belief that animal operations are motivated by no purposes. He has perhaps spent his spare time writing articles to prove that human beings are as other animals so that purpose is a category irrelevant for the explanation of their bodily activities, his own activities included. Scientists animated by the purpose of proving that they are purposeless constitute an interesting subject for study.[3]

I have quoted the above passage at length because in it a distinguished contemporary intellectual sets forth in moving terms the moral options legated to us by our more or less taken-for-granted metaphysical frame. While most scientific thinkers rarely confront the issue as honestly and forthrightly as does Daly—often tending, with evident awkwardness, to blur the lines of confrontation, seeking to have it both ways, when they feel compelled to address the issue at all—they almost inevitably come down, in effective practice at least, on the side of that scientific materialism that leaves no place for freedom, purpose, or value. Finding this conclusion unacceptable, Daly feels he has no choice but to opt for a transcendent religious belief, for which he then grasps for the seemingly most plausible philosophical framework with which he can maintain its rational coherence with the most advanced results of modern science. What other choice does he have with which he can preserve a place for freedom and value in a world of materialistic determinism? Given our culturally legated metaphysical frame, the answer is clearly and emphatically, *none!*

Confronting Reductionism

In a practical expression of the prevalent taken-for-granted scientific worldview, we frequently hear researchers say or only suggest that they have found a chemical or neuronal pathway that causes a specific behavior; therefore, by implication if not explication, the behavior is not caused by attitudes or personal psychology. There is a growing tendency among researchers in the natural sciences (not to speak of medical practitioners and the lay public) to assume that if they find chemical or neurological factors that influence behavior (for depression, schizophrenia, hyperactivity, aggression, and the list goes on), this proves that the behavior is materially caused, and that attitudes and values, psychology and sociology, are at best epiphenomenal explanatory systems—products of an incomplete scientific reduction.[4]

Underlying such an approach is an almost universally shared perspective that an event is either materially determined or psychically determined, but not both—for otherwise, how would they interact? For most scientific observers, these alternatives are usually only explicitly posed in order to better refute the dualist and idealist alternatives, thus establishing the sole priority of a reductive materialist interpretation.[5]

As witnessed by Daly and colleagues, but having much broader (and usually less sophisticated) appeal, there is, of course, the alternative move of religious, spiritual, and "new age" thinkers who seek to discredit the materialist interpretation in order to instantiate an opposed transcendent and spiritual one. They seek to defend an essentially idealist interpretation of the world that will justify anything from individual freedom and the objective reality of purpose and values to reincarnation, eternal life, and even psychokinesis, telepathy, and teleportation. Of course, at its philosophical root, Christianity, Judaism, Islam, Hinduism, and (to a major extent) Buddhism are all rooted in a similar metaphysical idealism. (In a lecture on cognitive science, John Searle reports being surprised to hear the Dalai Lama present a Buddhist view of the world that was straight Cartesian dualism—without any reference to Descartes himself.)

Thus, either we find the world divided between two completely incompatible metaphysical orientations, each of which is essentially monistic and reductive, or we are left with a completely implausible dualistic amalgam. The vast majority of the world's people believe in a religio-idealist interpretation that is fundamentally inconsistent with the scientific worldview that provides the foundation for the technological developments by which we all increasingly live. But it is this very spiritualistic approach that grounds the world's ethical systems, and sustains human beings' sense of the meaning and dignity of their lives and the possibilities of their having some effective control over their daily life.

On the other hand, it is quite clear that the world's institutional, economic, political, military, and scientific activities are increasingly guided by a scientific/technical worldview that is essentially materialist and reductionist, effectively denying personal choice and human freedom, while practically developing increasingly refined ways of manipulating and controlling human experience and subtly denying it the philosophical legitimacy to resist.

We see this in every sphere, from the approach to mental illness to the explanation of the nature of life. But is this polarized perspective necessary? Are the theoretical alternatives posed by Daly the only ones possible? Or may they not be the dead-end box into which that metaphysic has unjustifiably placed us? Daly has made poignantly clear some of the fundamental issues that are at stake. I have already suggested some crucial fault lines in the theoretically dominant perspective. It is for me now to pick up this line of argument and directly address the problem and offer an alternative metaphysical frame for its possible solution. That frame will involve the development of a naturalistic and nonreductive field theory, providing the foundation for a doctrine of emergent qualities and powers that can place our understanding of the world on a more sure and productive foundation. Somewhat in the spirit of Richard Rorty, let me suggest that we "try thinking of [the world] this way."[6]

Addressing Purpose in Nature

The first thing to note is that human behavior is apparently purposeful, while objective nature has long been thought to operate in accordance with mechanical laws. Certainly in the post-Newtonian world, the mechanical clock was long taken as the model for physical interactions. David Hume often had recourse to the similar operating system of interacting billiard balls, with their resultant behavior being a completely determinable consequence of their inertial mass and momentum, modified by the resistance of the medium.

There can be no doubt about the experimental and technical success of the Newtonian system, from industrial developments to war and space exploration. Yet it is human beings that develop these theories and implement their technical applications in accordance with thought processes that clearly do not seem to follow any such deterministic processes. It has, for example, never been clear how the Newtonian system can account for the purposeful scientific investigations of Isaac Newton himself. As Roy Bhaskar insightfully observes, "it is only a non-reductionist metaphysics that can bring itself within its own world view."[7]

Clearly human beings experience the capacity to think, weigh alternatives, make free choices, and even experience anxiety about the possible consequences of these alternatives. Jean Paul Sartre well captured this experienced duality with his phenomenologically descriptive categories of the "in-itself" and the "for-itself," by which he divided up *what is*. In updating the Cartesian dualism of extended substance and thinking substance, Sartre clearly eschewed any attempt to account for the origin of these two distinctive modes of being, simply asserting that we find these two opposed and irreducible qualities in experience. The task of his "phenomenological ontology" was to describe extensively and in detail their modes of interaction. In describing these modes of being, he claimed that the in-itself followed deterministic laws, being completely predictable, while the for-itself was essentially defined as a self-conscious freedom for whom the world appeared as a field of possibilities.[8]

Of course, at one level, Sartre is quite right. That *is* the way our experience appears. And that appearance needs to be accounted for. But does that appearance ultimately make theoretical sense as an adequate foundation? While traditional dualism has never been able to explain the manner of interaction between the fundamentally opposed substances of thought and extension (i.e., mind and body), Sartrean thought seeks to avoid that problem with its noncausal approach, thus also eschewing any investigation into the knotty problem of the origin of this dualism. Meanwhile, it still fails to deal with the original dilemma by fudging the question of the relation of the free conscious subject to the body that seems to be its material precondition. It thus leaves its freedom dangling in thin air, a metaphysical surd without roots or a home in the universe. Perhaps this is a historically appropriate expression of a culture whose preindustrial roots have been torn asunder by industrial development and the world market, but it is hardly a philosophically adequate theory of being.

If, on the other hand, we take seriously the astounding development of human technical and theoretical capacity that constitutes pragmatic proof of the power and essential validity of modern science, we must come to terms directly with its operative materialist assumption.[9] Either we need to accept it, and then show how thought can be reduced to the terms of a materialist science, or, since dualism won't do, we need to provide an alternative framework that makes sense of thought as an emergent property of nature itself.[10] The challenge before us will be to show why the prevalent materialist reduction is inadequate (and ultimately incoherent), while the doctrine of emergence can not only do justice to the facts, but also provide a means for coherently addressing the problem of freedom, and its relation to determinism.

The Problem of Calculation, Measurement, and Predictability

Let me first be clear. My concern is *not* with the practical or technical problem of the impossibility of now—or, almost certainly, ever—actually performing the necessary calculations to provide the definitive predictions that the deterministic model invites. I will first say a few words as to the reasons for that practical impossibility intrinsic to the deterministic model itself. But even showing that would provide no justification for emergent levels of being. It would only codify the limitations of our knowledge and our capacity to predict and control existence. Important as such chastened hubris may be, it would in no way diminish the conceptual plausibility of the reductionist project. My intent goes deeper—and seeks to recast the entire conceptual framework, thus providing coherent and rationally defensible grounds for, among other things, consciousness, freedom, and morality. But let me first briefly address the technical limitations to measurement and predictability. I draw upon the discussion of Brian Silver in *The Ascent of Science*.

It was the Enlightenment thinker Pierre-Simon Laplace who explicitly drew out the deterministic cosmological significance of the Newtonian worldview. Since "Newton's laws completely determined the motion of all bodies, if we could at any moment measure the position and velocity of every particle in the universe, we could use the laws of motion to determine their future motion completely."[11] Similarly, we could also specify the universe's entire past history, thus leaving nothing to either chance or ignorance. But how would one even begin to calculate the exact position of every particle? Consider, for example, the behavior of gas molecules.

> In one second a molecule in the air makes several billion collisions; a tiny change in the direction of our molecule at the beginning of its journey may only slightly alter the way in which it makes its first collision, but that will slightly alter the direction and speed with which it carries on after the collision, *and* slightly alter the subsequent movement of the molecule that it hits. After very few collisions our molecule, and the molecules in its vicinity, will have entirely different positions and velocities from those that we predicted. After 4 billion collisions the molecule is likely to be in an entirely different place from that originally calculated. It is easy to believe that the effect of an extremely small change in initial conditions will have an effect which is out of all proportion. What we are seeing is an extremely simple example of the fact that: *There are systems in which the outcome of a series of events is very sensitive to the initial conditions. So sensitive that the behavior of the system may be unpredictable in practice, even if it is predictable in theory.*[12]

Of course, with a body of enclosed gas we may be able to average out the behavior of molecules in order to produce an average behavior of the system (which has important implications pointing toward the stratification of science and reality), but this is clearly not possible for meteorological conditions. The problem is in fact far worse. As Silver reports:

> An extraordinary illustration of this sensitivity is provided by the calculations of the physicist Michael Berry, who considered a collection of oxygen molecules at atmospheric pressure and room temperature. He placed an electron at the edge of the known universe (about 10^{10} light-years away and asked: After how many collisions would a given molecule miss a collision that it would have had if the electron were not there? Now the electron is supposed to act only via its *gravitational* field, which as you know must be so incredibly small that any right-thinking scientist would completely ignore it. Bad mistake! After fifty-six collisions the molecule misses a collision. I find this result to be almost incredible, but you can see why any attempt to predict the microscopic future of molecular systems requires a macroscopic amount of optimism.[13]

Silver concludes his more extended discussion by noting "the impossibility of completely specifying the initial state of a system (in our case the position of a molecule) and the extreme sensitivity of the future development of a system (the path of the molecule), to its initial state (the position of the molecule)." It was considerations such as these that led to the development of chaos theory. "Chaotic processes are ... unpredictable *in practice* because of their oversensitivity to initial conditions," though "unpredictable processes need not be chaotic," like the toss of a coin. But "the fact that we have no hope of predicting the behavior of chaotic systems does not mean that they are not deterministic." Thus, chaos theory leads to "the collapse of *practical* determinism and the realization that there are insoluble problems within the framework of deterministic science."[14]

This problem is only exacerbated by Poincaré's demonstration that "*in principle* there is no analytical solution to the three-body problem ... For a problem involving three, or more, interacting moving bodies, there is no closed solution, no simple mathematical expression."[15] This might be taken as intrinsic theoretical substantiation of the fundamental inadequacy of linear causal thinking, and a practical exemplification of the indispensability of field-theoretic considerations, of which more will be explained later. We have, of course, said nothing here of the fundamental indeterminacy revealed by quantum mechanics, nor of the intrinsic incompleteness of mathematics as demonstrated by Kurt Gödel.[16] So much for the impossibility of practical determinism, but what of its theoretical foundations?

The Reductio of Reductionism

Let us take it from the beginning, in the simplest terms. We experience free choice and a world in which much is quite predictable. Our freedom provides the basis for our ascription of moral responsibility, and the justification for our punishment of those who violate laws and moral obligations. It also grounds our sense of dignity and self-worth, and provides the basis for hope that we may be able to contribute to making our life better. At the same time, we have increasing evidence of the power of science not only to explain but also to produce, reproduce, and transform the material world. It is this very power that provides our free choice with a vastly expanded terrain for action and aspiration. But that science also provides us with theories and strategies for intervention that can radically transform who and what we are and do. Medicine can repair broken parts, pharmacology transform our mood, thought, and behavior (without as of yet any definable limits), biological engineering reconstruct our very genetic constitution, and information processing possibly technologically reengineer human biology.

Further, this same science describes, on the macroscopic level, a material universe that has probably existed for some 13.7 billion years, vastly expanding to truly astronomical dimensions with little evidence for the existence of life, not to say, mind or spirit, throughout vast reaches of time and space. In fact, as far as we know at present, any life, not to say complex life forms or mentally developed ones, only exists on this relatively minor planet revolving around an ordinary star located far off center in an average galaxy that is but one of billions of galaxies that spread out from here well beyond a distance of 10 billion light-years. Certainly there is nothing special about our material place in the universe. Certainly there is little rational basis to claim that spiritual forces have had anything to do with those natural processes by which our Earth came into being some 4.5 billion years ago.

As General Relativity plays this development back to its origins, it supposes the universe to have emerged out of a gigantic initial explosion called "the big bang." At that initial moment of infinite mass-energy density and space-time compression, there were not even protons and neutrons, not to speak of atoms, molecules, light, things, minerals, plants, animals, or minds. Out of this "quark soup," literally everything has developed.

Now if we are to take the reductionist paradigm seriously, what it must be claiming is that "there is nothing new under the sun," or to be more exact, that everything—the Sun included—can be explained and in essence reduced to and, in principle at least, predicted from an analysis of that initial moment: the theory of that moment could in principle explain and predict everything that has followed. Thus, any qualities, properties, capacities, or attributes that have emerged to constitute the universe are "nothing but" versions of that initial "soup" that can be fully explained by using the terms and laws that explain that event. This must also mean that any concepts that describe emerging properties and powers must be capable of being completely replaced by concepts that only describe those initial events. For example, all thought processes must be completely describable in terms of the not yet developed but eagerly sought for theory of quantum gravity, or some equivalent thereof.

To add to this challenge posed to materialism, we must also take into consideration the problems posed by the Heisenberg Uncertainty Principle—to a very brief consideration of which we will return later—that rules out in principle the possibility of deterministic predictions of single quantum events. Its particular relevance at this point lies in the fact that the initial conditions of the big bang are probably best understood as a singular "quantum" effect, hence, in principle, indeterminate.[17] Thus, a complete materialist reduction, at best, must assert the complete randomness of the fundamental structure (and possibly laws) of the supposedly deterministic universe. The extremes of this position are suggested by investigations of the Cosmic Background Explorer Satellite (COBE) and the Wilkinson Microwave Anisotropy Probe (WMAP) that have tended to confirm the view that the very existence and structure of the galaxies is the result of initially indeterminate random quantum fluctuations at the moment of the big bang.

For reductionists, therefore, either everything is causally present at the initial moment of creation or something "new" has "emerged" at some later point. If the latter is the case, however, then we need a theory to explain how something fundamentally new and nonreducible (or initially predictable) can ever have emerged. And if that happened once, why only then, and never again? Otherwise, all we would in principle ever need to know is the nature and structure of the initial moment and its operable causal laws—the so-called theory of everything—and all else would follow necessarily. That is equivalent to claiming that the theory of quantum gravity will not only be the comprehensive unifying theory of everything, but it will also, at least in principle, be exhaustive of all possible explanations. All other theories would only be short-hand expressions of the laws of quantum gravity.

To be still more precise: any concept from any more "developed" science (or religion, art, culture, etc.) would have to be capable of being completely describable and explainable (that is, completely replaceable without conceptual remainder) by concepts and laws drawn solely from the theories of quantum gravity. Thus, qualities such as thinking, faith, love, care, aspiration, marriage, money, inflation, depression, trust, and, of course, consciousness and freedom would have to be in principle completely describable in terms of quarks (or strings) and explained as quantum events. In fact, the entire world of qualities would have to be treated as ultimately illusory epiphenomena.

Consider, for example, two further problems with this deterministic paradigm. As Werner Heisenberg liked to point out, if you heat a magnet sufficiently—to about 720 degrees—it loses its magnetic properties. When you let it cool again, it regains those properties, but there is *no way* to determine *in advance* which side will become positive, which negative. The result is a purely fifty-fifty random determination. Then there is the point made clearly by Heinz Pagels to the effect that the Second Law of Thermodynamics—the law of entropy—holds only for systems, and can say nothing about, and is not reducible to, the behavior of individual molecules. How can we explain either of these processes in a deterministic fashion and without referring to anything other than the laws governing quark soup and the big bang?

Reconstructing Scientific Logic

Let us look further into the problems posed by this *metaphysical logic* that secretly undergirds reductionism. It expresses what might well be called a linear causal deductivism. That means that it seeks to explain events by looking for the causal factors that not only produce but can also completely explain the "emerging" properties and powers in a step-by-step process without remainder. It understands those factors not only as the elements whose combination is completely responsible for the resultant events and structures but also as elements capable of completely explaining all of its properties and causal powers—thus providing the necessary and sufficient conditions for a complete explanation. Its research program implicitly assumes that to explain an event or structure is to reduce it to the logic of operation of its constituent elements. In principle, then, this resultant event or structure is *nothing but* the result of the activity of those causal elements, and its behavior can be completely explained by the laws that govern its constituent elements. Hence is reproduced the Cartesian program that framed the seventeenth century's Scientific Revolution by seeking to analyze complexes into simples, and then rationally (and mathematically) to reconstruct the initial complexes out of those simples.[18] In an important sense, however, this is "nothing but" the mathematization of the Aristotelian deductive logic that has provided the foundation for scientific inquiry since the fourth century B.C.E., of which more will be explained later.[19]

But why should we assume the adequacy of the Cartesian reduction—or Aristotelian deductive logic, for that matter? We have already seen that the logical conclusion of this process is the implicit claim that all was included and implicitly deducible from the initial conditions of the big bang. Thus, our problem with this logic is not solely the problem of adequately addressing the so-called mind-body problem—explaining the nature of consciousness and purposeful behavior in a deterministic physical world. It is in fact a more generic problem of explaining the *relative* autonomy of numerous realms of being from the most "primitive" to the most complex. Let's consider several examples where reductionism fails, and an alternative metaphysical logic is suggested.

We have already had occasion to refer to the Second Law of Thermodynamics and to Heisenberg's Uncertainty Principle, to both of which we need now to devote more attention. But let us first briefly consider some other problems with the prevalent model:

1. Consider the stabilization of the Earth's climate. The Sun provides 99.98 percent of the Earth's energy in the form of electromagnetic radiation, much of it in the visible range. The Earth is warmed by the approximately 70 percent of that energy that is absorbed—the remainder being reflected away by the Earth's atmosphere before absorption. After absorption, that energy is reradiated in the form of infrared heat, which itself tends to be trapped by the atmosphere until the Earth heats up sufficiently to increase the heat differential between the Earth and its surrounding space so that the heat is finally able to completely escape as infrared radiant energy. Ultimately, heat-in equals heat-out, and the Earth's climate reaches an equilibrium balanced at a specifiable temperature. The same is true of course for Mars, Venus, and the other planets—as well as for most hot bodies.

   One can rather precisely calculate the amount of energy coming to the Earth, and the amount leaving, and in principle trace the precise paths that energy takes in warming the planet and producing the so-called greenhouse effect. Further, that energy is a necessary condition for almost everything that happens on this planet—certainly for the development of life in its indefinite variety of forms. Practically nothing that happens on Earth can fail to be influenced by this energy cycle—and nothing can impede the laws of operation that determine that heat-out will equal heat-in at any specified temperature. But does this natural process *determine* what takes place on the Earth? Would it make *any* sense to treat this process in a reductionist mode? Of course not. The energy transfer provides a "boundary condition," it sets limits on the amount of energy available, and in what form. But it does not determine what is done with that energy, the quality, extent, nature, or direction of that activity. Rather, one might say that that resultant activity is an emergent property of the energy-transfer system. That system provides the necessary, but hardly the sufficient or determining, quantitative conditions of distinctive qualitative energetic activity on our planet.

2. Similarly with gravity. Gravity concerns itself solely with the issues of mass-energy and distance. Its effects can be calculated quite precisely, and are oblivious to any and all qualitative modifications of mass-energy. Considerations of quality, structure, internal processes, and values are irrelevant to calculations of gravitational forces, and can have no effect on them. But can gravity be said to determine them? Can gravitational laws predict what properties they will have? Or how they will behave? Of course not. What they can do—and with great precision and without exception—is set precise quantitative limits on that activity. As with climate and heat, gravity's causal relation is structural, being at the same time constraining and empowering. It channels activity without determining it. And thus offers a vital lesson in the appreciation of the relation of natural processes to emergent properties.

3. One way to think of this is in terms of "conservation laws." Rather than determining in a deductive causal manner the consequent reality, scientific forces are better understood as specifications of what cannot happen—of forces that must be conserved throughout all transactions, and thus provide inescapable quantitative limits and structural conditions that constrain and empower the processes that emerge. Clear examples of such fundamental conservation laws are those that govern mass-energy, position-velocity, electric charge, and atomic spin. These cannot be violated. But they are not determining. They provide, as it were, necessary, but not sufficient, conditions for explaining a particular event. They lead one to think of reality as composed of an indefinite number of structural levels, each of which contributes to, but limits, the nature and scope of the activity that can be built upon it at "higher" levels. This offers us a precious clue to an ontological model of reality upon which we will build in the discussion that follows.

4. Consider, for example, the operation of evolution. Clearly, acquired characteristics are not inherited. The vehicle of hereditary transmission is the genome, the carrier of the DNA. It is the transmission of the DNA from one generation to the next that determines the genetic

endowment of the offspring, determining some traits directly, and providing an indefinite range of possible capacities for many others. But the mechanism that determines the survivability of the resultant organism is natural selection, which functions primarily at the level of the phenotype, not the genotype. The relevant questions here are the adaptability of the resulting organism *in the particular environment* within which it finds itself. The point being that while the phenotype may be in whole or in part determined by the genotype, natural selection, itself a property of the environmental field, will ultimately decide which organisms and species—hence DNA sequences—survive or not. Thus, the long-term future of the genome will be decided by the wider field in which it operates but to which it is a relatively minor contributor. Hence, the causality of evolution cannot be explained by, or simply reduced to, the operation of the constituent elements that play such a vital causal role in determination of the inherited characteristics of individuals and species. Evolution must be understood as a process of transactional fields.

The Challenge of Entropy

A remarkable thing about the Second Law of Thermodynamics is that it cannot be deduced from any other law. It is a generalization from experience that is apparently universal in scope, and yet completely independent of any other natural law. Yet it ranks as one of the most fundamental theories of contemporary natural science, and poses basic challenges to a reductionist perspective.

There are many ways to state the law. When Sadi Carnot first formulated the law in the middle of the nineteenth century, he was concerned with the impossibility of converting all of the energy generated by a steam engine into useful work. Some energy was always lost. Thus, while the First Law states that the amount of energy in a closed system remains constant—the law of the conservation of energy, since revised in accord with relativity as the conservation of mass-energy—the amount of energy available to do useful work is continually being reduced.

Why is this, one might ask. Why does heat not flow spontaneously from a colder to a hotter body? Why do organized systems tend inevitably over time to become less organized—unless, that is, they receive energy inputs from without? It's like what happens to your house unless someone comes along regularly to clean it up. It seems that organized systems are ones whose internal organization is highly improbable, and thus can only be brought about—and maintained—by doing work, which requires a continual infusion of energy. Without the necessary input of energy, the work

cannot be done and the system tends on its own to move from a less probable (and more organized) to a more probable (and less organized) state.
The key being that organization requires work, which takes energy, and
that energy cannot be converted into work with 100-percent efficiency.
Some of its capacity to do useful work is inevitably degraded.

It is this property of closed systems to move from states of lesser probability (and order) to those of greater probability (and relative disorder)
that is the meaning of entropy. Thus, the Second Law can be formulated to
say that the entropy of closed systems is continually increasing. (In so far
as the universe is a closed system, its entropy should also be increasing, as
it moves toward an equilibrium condition (of maximum probability and
minimal order) in which there is no more available energy to do useful
work. How gravity may effect this process, and whether there are unknown
capacities available for the initial creation of sources of energy—which
might be suspected in view of the original "creation" of this universe, not
to speak of the "discovery" of "dark matter" and "dark energy"—remains
to be determined.) Thus, the statement that the entropy of a closed system
is continually increasing is equivalent to the statement that the disorder
of the system is increasing. In short, "entropy is probability in disguise."[20]
Living systems, on the other hand, are states of dynamic equilibrium that
constitute islands of high order and low entropy surrounded by realms
of increasing entropic disorder and dissipation. Of course, their existence
does not in any way conflict with the operations of entropy, since living
systems are essentially energy-transfer units open to, and drawing subsistence from, their environs. Thus, their survival is ultimately bought with
useable energy extracted from those environs, often with quite deleterious
effects on those environs.

In sum, as Silver notes: "No one has yet succeeded in deriving the second law from any other law of nature. It stands on its own feet. *It is the
only law in our everyday world that gives a direction to time.*" "The laws of
motion and Maxwell's laws are unchanged by reversing time. Any process described by these laws can be run backwards without violating the
laws."[21] The same is true for relativity and quantum mechanics. Entropy
is time-irreversible, and cannot be derived from the other fundamental
laws that are in principle time-reversible. Newton's laws of motion, for
example, are completely obeyed by the behavior of gas molecules, but they
would be as well obeyed if the process ran backwards. Only probability
seems to dictate that it can't happen.[22] The mechanical laws are being
obeyed with respect to the behavior of each individual molecule, but they
cannot alone predict the behavior of the collection. Thus, Silver concludes,
"*there is no law based on the behavior of individual molecules that indicates
that mixed gases cannot spontaneously unmix. And yet there seems to be a*

natural direction for spontaneous processes ... *the direction of spontaneous, irreversible processes is always the same as that in which we think that 'time' develops.*"[23]

Thus, "we can dispense with physical laws of cause and effect, such as the laws of motion ... the direction of spontaneous processes is determined by probability, and ... the direction of time is tied to the direction of increasing probability ... (But) *probability in itself gives no preferred direction for a system to evolve.*"

The implications of the Second Law are, of course, enormous, but here I wish only to highlight one. We seem to be confronted at the very center of modern physics with an emergent system, a structurally distinct level of being—with its own laws and causal properties—whose governing laws cannot be reduced to, or deduced from, those that govern the behavior of its constituent elements. This structurally distinct level of being—with its emergent properties, not the least of which seems to be the irreversibility of time, at least at macrolevels—constitutes one of the most fundamental contours of the real world.

Quantum Uncertainty

From a classical point of view, there are several things wrong with quantum theory. Predictions are always statistical, and never for individuals; there seems to be a fundamental indeterminacy in the behavior of ultimate entities; ultimate reality seems to be both wave and particle—it acts like a wave but reveals itself only as a particle; it is fundamentally impossible to separate the observer from the observed; and some of the ultimate particles (quarks, possibly strings) seem to be completely unobservable and only to function in structured relations, never alone, while each type of ultimate particle (also including electrons and neutrinos) seems completely identical to other members of the same group,[24] without any singular properties that alone can explain the forces between them and the structures (of the universe) to which they ultimately give rise. In short, the project of classical metaphysics seems to have come up against a dead-end with quantum theory—however much it may continue knocking its head against the wall of larger and larger accelerators in its search for the ultimate constituents of reality.

"In classical physics," observes David Lindley, "we are accustomed to thinking of physical properties as having definite values, which we can try to apprehend by measurement. But in quantum physics, it is only the process of measurement that yields any definite number for a physical quantity, and the nature of quantum measurements is such that it is no longer possible to think of the underlying physical property (magnetic orientation of atoms, for example) as having any definite or reliable reality before the measurement takes place."[25]

Even more problematic than the famous collapse of the wave function, the problem of measurement, wave-particle duality, the essentially probabilistic and nonpredictable behavior of individual subatomic particles, and the fundamental equivalence of matter and energy is the problem of nonlocal causality. Nonlocality—which Einstein could never accept, but which now seems to have been experimentally confirmed—has been described as "one of the most surprising and paradoxical aspects of quantum theory in that parts of a quantum system that have been connected in the past retain an instantaneous connection even when very far apart."[26] It suggests that "two parts of the same system separated in space are linked by a quantum field."[27]

An Emerging Alternative

It is instructive to recall that the Scientific Revolution practically begins with an attack by both Descartes and Bacon on the Aristotelian notion of final causality. To explain something in terms of its final cause was to seek to explain its nature and behavior by reference to its "telos" or purpose, the reason for its existence. The emerging mechanical science of the seventeenth century is resolutely antiteleological. The behavior of things was to be explained solely by reference to their "efficient cause," those mechanisms or structures that "caused" them to behave as they do. There was no place in such descriptions or explanations for appeal to any final cause or purpose. It was precisely this approach that provided the philosophical foundation for the determinism of the emerging mechanistic science.

But this research strategy is a perfect expression of the purposeful structure of intentional thought. The logic of scientific inquiry that gave birth to a reductionist system of mechanistic determinism was itself a perfect expression of precisely that purposeful logic whose reality it was denying. As we investigate and seek to reduce mental to brain processes, we must demonstrate how physical processes can acquire those intentional capacities that are one of the most astounding characteristics and powers that mark the emergence of the mental. Nothing, at least, would seem to be more clear than that these two systems—the physical and the mental—operate in accord with distinct and opposing logics.

We may draw a clue on the nature of emergent phenomena, however, from the examples of quantum mechanics and thermodynamics. In both cases, it is the *organizational structure* or field properties of the situation that determine its mode of operation and governing laws. They provide the explanatory framework and causal nexus that is required to make sense of the nonreducible properties of the resultant behavior. In speaking of the charge of the electron, Nobel Laureate Robert Laughlin writes:

> We are accustomed to thinking of this charge as a building block of nature requiring no collective context to make sense. The experiments in question, of course, refute this idea. They reveal that the electron charge makes sense only in a collective context, which may be provided either by the empty vacuum of space, which modifies this charge the same way it modifies atomic wavelengths, or by some matter that preempts the vacuum's effects. Moreover, the preemptive ability of matter requires the organizational principles at work there to be the same as those at work in the vacuum, since otherwise the effects would be miracles.[28]
>
> The electron charge conundrum, as it turns out, is not unique. All the fundamental constants require an environmental context to make sense.[29]

This relational causality contrasts with the reductionist logic that would claim to explain the behavior of all complex systems solely by the causal properties and governing laws of its constituent elements. But what has given such initial plausibility and pervasive theoretical hold on our imagination to that reductionist paradigm? I think it is the conceptual structure classically articulated first in Aristotle's deductive logic and corresponding metaphysics, to which reference has already been made.[30]

Central to the Aristotelian analysis of rational thought is the notion of the syllogism. It has long been known that nothing objectively new can emerge out of a syllogistic argument. It is precisely the fact that the conclusion can never contain more content than is at least implicitly included in the premises that provides the syllogism with its demonstrative certainty. (This does not, of course, deny that the deductive conclusions may provide useful and informative claims that are psychologically new, but one must not confuse the order of thinking with the order of being and truth.) Syllogistic reasoning may set a standard for the structure of valid arguments, but it leaves much to be desired when it comes to creativity, imagination, and novelty. It provides a means of demonstrating the truth of a position on the basis of initial positions already agreed to, but it provides little assistance in the search for the new.

It should be obvious, therefore, that to the extent that the syllogism provides the model of rational thought, such thought must always find nonreductive theories intrinsically inadequate.[31] It is a box from which we can never exit. But on what basis can we be so sure that the world is structured along such deductive "syllogistic" lines, and that Aristotelian metaphysics reveals the structure of being. If quantum theory had done nothing else, it has provided a fundamental challenge to this reductive mode of analyzing individual behaviors, to which Symbolic Logic has added the irreducibility of relations to their constituents.

Certainly creativity and scientific innovation cannot be generated or explained by syllogistic paradigms. That was, no doubt, the point Einstein had in mind when he referred to scientific theories as "free creations of the human mind,"[32] a point to which numerous theorists have been sensitive even if they have often failed to draw this more important metaphysical conclusion.[33]

Some Additional Emergent Properties

Consider a brief exchange between two people. (The example is Bhaskar's.) Person A tells person B to give thing C to person D. B follows suit. Clearly this behavior was "caused" by the communication. Something "really" happened, that would not have happened had it not been for the verbal communication. That communication was "intentional" and "purposeful," and it had an effect in the real world. It makes no obvious sense to suggest that the physical movement of the sound waves alone could have had that causal effect.

In fact, that intentional behavior could not have taken place had there not already existed an operative language that was shared by both A and B. The private and individualized intentions of both A and B presupposed the prior existence of a socially shared set of meanings that permitted them to form those intentions, and then articulate them in a language that each could understand.

Now, we may well suppose that A, B, and D are physical systems with physical properties that can be well and accurately described in the terms of physics, chemistry, biology, physiology, neural physiology, and brain chemistry. I am quite willing to suppose, in accord with the best of current science, that there is "nothing more" than such physical systems at work constituting A, B, and D. But can one then suppose that these systems can *on their own terms* adequately account for the behavior in question. Where comes the intentionality of the individuals in question? And where comes the linguistic meanings that the individuals presuppose? In short, the meaningful behavior of the individuals presupposes a relatively autonomous social realm, while the intention to communicate presupposes a relatively autonomous individual realm, none reducible to the other.[34] Our challenge is to make sense of these relatively autonomous realms as emergent properties of natural systems—subject to, but not determined by, the original conditions set down by the big bang.

In this last example, we have suggested the existence of at least three distinct and nonreducible causal structures: the psychological-individual, the sociological-linguistic, and the neurophysiological and biochemical.

The first is in general the realm of consciousness; the second, the realm of mind and meanings; and the last, the realm of natural processes, including living things, which, no doubt, deserve their own realm, of which more will be explained later.

The Nature of Emergence

In the foregoing discussion, I suggested problems intrinsic to the reductionist paradigm, and offered several examples of areas in which it seemed to fail. I want now to attempt to elucidate more precisely what I mean by emergence, and to provide criteria for the determination of emergent structures and phenomena.[35]

Emergent phenomena are ones whose nature and operation cannot be completely explained by a description of the behavior of their constituent parts. They are systems of structured networks of relationships that have properties quite different from those of their "constituent elements." This means that the emergent has properties, powers, and modes of operation[36] that: (a) are not possessed by the elements that make it up and (b) cannot be completely explained by, or reduced to, the properties and causal powers of those elements alone. Rather the properties and causal powers of the emergent are systemic. They are properties of the structure of the system. They operate in accordance with a causal logic that is particular to the emergent structures, and that requires the use of concepts and principles that cannot be completely replaced by those that describe the behavior of its constituent elements. Furthermore, the emergent's systemic properties and causal powers will usually have consequences that can actually determine the behavior of the very elements that compose it.[37]

To think of this in very specific terms, consider an effort to provide a reductive explanation of a purportedly emergent phenomenon. It would have to use only terms and theories that were drawn from the levels of explanation that were appropriate to the constituent elements. The only new terms it could use would be ones that served as shorthand expressions for complex processes that were "nothing but" the logical and/or causal consequence of the activity of the elements. It could not create new terms for properties or causal powers that were not directly applicable to—or explainable in terms of—its original domain. An example of a completely adequate theoretical reduction would seem to be that which explains heat as "nothing but" the expression of the average speed of the motion of the associated molecules. "Heat" is generally claimed to be only a shorthand expression for the impact of that average molecular motion.[38]

In a preliminary discussion of explanatory reductions, Searle distinguishes between eliminative and noneliminative reductions.[39] An eliminative reduction is one like that which explains (and thus explains away the apparently autonomous reality of) sunsets, which are simply the result of our stationary location on an Earth that is rotating on its axis as it revolves around the Sun. On the other hand, a noneliminative reduction is one that causally explains the real emergence of a new property. Such an emergent property is explained by the behavior of its lower level elements—but it is not itself a property of those lower level elements, for example, solidity or liquidity, the atoms of which are neither solid nor liquid, or color as the expression of distinct frequencies of light that are not themselves colorful. But the question here is, are the higher-level qualities and behaviors completely explainable in terms of the structure of the constituent elements? Or do we have to smuggle in the concepts of solidity and liquidity into that underlying level in order to carry out the explanatory reduction?[40]

Of course, the discussion of the reality of emergence is not meant to deny the dependence of emergent phenomena on the processes out of which they emerge. Quite the contrary. It would be appropriate, at least at first, to think of this as a process of layering, in which emergents build up and are constrained by the powers of the underlying structures. In fact, emergent phenomena are best thought of as themselves elements of emergent structures that express the unique organizational properties and powers of distinctive fields or levels of reality. When one speaks of these powers as being systemic, what is meant is that a structured field emerges with its own distinctive properties and causal powers. This field emerges out of the elements that, in constituting it, condition both its appearance and its mode of operation, providing both enabling conditions and operative limitations. The emergent cannot violate the laws that govern the underlying field, but those laws are not sufficient to explain or initially predict the behavior of the emergent field. Thus, gravity conditions life, and no life can violate gravitational laws, but gravity does not determine what living things do. "For a *diachronic* (that is, temporally causal) *explanatory reduction*, in which the processes of the formation of the higher-order entities are reconstructed and explained in terms of the principles governing the elements out of which they are formed, is compatible with *synchronic* (that is, contemporaneous) *emergence,* in which the higher-order principles cannot be completely explained in terms of the lower-order ones. Note that it is to the former that biologists are committed in investigating the origins of life (or engineers in constructing machines), but it is to the denial of the latter that the materialist is committed."[41]

Language, for example, requires brain cells to transmit electrical signals, but none of those cells have or understand language. Their behavior operates in accord with the causal structures of neurological networks, but when involved in language activity, their behavior follows the patterns dictated by the embedded meanings, none of which can be at odds with those neurological structures, but the meaning patterns of which can only be adequately explained by drawing upon the mental structure of meanings—including the syntactic and semantic structure of language, and the socially rooted psychic intentions of the language user. Hence, a scientifically adequate causal account will have to incorporate explicit consideration of the structured field of objective meanings embedded in the culture as well as the unique personal concerns of the individual.[42]

An emergent property or structure thus functions primarily in accordance with its own logic of operations. It requires a specification of the structural boundaries that determine what is and what is not within the domain in question. The emergent field operates in accordance with a causal logic that is to some extent *sui generis*. It determines and partially explains the behavior of *its* constituents, but only on its own terms—even though it will undoubtedly and of necessity draw upon the causal powers of the underlying fields.

Emergent properties are nowhere more evident than in the phase transformations that naturally abound in daily living. In phase transformations, the underlying atoms undergo a structural transformation in the chemical bonds that gives rise to complex substances with distinct properties and modes of operation that are not characteristics of the underlying material. Nothing is more pervasive than the regular transformations of water occasioned by changes in temperature (and/or pressure) from ice to steam, or even plasma. These transformations occur at specific conjunctures of temperature and pressure that occasion the organizational restructuring of the same chemical molecule, thus realizing different properties and modes of interaction. Another graphic example is that provided by graphite and diamond. The former is one of the softest materials known, used as a lubricant and as the writing element in pencils, while the latter is one of the hardest materials known, yet both are composed of the same element, carbon, in which only the structure of the chemical bonds is different. Clearly, then, the resultant emergent properties are not properties of the isolated carbon atom, but of the structural organization of that element into these distinct substances.[43]

In most all of these cases, the (diachronic) causal conditions that lead to the phase transformation can be spelled out with great precision, but the resultant (synchronic emergent) properties are not logically deducible from the properties of the constituents, but are systemic properties of the emergent substance, subject only to the boundary conditions or conservation laws for the constituent elements.

Laughlin makes this point quite nicely:

> The phases of matter—among them the familiar liquid, vapor, and solid— are organizational phenomena. Many people are surprised to learn this, since phases seem so basic and familiar, but it is quite true. Trusting the ice [when skating] is less like buying gold than buying stock in an insurance company. If the organizational structure of the company were to fail for some reason, one's investment would vanish, for there is no physical asset underneath. Similarly, if the organization of a crystalline solid—the orderly arrangement of the atoms into a lattice—were to fail, the rigidity would vanish, since there is no physical asset underneath it either. The property we value in either case is the order. Most of us would prefer not to think we are entrusting our lives to an organization, but we do it every day. Without economies, for example, which are purely organizational phenomena, civilization would collapse and all of us would starve.[44]

A Metaphysical Caveat

I have been arguing for the existence of completely emergent fields that are logically irreducible to their constituents. It is important to note, however, that there would also seem to be many situations for which field theories would be the most appropriate tools to describe a reality that *is* in principle reducible to the operation of its constituent parts, though in practical fact too complex to be so described. Examples of the latter might include anything from aspects of the reduction of chemistry to physics, to strategies for playing chess. For example, Steven Weinberg has written that:

> after the development of quantum mechanics in the mid-1920s, when it became possible to calculate for the first time … the spectrum of the hydrogen atom and the binding energy of hydrogen, many physicists immediately concluded that all of chemistry is explainable by quantum mechanics and the principle of electrostatic attraction between electrons and atomic nuclei … Experience has borne this out; we can now deduce the properties of fairly complicated molecules—not molecules as complicated as proteins or DNA… But chemical phenomena will never be entirely explained in this way, and so chemistry persists as a separate discipline.[45]

To which, however, we might well counterpose the previous quotation (and extensive endnote) from Laughlin on the irreducibly structural nature of these levels of reality. The resolution of this issue is unclear to me.

An extremely interesting example of this "metaphysical caveat" is the so-called cellular automaton phenomenon, in which the logical behavior of the elements can be spelled out in complete detail, but the resulting behavior of the complex system expresses "emergent" properties that can neither be predicted nor anticipated.[46] Thus, the behavior of such systems would seem to be logically predictable in principle, not revealing any relational properties that are themselves emergent, and yet in practice completely unpredictable on its own terms and in need of a distinct field-theoretic interpretation.[47]

Only empirical inquiry joined to careful philosophical attention to the logical status of the employed concepts can determine the truth of a particular theory, and hence the appropriateness of a particular approach—whether structural and field-theoretic or not—in each specific field of inquiry. Our primary argument is to the effect that there seem to exist quite important nonreducible relational fields that require a distinct field-theoretic metaphysic for their interpretation. But such field-theoretic frameworks would also seem to be called for by the internal complexity of many areas, such as gliders, that are not themselves logically emergent. Each of these two types of systems would require in practice the application of an ecological vision and field-theoretic framework, although they would ultimately pursue different fundamental logics, thus pointing toward distinct research agendas and explanatory frameworks, and bearing quite distinct metaphysical and ethical import.

The Metaphysics of Historicized Fields

If there is something fundamentally wrong with the "classical" substantive metaphysics, what then is/are the alternative(s)?[48] It would be presumptuous to claim that there can only be one alternative. Certainly I have no intention of trying to offer a "transcendental deduction" of any such Truth. My intent is only to present a theoretical framework that seems to be suggested by, and to make coherent sense of, the converging results of modern theory and practice. First, I wish to set forth that alternative metaphysical frame. Then, I will suggest how by reposing fundamental conceptions of theory and practice, it may offer a more constructive way to address pervasive concerns of the contemporary world.

I can begin with the aforementioned Einsteinian identification of matter and energy, as spelled out in that most famous equation, $e = mc^2$. If matter and energy are equivalent, then clearly from the perspective of relativity, either can be expressed as a function of the other. Energy can be understood as matter "unleashed"; or matter as energy "congealed." But neither is "basic" or fundamental—or both are![49] Thus, it would be as appropriate to see the world as "made up" of patterned energy as of structured "things." In the words of Nobel Laureate Leon Lederman, "The physical world is a fabric of events."[50]

"It was Einstein who radically changed the *way* people thought about nature," continues Lederman, "moving away from the mechanical viewpoint of the nineteenth century toward the elegant contemplation of the underlying symmetry principles of the laws of physics in the twentieth century."[51] Consider Einstein's own statement of the problem:

Matter represents vast stores of energy and ... energy represents matter. We cannot, in this way, distinguish qualitatively between matter and field, since the distinction between mass and energy is not a qualitative one. By far the greatest part of energy is concentrated in matter; but the field surrounding the particle also represents energy, though in an incomparably smaller quantity. We could therefore say: matter is where the concentration of energy is great, field where the concentration of energy is small.... . There is no sense in regarding matter and field as two qualities quite different from each other. We cannot imagine a definite surface separating distinctly field and matter.

The same difficulty arises for the charge and its field. It seems impossible to give an obvious qualitative criterion for distinguishing between matter and field or charge and field ... [Thus] we cannot build physics on the basis of the matter concept alone.... . Could we not reject the concept of matter and build pure field physics? What impresses our senses as matter is really great concentration of energy into a comparatively small space. We could regard matter as the regions in space where the field is extremely strong. In this way a new philosophical background could be created. Its final aim would be the explanation of all events in nature by structure laws valid always and everywhere ... There would be no place, in our new physics, for both field and matter, field being the only reality. This new view is suggested by the great achievements of field physics, by our success in expressing the laws of electricity, magnetism, gravitation in the form of structure laws, and finally by the equivalence of mass and energy.[52]

But this is still not the quantum world. In fact, contemporary physics speaks sometimes of fundamental particles, sometimes of basic energy packets, and sometimes of waves and frequencies of energy. It even speaks of the basic reality of possibility, as, for example, of the possibility of finding a particle at a specific location or with a specific velocity. But, note, not of finding both the precise velocity and location of the same "particle" at the same time, due to the Uncertainty Principle. That Uncertainty Principle itself is open to many interpretations, not unrelated to the fact that the reality being tested for seems to have properties that approximate waves of probability in which velocity and location are two of many pairs of complimentary properties. This also suggests the possibility of seeing The Real as patterned waves of energy, described in terms of frequencies and amplitudes. But then the greater and more frequent the amplitude—and consequently, the more discrete the appearance of its energy packet—the more its appearance approximates a discrete object or atomic thing.[53]

I will return to these considerations and their significance later. At present, my concern is simply to use them as a jumping-off point that not only underscores the inappropriateness of the traditional metaphysics but also begins to suggest an alternative.[54] What a focus on the fundamental nature of energy makes clearer than does the exclusive focus on matter is the need to step back from an excessive concentration on the individual entity in order to grasp the dynamic pattern that is being displayed. It is fairly clear with respect to energy that it expresses itself *temporally* as well as spatially, and that it is not *static*. It changes regularly in space and time. In fact, for Einstein, the relativity equations require appeal to a "fourth dimension," that of space-time, thus underscoring their essential unity. But as soon as one takes time as fundamental too—as Newton and classical physics did not—then the dynamic pattern of change (even perhaps of the basic "laws" and "forces" themselves) comes to the fore.

An energy pattern is spread out over space and time. It is not a point particle, nor does it exist at a single location. It would be as true to say that the things that appear are as much a result of the pattern of forces as that the forces are an expression of the action of the things. In fact, there seems to be no need to reduce one to the other. The equivalence of matter and energy is just another way of expressing the essential unity of matter-energy as of space-time. We might thus begin to reconceptualize the reality of matter-energy as a dynamic force field. By field we understand a dynamically structured temporally unfolding pattern of activity and events.[55] As we will see, such fields can be causally and empirically layered, with qualities being primarily determined by the space-time field, only secondarily attributable to the things that emerge themselves as field qualities. Thus, fields themselves have emergent laws that describe their mode of operation, distinct from, and nonreducible to, the qualities and laws of their generative "parts."[56]

> Since principles of organization—or, more precisely, their consequences—can be laws, these can themselves organize into new laws, and these into still newer laws, and so on. The laws of electron motion beget the laws of thermodynamics and chemistry, which beget the laws of crystallization, which beget the laws of rigidity and plasticity, which beget the laws of engineering. The natural world is thus an interdependent hierarchy of descent.[57]

Another way of expressing these ideas is to say that we are dealing with a world of patterned and layered fields of matter-energy in space-time. These may be conceptually reconfigured by perspectival intentional interventions, that is, as seen from different perspectives and in accord with diverse intentions. In such cases, the more concentrated the field, the more distinctly individualized its "elements" will appear—taking the form of things—and the more distinct the being and action of one "field" is from that of another; the less concentrated (or more dissipated or diffuse) the field, the more it merges with neighboring fields, or things.[58]

By perspectival intentional interventions, I mean to highlight the integral relation between the perspective or space-time location of the thinking subject and the meaningful structure of the intended objective field being described. This must not, however, be taken to suggest either that the subject simply constitutes the meaning of the object or that "everything is relative to the 'observer.'" Rather it should be taken at least in part as a restatement of Einstein's discussion of "frames of reference," the import of which is that, while the values of variables such as position in space and time may be different for different observers, the fundamental laws of nature are invariant between frames of reference. But the frame of reference must be self-reflectively included in the description of the situation in question. Of this, and its relation to metaphysics and social theory, more will be explained later.

These thoughts are just initial suggestions or outlines of the plausibility of an alternative metaphysical paradigm. That paradigm means to suggest that we should no longer view The Real as essentially "thingafied," as a coordination of objectified nouns engaging in "verbal" interactions. Rather, we have to replace the metaphysics of "things and persons" with one of the dynamically structured patterns of matter-energy in space-time.

To get an initial sense of the significance of this change, consider traditional Indo-European languages. What would be the metaphysically appropriate alternative to "'it' is raining?" John Dewey had once suggested replacing nouns with verbs and adverbs in order to express the processive nature of reality, but clearly that will not do. It is not a question of reducing things to activities, however much that does assist in breaking the conceptual (and perceptual) stranglehold of the substantive metaphysics. We need to appreciate the experienced reality of space-time that William James captured with his famous description of the experience of "thunder-crashing-in-on-silence-and-contrasting-with-it." James understood that our traditional conceptualizations made nonsense of this lived experience—however inadequate his own first "pragmatic," and then "radical empiricist," efforts at reconceptualization.[59]

It is not for an activity to replace an object or event, but for a "patterned whole" to be constituted by the active emergent field elements. It is, of course, essential, however, to see that the logic of the operations of that "whole" includes, as well as is expressed and transformed by, the existence and activity of those "things" that are intrinsic to its existence. "The world," comments Heisenberg, "appears as a complicated tissue of events, in which connections of different kinds alternate or overlap or combine and thereby determine the texture of the whole."[60]

> "What are these corpuscles really?" Schrodinger answers " … at the most, it may be permissible to think of them as more or less temporary entities within the wave field, whose form [Gestalt], though, and structural manifold in the widest sense, ever repeating themselves in the same manner, are so clearly and sharply determined by the wave laws that many processes take place as if those temporary entities were substantial permanent beings."[61]

Harris develops this point:

> What is here making itself felt is the effect of the transition from classical to quantum conceptions. The abandonment of the notion of hard, point-like, particulate constituents of matter is forced upon us by the quantum approach, and many eminent scientists have expressed the view that the explanation of physical phenomena is not to be reached by analysis of them into separable, additive entities, events and forces, but only through the recognition and study of structured totalities, which are neither simple unities nor dissectible aggregates, but are diversified wholes of distinguishable though inseparable constituents. Max Planck writes: "Modern physics has taught us that the nature of any system cannot be discovered by dividing it into its component parts and studying each part by itself, since such a method often implies the loss of important properties of the system. We must keep our attention fixed on the whole and on the inter-connection between the parts."[62]

Lindley elaborates:

> In classical physics, we are accustomed to thinking of physical properties as having definite values, which we can try to apprehend by measurement. But in quantum physics, it is only the process of measurement that yields any definite number for a physical quantity, and the nature of quantum measurements is such that it is no longer possible to think of the underlying physical property (magnetic orientation of atoms, for example) as having any definite or reliable reality before the measurement takes place.[63]

He further comments that in view of the Stern-Gerlach experiment, it would seem that the property of spin cannot simply be an intrinsic property of the point particle electron but somehow a property of its interaction with the electromagnetic field.[64]

In other words, to reinforce the point we already made, an electron by itself is not described by one unique wave function; the way you describe it, the wave function you use, depends on what you plan to measure. And although the wave function obviously depends on the state of the electron, and on what you know about it, it can be misleading to think that the wave function somehow "is" the electron. It's better to say that a wave function describes a system—the thing being measured and the measurement being made—rather than being an independent description only of the thing being measured.[65]

In sum, in the words of Professor Stephen Pollack, "Every particle in nature can be thought of as a ripple in a field."[66]

Further, that field or "whole" is not itself completely set off from its surrounding fields. Here is one place where the importance of the above-mentioned notion of "intentional interventions" comes into play—and this *is* precisely the deeper truth being reached for by James's "pragmatism" and Dewey's "instrumentalism." For every field is itself a "whole" that is but a thing-like emergent from the more encompassing field of which it is a "part." In a deep sense, ultimately there is only one field, and that is the entire universe. That is the point of discussions of the gravitational attraction among planets and galaxies, and of the significance of questions about the expansion, stability, or contraction of the universe. But different "forces" have different effective ranges, qualities, and logics. And that refers also to the structure and properties of the field of which they are the forces. Such was the import of our prior discussion of the distinct but related questions of the perspectival nature of intentional interventions and of the objectively layered structures of forces and processes. It is precisely that analysis that provides the framework for an approach to the problem of freedom.

Freedom

The establishment of the semiautonomous reality of emergent structures provides the framework for a solution to the so-far intractable problem of the relation of freedom and determinism. To put it concisely, freedom is precisely such a nonreducible power of an emergent field constituted by complex, highly integrated energy exchanging self-maintaining and replenishing self-conscious life forms. It is thus subject to all of the deterministic causal forces that operate at the underlying levels, while drawing upon, and being empowered by, them in its own operation. But it is responsive to the imperatives of its own constitution, the experience of which is an objective and intrinsic property of the constituting field, and is neither reducible to the operation of its members nor explainable solely in terms of the behavior of its constituents. Thus, freedom is a property of the system, and not of any or all of its elements. It is realized by being it—and thus its reality is grounded in the *sui generis* experience of subjectivity. Let us now explain this more clearly and in greater detail, beginning with a definition of determinism, with which it is to be contrasted.

"A theory may be said to be deterministic if, using only the theory and a complete description of the state of the system, every subsequent state of the system is logically inevitable." Thus, "for every event there must be a cause, and so, given the conditions preceding the event, and the laws of nature, every event must be in principle predictable and in practice inevitable."[67] If freedom is to be anything other than a misleading illusion, it must involve the capacity of the organism to act in ways that are other than simple logical consequences of the preexisting conditions and operative natural laws. Hence, the free being must be able to initiate a causal chain that in principle is not simply the predictable causal consequence of the prior situation, and thus for which it is ultimately responsible.

It should be clear from this that freedom is the capacity of an organism to formulate by and for itself plans of action and to select from among them, and thus be responsible for what it does. It is thus clear how freedom is the foundation of moral responsibility and human dignity. What makes human freedom ontologically possible is the existence of self-consciousness, the capacity to treat oneself as an object of one's own reflection, placing oneself conceptually within the field of meaningful objects and possible activities. (We are not here addressing the issue of the relation of human freedom to the wider biological context of the capacities for self-determination of less complicated conscious living systems.)

No doubt, the possibility of the emergence of self-conscious beings is conditioned by the development of highly complex and internally networked biological systems. All the laws that govern such systems no doubt govern (and constrain the possibilities of) the activity of self-conscious beings. But self-consciousness is not a property of the elements of the living system of which it is composed, any more than information is contained in any one of the neurons that compose a neural network. Rather, in both cases, the emergent phenomena are field properties of the system. Consciousness is the subjective experience of a system with a sufficiently complex and adequately integrated biological network.[68] Such a system acquires properties and powers that its constituents do not themselves possess. In the words of Bennett and Hacker:

> What neuroscience can do is to explain, for normal human beings, how it is possible for them to be open to reason. But it cannot explain the rationale

of human actions in the particular case, or elucidate what makes a certain reason a good reason. It can identify necessary conditions for the exercise of human capacities. But it does not follow that it is, or ever will be, in the position to specify a set of neural conditions that are sufficient conditions for characteristic human action in the circumstances of life. To explain typical human behaviour, one must operate at the higher, irreducible level of normal descriptions of human actions and their various forms of explanation and justification in terms of reasons and motives (as well as causes). These descriptions will cite multitudinous factors: past and prospective events that in given circumstances may constitute the agent's reasons for action; the agent's desires, intentions, goals and purposes; his tendencies, habits and customs; and the moral and social norms to which he conforms.[69]

Such emergent field properties of the constituent natural elements require no appeal to nonnatural elements. Thus, we can say, with Searle, "that brains cause minds," and "that minds are features of brains." (There is no reason in principle why such self-conscious natural beings could not be "artificially" created in the laboratory—or in any other appropriate venue—once sufficient knowledge of the constituent elements has been acquired. But any being so "created" would then possess a comparable degree of self-conscious autonomy.) But Searle's definition of features leaves the issue ill-defined, because he fails to adequately address the issue of emergence—and thus, also, he remains incapable of adequately addressing the issue of freedom. Instead, his "biological naturalism" looks suspiciously like a sophisticated biological reductionism that encounters freedom as an embarrassing surd.[70]

If we take our emergent naturalism seriously, however, it is to be expected that for each and every activity of consciousness, there will be a corresponding activity of the brain. This no more justifies the claim that minds are "nothing but" brains than would the claim that life is nothing but the activity of atoms since living beings are not made up of anything but atoms. The point in each case is that the emergent system has properties and powers that determine a mode of operation that the elements themselves do not possess.[71] This resultant mode of operation has objective and distinctive effects in the real world that cause its constituent elements to behave differently. The logic of its operation produces objective laws that are distinctive to its field of being. Of course, intervention is always possible at the underlying levels, and such intervention, in effecting the constituent elements, will obviously affect the consequent operation of the field. Thus, life can be deranged by changes in types and levels of radiation, and consciousness can be similarly affected by hormonal changes. But to establish that such biological processes are necessary preconditions of the operation of conscious activity is not the same as equating or reducing one to the other.[72]

It is further to be noted that there is no reason to suppose that any specific mental event is correlated with any particular neuronal or brain event. It is perfectly conceivable that very different brain events in the same or different persons can be identified with the same mental event. "Not only is it the case," observes Bhaskar, "that the same social or psychological states can be realized in a number, probably infinite, of different ways, but (worse) the reverse, viz. multiple social or psychological correlates of psychological or physiological states, also seems to hold."[73]

This is quite similar to the conception among cognitive scientists of "multiple realizability." That notion holds that a computer program can be carried out by an indefinite number of physical systems, so long as they have certain minimal properties. But that means that there is no necessary causal relation between the physical system and the operation of the program. Rather the system provides the necessary conditions for the implementation of the program, but the program provides the "logic" that determines the "meaning" of its operations. This provides a good model for the relation of the brain to the mind.[74] The brain makes possible mental operations but does not determine their meaning. Their meaning is intrinsic to the system of language in use—which system only "uses" the brain as the apparatus for implementation—as well as to the wider social, biological, and natural world by which its activity is constituted as a nodal point. Thus, analysis of the hardware would not explain the meaning of the operation.

The point here is that there is no one-to-one correlation between brain states and mental states. The same person may have the same idea at different times, or different people may have the same idea, or the same thought may be expressed by the same person in different languages. The logic of the thought and the biology of the system operate in accord with different logics. Most centrally for the issue at hand, conscious beings engage in purposeful behavior, operating in accord with principles and meanings to which their biology is deaf.[75] But that behavior can have profound effects on the very possibility of that biological system to survive—as our prior discussion of evolution made clear.

> Cognitive processes would seem to be differentiated from non-cognitive ones in that they are at least typically (but not necessarily) *conscious, referential* (that is about something), and *intentional* ... But ... it cannot be said that brain processes are *about* anything, that they are meaningful, or that they are true or false, or that they are *of* or *for* something (as is the case of beliefs and desires respectively.)[76]

There are, of course, important disanalogies between computers and programs, brains and minds. Most crucial, of course, is the existence of consciousness and purpose. Those are properties of the particular "hardware" that brains seem to be. The argument for multiple realizability seeks only to show the distinction between program and machine implementation. The quality of the implementing machine will determine not only its capacities to carry out the program, but also its relation to that program and the wider environment within which it operates. At this point, we are beginning to address the systemic field and the logic of *its* operation.[77]

Self-consciousness is itself an emergent property of consciousness and minds, each of whose terms refer to distinctive and complexly interrelated field properties. But it is important now to be quite precise in our use of words. We must clearly distinguish minds from consciousness, and the latter from self-consciousness. Very briefly, consciousness refers to the remarkable capacity of numerous living systems not only to be sensitive and able to respond to external (and internal) stimuli, but also to maintain the experienced presence of, as well as integrate from several distinct sources, those stimuli through time. Thus, a quality of subjective awareness of an experienced field of objects and activities emerges. While subjectively experienced as essentially unified, with its own distinctive affective quality, this emergent field is perceived as a patterned and bounded series of colors and shapes, with more or less distinctive elements appearing within a sustaining background—as with the famous figure-ground relation so familiar in Gestalt Psychology.

By consciousness we thus refer to the capacity of some living systems not only to be sensitive to stimuli but also to be able to sustain the presence of such sensitivity through time, beyond the moment of stimulation. It is in the "internalization" of the stimuli wherein lies the emergence of consciousness beyond the simple capacity for response. Clearly, this is a process that allows for vast and subtle degrees of difference, which have emerged and developed over time.[78]

With this internalization, a field of awareness begins to emerge. Elements take on relations for the subject within its field of awareness that their initiating stimuli did not initially have among themselves, including relations between present stimuli and recalled echoes of previous stimuli. With the expanding range and complexity of the organism comes an increased range, complexity, and potential sophistication in the experience of consciousness. Furthermore, instead of responding directly to the initiating stimuli, the organism can respond to the elements of its awareness, reorganizing them in accordance with its organismic demands. Consciousness thus refers to this capacity of certain living systems to experience an "inner" world as well as an "outer" world, and to reorder that "inner" world in a manner different from that of the "outer" one. Thus, we encounter two distinct operative "logics," with the emerging "inner" one responding to demands initially dictated by the makeup of the experiencing subject. It is here that we begin to see the emergence of the ultimately profound gap between the object of experience and the experience of the object. Furthermore, there is no reason to assume that the order and weighting of the elements of the subject's awareness will be the same as they would to another who was viewing or recording those same elements, but not experiencing them—or even to the same subject who is experiencing the exact same sequence of external events on two or more different occasions.

Such consciousness is clearly distinct from, but would seem to be a necessary precondition of, the emergence of mind. By mind is meant the capacity of living beings to "make sense" of their experience. "Making sense," in the most rudimentary sense, involves one aspect of consciousness suggesting or being linked with another. Initially, it might have involved something as simple as the kind of quasi-automatic associations discussed by Hume, namely those connections of images generated by resemblance, (spatial or temporal) contiguity, or causality. Any kind of juxtapositions from one or several senses might have suggested connections, where one "image" suggested another. Meaning would seem to have emerged out of experienced linkages, becoming an independent reality to the extent to which the "mental" connections were not biologically fixed and determined. As one "idea" becomes "linked" first with one, then with several ideas, and then with increasingly complex networks of ideas, it gains "meaning," that is, the capacity to suggest, refer to, symbolize, implicate, stand in for, prepare for, predict, or "prime," and therefore increase the likelihood of ideation in the immediate future, et cetera.

Meaning, however, does not reside in the idea itself, but in the network of connections. It is a property of the system more than of its elements. The systemic field determines its range, scope, complexity, sophistication, functionality, and affective tonality. As the field becomes structured, so does the range and sophistication of its capacity to generate meanings. Language is precisely such a structured field of meanings that determines the capacity of the participating consciousness to entertain and relate meaningfully to itself and its environment. Thus, while there can be no meanings without conscious beings for whom meaning exists—those, for example, who are the "bearers" of the language—the structure of the language or meaning-field predetermines what and how those consciousnesses can think. In short, the reality of language is not reducible to, or explainable solely in terms of, the operative reality of the conscious beings who real-ize the language. Thus, while consciousness is irreducibly subjective, meaning (and language) is irreducibly social in nature, while "mind" is simply the capacity to be aware of, to employ, or to operate on or with, meanings.[79]

Self-consciousness involves the capacity of an organism to be at the same time—in one unitary act—both the subject and object of its own awareness: to be an object "for itself." Little is more commonplace and yet mysterious than this taken-for-granted experience of everyday human existence. I will, of course, have much more to say of the existential significance of this experience later on. Here I simply wish to be clear about its nature and essential relation to consciousness and mind. It would seem that self-consciousness presupposes the existence of at least a rudimentary language or structured meaning-field. For it would seem to require some minimal sense of self about which to be reflexively conscious. And that would seem to require at least some quasi-linguistic capacity to use signs that would allow for the designation of an object such as one's self. Here is not the place for a discussion of the significance of the self, and its relation to its ambient biological and social field. But it is important to see that the capacity for self-consciousness seems to require that the conscious subject be able to have some more-or-less clear and articulate sense of its being, specifiably distinguishable from the other beings within its field of awareness. In short, self-consciousness would seem to be consciousness mediated by mind, however elemental, and thus irreducibly social.

We are thus confronted with a unique emergent field characterized by both irreducible subjectivity and sociality, neither of which, furthermore, are reducible one to the other. Consciousness *is* the subjective structure of that experience. Self-consciousness is the meaningful organization of that experience as it locates itself within its own meaning-field. This field, by a necessity that is social as well as biological, must overlap with other such fields, and thus is, in principle, to some extent sharable—that is, it is the objective basis of the possibility of communication. But it is, at the same time, inescapably subjective—and, where self-consciousness is in question, quite personal—and thus inevitably private, and to some extent inaccessible to the thought of another. We might well observe the (brain) processes that make this experience possible, but not the experience itself. We can observe the causal conditions but not the qualitative reality. We cannot experience the experience of the other—we cannot *be* the other, only *know* what natural processes are taking place—and hence, we cannot know the meaning that that experience has for the other. The other's intention—what it "means" and what it proposes to do—is an intrinsic property of its field of conscious awareness. It is *not* a property of the causal conditions of its awareness. Thus, an objective knowledge of those conditions is not equivalent to a subjective awareness of their meaning. Hence, from a knowledge of those conditions, nothing necessarily follows about the meaning, intentions, or likely behavior that will emerge from that experience.[80]

We can see the profound significance of this emergent reality by contrasting the operative logics of natural or biological processes with that of
human intentionality and purposeful behavior. To take but the simplest
case: billiard balls operate in accord with fairly straightforward principles
of causal determination—using Newton's laws of motion, calculate the
force acting and the inertial mass being acted upon along with the coef-
ficient of friction and the resultant behavior can be fairly accurately
predicted. The event follows rather straightforward causal principles,
without any consideration of purpose or goal. It might be suggested that
certain biological reflexes operate similarly—and perhaps, even certain
mental associations might follow a similar law of quasi-automatic causal
connection.[81]

Contrast that situation with the linguistic (and behavioral) pattern
determined by the desire to create an articulate sentence, however rudimentary. Here the connections between words are determined not by
their physical or causal properties, but by their meaning. The operative
logic of discourse "makes sense"; it organizes thoughts, feelings, images,
and projects in accord with a logic of intention, determined both by the
purpose of the subject and by the structure of the language. This intention,
while in no sense violating the laws of physics or biology, can determine
a distinctive course of action that will causally redirect those very natural
processes that are the conditions of its possibility. The behavior of the
natural scientist operates in a manner quite different from the causal laws
he or she is seeking to unearth. In fact, the organization of an experiment
presupposes the capacity of the inquirer to reorganize experience and
restructure events in accord with a coherent set of meanings that is meant
to produce an expectant result—one that would not have occurred but for
the organized experimental situation that reflects the coherent application of a theoretically based system of elaborated meanings. The inquirer
will "mind" the results to see whether or not the anticipated structure
of meanings is confirmed by the causal behavior of the experimentally
produced result. Thus, two quite distinctive operative logics are at work.
The distinctive logic of intentionality is grounded in the unique being
of self-conscious mentality, itself the ground and possibility of freedom.
Freedom is thus precisely the nonreducible determination of intention,
meaning, and actions that emerge from the uniquely personal reality of
self-conscious subjectivity.[82]

This discussion prepares the ground for the reframing of the social
sciences as dealing with an emergent, nonreducible field that must be
addressed primarily in terms of socialized meanings, that is, hermeneuti-
cally. Thus, any potentially adequate social theory will have to consider the
manner in which the subjects "tell their story," thus scientifically grounding

a dramatic and existential interpretation of individual and social life. Such a life can only take form, structure, meaning, and direction within the meaning frame of the ongoing drama of a specific historically institution-alized culture. But of this, more will be explained later.

A New Causal Paradigm

No doubt, the effort to offer an alternative causal logic strikes deep at the core of our inherited metaphysic. And rightfully generates much resistance. It seems so strange and counterintuitive. It seems to leave much wanting. I am claiming that the causal deductive logic that has undergirded Western thought for more than 2,500 years is inadequate, has led us down numer-ous blind alleys, and has left us knocking our heads against the proverbial brick wall in countless theoretical and practical domains, of which the free will or determinism conundrum is only the most obvious and intractable. "Like other things one does not talk about, unclear thinking about what is fundamental can come back to haunt us later on. Its most insidious effect is to lead us out into the desert by inducing us to search on smaller and smaller scales for meaning that is not there."[83] But the proposed alternative will no doubt leave many people scratching their heads, and feeling that something is missing. Where is that tight deductive causality that predicts the behavior of the event as the logical consequence of the statement of existing conditions and specification of operable laws? Where is that dis-section of complexes into self-evident and indubitable atomic simples out of which we can step-by-step reconstitute and thus fully and completely explain the resultant complex? What kind of determination can the past provide to the future? Haven't we simply waved our wand, overlooked the practical details, and created an illusory and quasi-magical field that none can see, or "sink their teeth into," and offered that as a new causal structure? Haven't we just obtained our results—and "solved" our meta-physical and practical problems—by giving up all pretension of seeking to completely understand the processes at work?

We might well recall here the now classical argument between Einstein and Neils Bohr over the adequacy of quantum mechanics. Einstein was convinced that quantum mechanics was an incomplete theory of reality because it was incapable in principle of predicting the behavior of a single quantum particle. Its theories only allowed statistical predictions for the behavior of aggregates. It was this situation that led to Einstein's famous remark that "God does not play dice with the universe." He was convinced that there were "hidden variables" that the theory failed to include that, if included, would complete quantum mechanics by allowing for precise predictions of the behavior of each individual particle.[84] For it was clearly

Einstein's view that only such a classically deterministic theory could possibly be adequate. Much of the last thirty years of his life was dedicated to the design of thought experiments—the most famous being the Einstein-Podolsky-Rosen experiment—that sought to show, without success, the fundamental incompleteness of quantum theory. Einstein's metaphysical faith in the priority of Aristotelian logic is one of the key reasons for calling him the last of the classical physicists.

The purpose of these remarks has been to suggest the fundamental inadequacy of that classical way of thinking—first systematized by Aristotle more than 2,300 years ago and which has dominated Western thought ever since—and to offer a conceptual frame for an alternative with which to replace it. It is clearly well beyond my powers or intent to claim to have proven the correctness of this position, or to claim to have definitively demonstrated the nature and structure of this metaphysical field theory and to have provided a detailed and convincing description of its operation in a vast range of domains. Rather I have sought to set forth what might be called a metaphysical research program—inviting and challenging others to seek either to refute my critique or to carry out the investigations that will instantiate my claims. An alternative paradigm can invite inquirers to ask new questions, look to new places for information, and use new models for the framing of theories—but the facts will have their say.

It is, of course, always appropriate to try to find linear causal pathways wherever the facts warrant—but we must avoid getting caught in that dead-end box. More and more people and investigators in different fields are coming to realize the need for a systems approach—both because of the inherent complexity of serious problems and because of what I take to be the fundamental, pervasive, and nonreducible reality of structured fields or levels of being. What I propose to show throughout the remainder of this work is the theoretical and practical fruitfulness of recasting some social and cultural studies in field-theoretic terms.[85]

Part II

Remaking the World

5

Telling Our Story: Myths for a New World

We enter upon a stage which we did not design and we find ourselves part of an action that was not of our making. Each of us being a main character in his own drama plays subordinate parts in the dramas of others, and each drama constrains the others. [1]

"[We want] a sense of purpose, a narrative arc to [our] lives."[2]

The Role of Philosophy

It is appropriate here to think again about the nature and function of philosophy. What purpose can a philosophical analysis serve? Of what relevance and significance is the analysis to which Part I of this book was devoted? What can one rightfully expect of, and draw from, such a metaphysical analysis? What was I trying to accomplish, and what can that contribute to an understanding of the contemporary world? These are the issues I would like to address in the opening section of the second part of this work. (Those not interested in the technical analysis may simply skip to the following section, Self-Consciousness and Death.)

A metaphysical analysis can serve essentially two distinct, but closely related, functions: the transcendental and the programmatic. By the former, I mean an inquiry that takes the form of an answer to the following type of question: "What are the (theoretical) preconditions of the possibility of 'x'?" The point being that certain facts and theories are believed—or claimed—to be true. These may be facts and theories about the nature of the "objective" or "real" world, about our beliefs about that world, or about our manner of acting in that world. An example of the latter would be the so-called scientific method, which assumes, among other things, that there are objective causal structures at work in our experience that reproducible experiments can capture and of which practical activity can make use.

A transcendental inquiry seeks to make explicit the essential metaphysical structure of the world presented usually in hidden form in the theories and practices under consideration. By making explicit those transcendental conditions, they may then be subjected to scrutiny for possible incoherence, inner contradiction, or implausibility, thus offering the possibility of critically recasting the given theoretical framework. It was just two such criticisms that were initially and quite incisively directed at Newton's theory of universal gravitation, though not adequately addressed for more than two centuries. The Cartesians criticized Newton because he postulated instantaneous action at a distance, which they said was unintelligible and smacked of magic. Leibniz, on the other hand, criticized the theory because it assumed the existence of absolute and uniformly structured space and time. Not until the development of Einstein's General Theory of Relativity, however, were these issues adequately addressed.

It was precisely the intention of our prior analysis to undertake a transcendental analysis (not to be confused with a transcendent one) that would reveal what I take to be essentially mistaken dimensions of the prevailing reductionist metaphysic.[3] But this being done, the second, and often far more difficult, task is programmatic: to provide the conceptual framework within which to reconfigure theoretical and practical inquiries. The challenge of such a "framework" analysis is to "change the terms of the debate." It is to provide an alternative set of categories, a different intellectual frame of reference—paradigm, model, set of assumptions, "preanalytic vision," conceptual matrix, or worldview— within which to interpret the events of our experience, whether scientific or practical. My attempt to outline a field-theoretic metaphysic is precisely such an effort, the purpose of which is to contribute to rethinking both scientific inquiry and social practice in the service of human betterment.

In the words of Joseph Schumpeter:

> We all start our own research from the work of our predecessors, that is, we hardly ever start from scratch. But suppose we did start from scratch, what are the steps we should have to take? Obviously, in order to be able to posit to ourselves any problem at all, we should first have to visualize a distinct set of phenomena as a worthwhile object of our analytic effort. In other words, analytic effort is of necessity preceded by a pre-analytic cognitive act that supplies the raw material for the analytic effort. In this book, this pre-analytic cognitive act will be called a Vision. It is interesting to note that a vision of this kind not only must precede historically the emergence of analytic effort in any field, but also may reenter the history of every established science each time somebody teaches us to *see* things in a light of which the source is not to be found in the facts, methods, and results of the pre-existing state of science.[4]

It is important to be further reminded here of several key distinctions. We must distinguish those conditions that are *necessary,* and hence inescapable, in any field of endeavor, from those that are *sufficient* to fully account for that field of endeavor. Oxygen is a necessary condition for human life as we know it, but it is hardly sufficient. In the hierarchically layered field-theoretic metaphysic, the outlines of which I have sought to sketch, I have sought to distinguish the constitutive role of the grounding structures that provide *boundary conditions* to the higher level inquiry from the semiautonomous systemic logic of the emergent fields that those conditions both constitute and constrain. Those conditions often provide the emergent fields with *conservation laws* that cannot be abridged, but do not in any way determine the content of the action within that emergent field.

A good example of what I mean can be provided by briefly considering the phenomenon of language. Language operates primarily by means of audible sounds, written signs, and physical gestures and expressions. These operate in accordance with the laws of physics and biology, which are quite adequate to explain their physical properties. The body can only make those sounds and movements that its biological constitution permits. But these boundary conditions can say nothing about the *meanings* carried by and expressed in and through those physical movements. The *way* the body is used to express meanings is determined *not* by its physical constitution, but by the logic of the language and the intentions of the speaker. These cannot be deduced from the natural science of the body, but require the importation of categories drawn from the emergent fields of sociology, psychology, and phenomenology, among others.[5]

Hence, Part I sought, first, to undertake a transcendental critique of our prevailing object-oriented reductionist metaphysic, and then, second, to develop from that critical analysis the programmatic outline of an alternative field-theoretic metaphysic. The task of Part II will be to show how that alternative metaphysic provides a constructive framework within which to reconceive or reframe and reorder the theory and practice of the social world and of human action.

Self-Consciousness and Death

Self-consciousness changes everything—even biology. What could be more ordinary—more matter of fact—and yet more radically significant, than our ability to ask "what should I do now?" Yet, this simple, mundane question reveals a capacity that brings meaning into the world, opening up a realm of possibilities that radically transforms the very character of human existence.

Just consider for a moment what is involved when I ask this question. At one and the same moment, I am the being asking the question and the one about whom the question is being asked. I am the subject and the object of the same act of awareness. As subject, I pose a question to the world. As object, I am the one about whom the question is being asked. It is my fate or choice as an object in the world among others that is being questioned. But it is I as the inquiring subject and center of conscious decision and choice that is asking the question. In a certain sense, I stand outside myself as active being and view myself as an object among others—to assess my needs, capacities, wants, possibilities, and the probable responses of other people and things to my actions.

Thus opens up before me a future that is not yet, a past that is no longer, and a present that is peopled by others—along with my awareness that I am an "other" for those others. I confront that future in anxiety and uncertainty, as hope, fear, and expectation; that past in satisfaction or regret; and that present by way of those others whom I encounter in pride, shame, love, or hate.

In all these experiences, I partially stand outside of myself, viewing myself as an object in the world, among others; but a very particular object with which I identify and to which I experience a deep emotional attachment. What is the nature of that "me" that "I" see before me, but which, at the same time, I am? What do I think others think of that me? How do I feel about that? How would I like them to think about me? And what can I do about it? These questions inevitably emerge in that existential space opened up by our self-consciousness.

At a still deeper level, I cannot help wondering where I came from and what will become of me. No wonder children ask these questions as soon as they begin to develop a reflective awareness of themselves, usually somewhere between the ages of three and five. No wonder that ethnologists have considered evidence of the burial of the dead as a clear sign of the presence of *Homo sapiens*.[6] Religion emerges directly out of the concern for our origins and destiny that is the inevitable expression of an emerging self-consciousness.

To be human is to be self-conscious, opening up the existential sphere of past, present, and future so as to place concern for the *meaning* of our life at the center of our experience. That is the ontological root of the biblical observation that "man does not live by bread alone." Humans live by confronting a world of meanings, filled with possibilities and uncertainties, in which our actions contribute to the determination of our destiny. No wonder Søren Kierkegaard spoke of facing our future in "fear and trembling." For that future is not completely determined, and is dependent at least in part on the choices we make, awareness of which cannot help but give us pause: "thus conscience doth make cowards of us all; and thus the native hue of resolution is sicklied o'er with the pale cast of thought; and enterprises of great pith and moment, in this regard, their currents turn awry, and lose the name of action."[7]

For those who doubt the importance of the future in determining the present meaning of our life, let them consider the significance of the following. You go to a doctor because you have been suffering from headaches. The doctor diagnoses a malignant tumor and says you have two years to live. Is that only a statement about your future, or does it not occasion a radical transformation of your present, transforming the meaning of that existential future that gave meaning and purpose, hope and expectation, to present activities? Present efforts take their significance from that to which they are seen as leading. Destroy their horizon of possibility and consequence, and you evacuate them of most of their significance—and with them goes much of the meaning of our lives.

This suggests an often overlooked, but quite significant existential dimension to the experience of aging. Slowly, almost imperceptibly, the future that spreads out before the young, often filled with infinite plans and prospects, contracts into a far more limited and ever-diminishing horizon of opportunities. Meanwhile, the past expands behind us, weighing us down with the consequences of what we have done. Less and less can we trust in making something more and better of our life; more and more have we to come to terms with what we have already made of it. There is thus a clear existential basis for the enthusiasm of youth and the resignation of age.

At the edge of this contracting horizon looms the specter of death, gaining in size and urgency as aging brings us nearer to it. But its reality did not emerge with aging, nor does it gain significance only for the elderly. Rather, death emerges with self-consciousness—they are inescapably bound together. Awareness of death follows directly from the recognition that I am an object in the world with others. Immediately, questions of origin and destiny arise in the obviousness of the fact that there was a time in which I did not yet exist, and there will be a time in which I no longer exist. No one who has emerged into self-consciousness can escape confronting this reality—however unpalatable. And none can fail to sense, if not directly realize, the challenge it poses to the meaning of personal and collective existence. No wonder the universality of concern with the burial of the dead. And no wonder the somewhat awkward responses adults tend to give children who ask naive questions about birth and death.

It is important to recognize the existential uniqueness of the problem of death. All animals die. But only self-conscious animals confront their own death as an existential problem. Death emerges within that lived space opened up by reflective awareness of ourselves as distinct and finite beings.

It is only because I am aware of myself as an object in space and time that I become aware of the inevitability of my death—that is, of the very finite extent of my duration. This awareness complements appreciation of the spatial boundaries of my self—the limitation of the infantile experience that Freud referred to as the "oceanic awareness of self." Delimitation of self-awareness is the precondition of my being able to meaningfully organize the world around me, and to develop and coordinate my own powers so that I may be able to effectively intervene in that surrounding world. Practicality and survival require delimitation and discrimination. They also augment self-awareness, accentuating appreciation of finitude. No wonder the continuing and practically universal appeal of religions that promise their adherents the possibility of merging with the infinite or divine.

Contrast this with the attitude of animals, even the most "advanced." Not only do they die but they kill and view death. But there is no reason to believe that they confront the inevitability of their own death as an existential problem. Not only is there no empirical evidence, such as religion and burial of the dead, but there is no philosophical reason to think they could do so without possessing the complex self-consciousness that would allow them to take themselves as the object of their own awareness—of which the possession of an objectifying language would seem to be a precondition—thus objectively placing themselves in a spatial and temporal setting with evident finite boundaries. Rather, animals seem to respond both to immediate threat and to habituation—but to live existentially in a world that expands little further than the field of the effective presence of objects and persons, colored by the habits and feelings carried forth biologically and unselfconsciously from the past.[8] They are spared the "fear and trembling" of which Kierkegaard spoke, as well as the pride, shame, hopes, and plans for future accomplishments, and regret for past failures, that so mark human experience, providing the foundation for the development of culture.

But confront death we must. Nothing so remarkably concentrates the mind's attention as a life and death struggle. No wonder our perpetual fascination with war and crime—and our perpetual celebration of the warrior. In fact, the warrior is the archetypal hero—the one who confronts death and returns to tell the tale. Before such demigods, all other heroes pale in comparison. It is as if confronting death gives meaning and significance to life. It certainly adds intensity to combat.

And that is the point. The moment takes on significance precisely because it is precious and irreplaceable. Without death, time would be infinite and nothing would make any ultimate difference. But death puts a limit to time, and makes the moment matter. It forces us to confront that moment as the precious and fleeting instant that it is. It charges us to make the most of it while it, and we, are here. We are thus turned back from vague thoughts about the infinite, and focused on the finitude and fragility of the present. Death is the ultimate horizon within which the drama of our life is played out. We sense that we must make something of that opportunity before it is too late.

Death as horizon emerges at the outer limits of the experience of my personal future. It casts its retrospective urgency over the present, however much practical experience hides or mitigates its presence. It calls upon each of us to make sense of the present in a way that will be sustaining. We cannot simply live our life on the basis of physiological need and satisfaction. Our self-awareness precludes that. Such is the existential meaning of the biblical story of the expulsion of humans from the Garden of Eden. We are condemned to have to make sense of our life in order to live it, and to have to bear that burden and challenge in the face of death's inevitability. *This* is the metaphysical cross we bear and the reason why efforts to understand and constructively address the problems confronting humanity are condemned to failure if they do not adequately address human beings' metaphysical needs.

Telling Our Story

Self-consciousness provides us with the inescapable challenge, and opportunity. We must speak to the inevitable reality of death, and do so in a way that motivates action beyond simple pleasure seeking and pain avoidance. This is the story of human history. And "story" it is—or rather stories, for they are as innumerable as are the storytellers. It would be better to call humans "*Homo dramaticus*" rather than "*Homo sapiens*," for it is hardly our wisdom that distinguishes the majority of our race. Rather, it is our need to have a story, possibly our own story, but more certainly that of our group, clan, tribe, or people. Whether real or imagined, we cannot live without a story of who we are, why we are here, and where we are going.[9]

Metaphysics may be the foundational philosophical inquiry into the nature of the real, and into the basic structure of our beliefs about it—what is "real for us"—but it hardly addresses the *way* we *live* that reality. What "turns us on" is the dramatic structure of our experience—what it *means* to us, personally, day in and day out. The goals we strive for, based on the needs and wants we experience and our grasp of the world out there—the values it makes possible and the obstacles we must confront—this is the stuff of daily life. We live for the most part unreflectively within the confines of a taken-for-granted meaningfully structured world that frames our practical undertakings and our most intimate sense of who we are and what we can hope for and strive after. This need seems to date from the earliest days of our prehistory. There is hardly a known civilization that did not tell itself mythic stories of origins and destiny, of heroism and tragedy, which provided a dramatic frame to their lives.[10]

Thus, the pervasive dramatic structure of our lives is the experienced ground of our metaphysics. We encounter it in the stories we tell about ourselves, our transactions with others, our community, and its organized collective effort to meaningfully structure our temporally unfolding journey into an ever-uncertain and always at least partially threatening future in which (some) others are possible impediments, if not actual antagonists. Yet, it is precisely those stories, incessantly created and indefinitely reworked, that deepen the significance and reenergize the determination of our efforts. Let me first provide a more systematic foundation for this interpretation of the existential metaphysics by which we live, before returning in greater detail to a consideration of its dramatic development.

The Human Need to Feel Good

Almost any trait that has been associated with people has been attributed by someone to "human nature"—from selfishness to benevolence, from aggression to sociability. Almost as surely, some inquiring spirit has shown a people or a culture in which that trait was absent or greatly diminished. Making claims to universal human traits is a hazardous business, more often than not revealing cultural prejudices rather than illuminating the issue. Yet generalizations from experience are always appropriate. When they are supported by a sound theoretical framework, they may be offered as legitimate claimants for general assent. Such, I believe, is the suggestion of Ernest Becker concerning the human need to be "a locus of value in a world of meaning." Drawn from his studies of cross-cultural anthropology, and grounded in his reflections on sociological and psychoanalytic theory and existential philosophy, Becker's suggestion of a quasi-universal structure of human motivation deserves serious attention. Let me explain its meaning, and then ground it in human self-consciousness and sociality.

All things being equal, human beings prefer pleasure to pain. In fact, it would be more appropriate to say that pleasure is what people feel when they are satisfied with an event or situation. It is not that pleasure is some one thing, that one can have more or less of. That nominalization is the key error of hedonists, who then assert that all people seek pleasure. No, one cannot seek pleasure, for then you would not know where to look—unless you first determined *what* gave you pleasure. But that *what* is precisely what needs to be determined. Rather, we seek for what we want, or think we want, and when we get it we are, or expect to be, pleased. For we use the word "pleasure" in the generic to denote the situation—any situation—in which we obtain what we want.[11]

The point of this is that while it is seriously wrong to make the hedonist claim that people seek pleasure, it is right to observe that we use the word to refer to situations that make us feel good. And we do want to feel good. It is of course evident and highly important that people have very different and often opposing wants—that what makes some people feel good makes others feel awful. But if people want to feel good, however devoid of specificity that word "good" might be, that is an important fact about human beings—which, I might add, probably does *not* distinguish them from sentient beings in general.

But humans are uniquely self-conscious and social. In fact, their self-consciousness seems only to develop in an intimate social or familial context. Although a biological trait, rooted in the helplessness of the human infant as well as in the fact that its brain is not fully developed until well after birth, this intimate social context of extended infancy provides the necessary "cultural" condition without which articulate self-consciousness cannot emerge. It also makes possible the cultural transmission of character traits, values, beliefs, habits, and practices that make possible historical development. This social transformation of the biological creature constitutes a radical alteration of its nature. So much so that we would hardly recognize as human a biological creature that had not been thus "socialized."

Thus socialized and incipiently self-conscious, the conditions under which such a being can feel good are transformed. Feeling good can no longer simply be the unmediated bodily encounter with environing conditions. Rather, consciousness must mediate that interaction, as it must mediate even our attitude toward our own body. And it must involve reflexive reference, whether or not articulate, to itself. In order to feel good, I must feel that what I am doing is all right. And that some significant others approve.

So far, we are still at the level of feeling rather than of articulate expression. We have not clearly distinguished developmental issues from ontological ones, that is, questions of the manner in which the self is initially formed from the structural conditions that ultimately must obtain for such development to be possible. It is not my intent to dwell on the process of self-formation in early childhood, though discussion of ontological issues will shed light on preferential strategies for upbringing. But my concern here is with suggested universal characteristics of "self-esteem" as they speak to the "demands of human nature."

Self-consciousness transforms the conditions of "feeling good." But such awareness is hardly more than incipient unless and until it becomes articulate, through the development of language.[12] Thus, objects get delineated, and self and world get named. Practical social interactions require coordination, essentially through articulate language. Objects emerge with specified names, and theories develop to explain how they behave. Similarly with "human objects." Reflective awareness incorporates "me" and "us" into this objectively defined world, giving us spatial and temporal location, and practical direction. These are universal parameters of civilization as we know it. By setting conditions for the individual's ability to act and to know himself or herself, they determine the preconditions of one's feeling good about oneself. That is Becker's point. Let me explain.

A Locus of Values

In order to feel good in general, one needs to feel good about oneself. But that is not possible unless several things happen. Significant others have to communicate a positive regard for you. You must be able to identify with and accept their regard. That regard must be consonant with your ability to act effectively in some aspects of your life. And those actions must be consonant with some self-transcending purpose that hopefully is shared by at least some of your significant others. All of this needs to find at least limited expression in some theoretical framework that describes the dramatic significance of the community's life, thus giving location, meaning, and purpose to the activities of its members.

These demands can be summed up by reformulating Becker's notion about being "a locus of value in a world of meaning," to say that human beings need to experience themselves as "centers of value and power in a socially rooted cosmic drama." In short, we need to be meaningful participants in some self-encompassing story.[13] Let me comment briefly on each of the components of this statement, and then suggest a more comprehensive interpretive framework. My aim is not to prove their truth, but rather to so describe them that their claim to our acknowledgment emerges from their elaboration.

Value

To be valued is to be worthy of respect. It is to feel that you have a right to be and to do, and that others cannot simply do with you as they please. You are not solely an instrument in the world or the plans of another. You can make demands that others ought to acknowledge. You can hold your head up, look others in the face, feel there is a place for you that does not have to be defended, and that others ought to acknowledge and support your right to be. It should be clear that such an experience of self-validation is a precondition for feeling good about oneself. It is practically impossible to feel good about yourself in a context in which everyone else is treating you with disrespect or contempt.

Irving Goffman speaks of "degradation ceremonials" by which "total institutions," such as prisons, asylums, or monasteries, initiate new inmates into the new identity that the institution demands.[14] These ceremonies are consciously orchestrated to give an immediate and powerful message that the institution will now determine who you are and what worth you have. They do it by totally controlling the social (and physical) context of the inmates' existence. Nothing is left to chance, and a careful effort is made to remove all social supports for alternative identities. The success of such comprehensive "reeducation" provides striking and unmistakable confirmation of the extent to which even the most intimate and pervasive sense of our personal identity is rooted in the social fabric of our lives.[15] It seems as if it is only those who have the deepest sense of being directly connected and personally belonging to an alternative community that transcends their explicit surroundings who have any chance of sustaining their prior sense of self before the onslaught of such a total institution.

Power

But it is hard to conceive how one could feel valued and valuable without some sense of a capacity to act effectively. As with validation, of course, so with effective action, I am talking of relative judgments and degrees of range and effectiveness.

The human being is invigorated by action, by mobilizing energies toward directed results. From the earliest days of infancy, there is a satisfaction gained from feeling your weight in the world, from seeing the world respond to your effort. We are born in symbiosis with the environment, from the mother's womb to the ecology of the biosphere. Being is transaction, and vitality is energetic. Total passivity would seem to be a concomitant of a deep depression that verges on death. It is difficult to conceive of a reflected sense of self that could approve of being completely passive, nothing but an instrument or consequence of the play of environing forces. What, it might be asked, would such a being be like? And how could it conceive of itself positively?

Action, on the other hand, means effecting change in oneself and in one's environs. It is the marshaling of energies to do something. It has a purpose or goal, however vague or inarticulate, and hence a direction.

Something is to be accomplished. Without it awareness would be only noninvolved observation, and the capacity for movement superfluous. The reality of our impotence would mean that we are no more than spectators of the world and of our selves. It would be difficult even to speak of our having a life to live. Rather, we might more aptly speak of "being lived" by other forces. But then it is difficult to conceive of our even having or being a self at all. Where would the "unity" of the self—whether actual or ideal—come from? Could there even be a self about which to have any self-reflecting thoughts or feelings? It is difficult to conceive of such.

We need not press the point. No deduction of the transcendental truth of these observations is required. Rather, the very strangeness of the situation suggests the force of the alternative claim, namely, that the experience of some degree of potency to act and effect changes in self and world is an essential condition for being a self—and thus for having any positive sense of one's self.

Social Rooting

Not only can the infant not even begin to develop a self apart from an intimate social or familial setting but also the very creation of the self involves the mutual and reciprocal sharing of perspectives, attitudes, values, beliefs, and practices. The self emerges as a distinct perspective and center of initiating (and receiving) activity within an encompassing social field. Self-consciousness begins with an emerging, and initially quite inarticulate, awareness of the individual as a being for others, responding to and appropriating their expectations, orientations, and behaviors. The self is immersed in that field, being formed by the differential and selective "interiorization" of key dimensions of the environing society. It is not by chance that we learn the language spoken by those around us. Similarly with attitudes, values, beliefs, habits, practices, and reflective appraisals. In the words of George Herbert Mead, "we become as we are addressed."

In reviewing *A Short History of Humanity* in the *New York Review of Books*,[16] William McNeill provides a suggestive overview of the historical stages in the development of human communication and reflective thought. He suggests that the emotional bonds of the community were probably initially established through dance and rhythmic expression, slowly giving birth from singing to speech. Then articulate language emerged in instrumental utterance required by the need to coordinate joint practical activity. These gave rise to increasingly regularized patterns of social activity and behavior, yielding explicit rules, customs, and regulations. With increasing size and complexity of social organization, along with the inevitable changes occasioned by the evolution of natural surroundings and social practices, critical revisions were called for that slowly led to the reflective evaluation, experimentation, and reconstruction of the tradition, itself the ground of an emerging articulate history, social theory, and science. For our current purposes, this quite brief overview simply underscores both the historically developing social field within which the human self emerges into reflective awareness and the ongoing affective bonds that nurture the adult self.

Hence, the self is essentially social from the very beginning. A non-social self is both an apparent contradiction in terms and as close to an empirical impossibility as can be. Of course, the way we live our sociality varies greatly—even to the extreme of complete rejection of any social contacts, as with hermits or certain religious "mystics," or in a destructive rage directed at that social world that gave one birth. But three points are worth noting here.

First, the rarity of examples of complete social rejection speaks strongly to the deep and intimate attachments that bind the human being to society. Second, those who leave society usually bring with them a belief system that is anchored around a self-transcending meaning system that focuses upon a relation with at least one highly significant other. Thus, their living solitude is "peopled" with imagined others. Lastly, the rejection of the social world—whether in destruction or in escape—is usually an emotionally charged way of relating to that which is rejected. The world is found repellant, disgusting, hateful, or sinful—but rarely, if ever, simply irrelevant. These are thus but quite unusual and extreme ways of living out a relation to "others," which, in bearing witness to the failure of social location, attest to the need of that which was found so painfully to be lacking.

The detour into the extremities of complete rejection of social place was undertaken so as to reinforce the claim that human beings need to be located in a sustaining social context. Not only self-esteem but also physical and emotional survival seems to demand it. We need but recall the numerous experiments that attest to the psychic withering, and even physical death, from which even the youngest suffer when "deprived" of a basic minimum of human nurturing. (The force of this truth is not limited to the human realm, as numerous other primarily mammalian species reveal similar affective and social needs.)

Cosmic Drama

The human need for others does not stop with the physical, affective, or interpersonal. Very quickly, this need becomes enmeshed with the conceptual significations embodied in the linguistic world that is increasingly constitutive of the emerging social self. For such a "self-conscious" animal, being part of a social world is little consolation unless that world is felt to be worth something. Our sense of self and its "worth" is inextricably bound up with that world of which we are, at least at first, an intimate part. We do not wish to identify with what is worthless. Its worthlessness could not fail to be felt as our worthlessness; its depression, our depression.

A society obtains its worth by doing something worthwhile. Its cohesion, purpose, and justification require seeing itself as an important, often central, player in an encompassing story. This may involve the creative activity of superhuman beings or a special purpose to which the tribe, clan, nation, or people are dedicated.[17] Something important must be felt to be at stake in the life of the group. That something becomes the central theme of the story of the group's life. It establishes the group's self-identity, and sustains its cohesion and purpose. Something is at stake in the group's activity that makes its collective effort worthwhile, and thus makes me an important person, if only because I belong to an important group. Have you ever wondered what is going on with those children who ape rock stars, join fan clubs, wear team uniforms, and proudly proclaim of the team—to which they do not belong, but with which they so passionately identify—"we're number one"? It's certainly not a long journey from there to racial, ethnic, and national passions, often of the most extreme sort.

The Objective Reality of Culture

The need to be a "center of value and power in a socially rooted cosmic drama" is prereflectively experienced in the care and attention we give to the practical concerns of daily living. Our commitment to tasks and projects, our comfortability with practices, techniques, and instruments, our observance and even respect for forms, norms, expectations, and institutions, our demand for justice and respect, and our attachment to persons, objects, and symbols, all express our "taken-for-granted" immersion in a "given" and ongoing culture within the meaningful contours and objective structures of which we seek to carve out a meaningful personal life.

We don't choose our culture, its institutions and expectations. We come to reflective self-consciousness as the person we have been chosen to be by those significant others by whom we have been more or less nurtured and "socialized" into a meaningful world. That world presents itself as an unquestioned fact: it's just the way things are. But careful reflection on that "cultural fact" reveals both its historically developed and continually evolving character and its "ontological" dependence on the very activity of those "others," oneself included, who constitute the processes of acculturation. Cultures are clearly not physical "things," whose existence would continue on without its continual reenactment by each new generation of adherents. We do not simply learn and assimilate into our culture, we reproduce (and subtly transform) it in the process of acculturation. Of course, that transformation is far more often than not unintentional, unacknowledged, and purposeless. It is rather the unforeseen but inevitable consequence engendered within the culture and its natural environs of the more narrowly personal goals we are pursuing.

In fact, culture is precisely that interpersonal historically evolving objective structure of values, beliefs, practices, and institutions whose ontological existence is only made possible by being reproduced and transformed by the day-to-day activity of its members. Its reality is *both* interpersonally objective and physically evanescent. We cannot see or touch it, though its physical marks are all around us, from its tools, "concrete" structures, and material transformations of nature to the symbols and distinct practices of social life. In fact, "the relations one is concerned with here must be conceptualized as holding between the positions and practices (or better, positioned-practices), [that is, norms and social roles,] not between the individuals who occupy/engage them."[18]

Nothing better expresses the objective but illusive reality of the cultural field than the phenomenon of language. Not only do we not choose our language, but we could not even form the concept of language if we did not find it already in existence. The very personal capacity for articulate expression presupposes the prior existence of an interpersonally objective field of linguistic meanings.[19] Another way of saying that, is that personal consciousness presupposes social mind, however much each linguistic enactment may itself (unintentionally) modify the linguistic space that made the enactment possible in the first place. Herein lie the objective ground, scientific significance, and essential irreducibility of hermeneutical interpretation and dialectical inquiry.

Bhaskar well summarizes the interpersonally objective existence of social, linguistic, and psychological structures, and their nonreducibility to each other or to the physical conditions of existence, when he observes:

All [human] activity presupposes the prior existence of social forms ... Society is a necessary condition of any intentional human act ... [C]onsider *saying, making,* and *doing* as characteristic modalities of human agency. People cannot communicate except by using existing media, produce except by applying themselves to materials which are already formed, or act save in some or other [meaningful] context ... Society is both the ever-present *condition* ... and the continually reproduced *outcome* of human agency.

[Thus] the properties possessed by social forms may be very different from those possessed by the individuals upon whose activity they depend ...

> [P]eople, in their conscious activity, for the most part unconsciously reproduce (and occasionally transform) the structures governing their substantive activities of production ... [They] do not marry to reproduce the nuclear family or work to sustain the capitalist economy. Yet it is nevertheless the unintended consequence (and inexorable result) of, as it is also a necessary condition for, their activity ... Thus we do not suppose that the reason why garbage is collected is necessarily the garbage collector's reason for collecting it (though it depends on the latter). And we can allow that speech is governed by the rules of grammar without supposing either that these rules exist independently of usage ... or that they determine what we say. The rules of grammar, like natural structures, impose *limits* on speech acts we can perform, but they do not *determine* our performances.[20]

Thus, society is an objective ensemble of social relations that are not reducible to the psychological attitudes or intentions of its members, though it cannot continue to exist without them, any more than it can continue without the natural conditions that make physical existence possible. Rather, society is a historically developed and regularly reproduced (and continually transformed) meaningful field of "positioned practices"[21] that are the institutions and norms that constitute, enable, and channel purposeful human activity. Its functioning illuminates our prior discussion of boundary conditions of systemic structures that both provide limits for, and the necessary preconditions of, "higher level" systemic fields of activity, of which, in this case, the psychological and personal are exemplifications.

Dramatizing Our Story

If that is the social world as seen "from without," however, it is clearly lived "from within" quite differently, as was already suggested by reference to the garbage collector's reason for collecting garbage. We live in terms of values, purposes, tasks, and responsibilities. We live with others, in complex interpenetrating networks of activities and social relations. We care deeply about our successes or failures, about the respect we obtain, demand, or have a right to expect from others, and our capacity to feel good about what we have done and how we are thought of by those others. We function like characters in a play, the seriousness of which often overwhelms us, and whose outcome is literally a "life and death matter." Unlike the more staged dramas enacted in theater, television, and movies, we are not simply observers in this drama, nor are we completely free to come and go as we please. Further, its script is not written in advance of its enactment, however much the basic structure of its roles—or "positioned practices"— and plotline are already delineated and generally understood. Even more remarkably, we are only one of the partial authors, though, from our point of view, one of the central characters, in its historical unfolding. But so is each of our fellow humans, each partial cocreators of the respective interlaced dramas of the self-importance of each. Our culture is thus a complex and only poorly coordinated collective creation through time. There is no complete agreement as to story line, main characters, or desired ending—nor even of our common history. Each individual or group author/ actor has a different "take" on the plot line and set of featured characters, in which our personal role is often usually quite diminished, if not actually marginalized, demonized, or negated by others.[22]

As dramatizing animals, our sense of self and significance clearly requires the collective elaboration of a meaningful world within which significant goals and values give purpose and direction to an individual's daily activities. The culture determines the thematic contours of that world, setting forth the imaginative space for personal aspiration, as well as the normal cast of characters and roles, and general range of acceptable actions and practices. Traditional cultures tend to be far more limited in the range of available "positioned practices" and less flexible in the ways in which individuals may choose to occupy those positions than modern industrial societies. Further, traditional cultural dramas tend to be clothed in auras of divine creation and ontological inevitability—they are far from inviting creative modification or pluralistic experimentation. The individual's dramatic character and social role is to all intents and purposes written in advance for him or her, only allowing for the most minimal individual variations—rarely celebrating originality—and having to adapt to the inevitable necessity of hardship and chance occurrences.

With the development of civilization, the elaboration of science and technology, the explosion of human capacities, the complex sophistication and diversity of human activities, the population explosion, and the increasing valuation of individual variation and personal experience, the awareness of individual opportunity and the challenge of practical possibility within a world that is both more open to individual variation and less supportive, or confining, of personal effort, all of these developments increasingly place the burden of our dramatic needs ever more squarely upon our personal resources. Thus, it becomes quite appropriate to view meaningful human effort through the metaphor of dramatic self-creation.

What could be more revealing of the structure of our life and activity than to ask: what is the dramatic staging of our culture? What are the goals that it invites us to pursue? That it offers to reward? What is the structure of the hierarchies of valued objectives that are available for the majority of "average" members, short of the "heroic" or celebratory? What are the pathways to those desired objectives, and what are the rewards for those who make their way upward? How widely shared is that dramatic scenario, and by whom? What are the other, alternative, competing, or actually antagonistic scenarios? Who sustains them, to what extent, and how threatening are they to ours?

What is our assigned place within that dramatic structure? By whom? What do "they" want and expect from and for us? To what extent do they expect or invite us to innovate our path? What other values are out there that might tempt us away from the "straight and narrow"? And what are the sanctions or rewards for such "deviation"?

Within that predefined dramatic structure—with its preassigned roles for us so insistently though subtly communicated by all of our most intimate and significant others—how does our sense of self emerge? Who do we think we are, and how do we begin to decide what we want to "make of ourself"? In Sartre's suggestive phrase, what is the "fundamental project" by which we choose the self we will become? Or more precisely, what is that becoming self we try to enact in the meaningful world that we try to (re)create within that world we have been given? What roles do we wish to assign to those others—significant or insignificant, intimate or impersonal—that people our world, and how do those assigned roles mesh with the roles they have chosen for themselves? Or those that the culture has designated for all of us? Here is the dramatic setting for a truly engrossing and completely uncertain historically open and dialectically developing cultural drama that, at least as far as each of us is concerned, has us at the center, if not actually in a starring role.

In sum, each of us finds ourself "on stage," literally playing the part of our lives. The general thematic lines of the script having been written by our culture, they are presented to us initially through the dramatic enactments of our "significant others." In contemporary America, far more than in almost any other society in history, we are called upon to "improvise," developing variations on the theme of our personal uniqueness and self-created individuality. No wonder jazz is the quintessential American musical form. By ourselves or in small groups, we are invited to create, be original, and experiment. We have to script our own story—"pull ourselves up by our boot straps," "make something of ourself." Such, at least, is the embedded message—however different may be the reality.[23]

But I do not here want to make too much, or too little, of the drama of American culture, to a more detailed investigation of which I will turn in a later chapter devoted to using the "story of America" as a case study in applying cultural hermeneutics. Currently, my purpose is more general. To offer a theoretical description by which to suggest that an adequate interpretation of human experience requires the invocation of existential categories that are nonreducible to those of the natural sciences.

Of course, this dramatic reading is not itself meant to be definitive, only suggestive.

"To show how natural it is to think of the self in a narrative mode," MacIntyre comments that:

> To the question "What is he doing?" the answers may with equal truth and appropriateness be "Digging", "Gardening", "Taking exercise", "Preparing for winter" or "Pleasing his wife". Some of these answers will characterize the agent's intentions, others unintended consequences of his actions, and of these unintended consequences some may be such that the agent is aware of them and others not. What is important to notice immediately is that any answer to the questions of how we are to understand or to explain a given segment of behavior will presuppose some prior answer to the question of how these different correct answers to the question "What is he doing?" are related to each other. For if someone's primary intention is to put the garden in order before the winter and it is only incidentally the case that in so doing he is taking exercise and pleasing his wife, we have one type of behavior to be explained; but if the agent's primary intention is to please his wife by taking exercise, we have quite another type of behavior to be explained and we will have to look in a different direction for understanding and explanation …
>
> We cannot, that is to say, characterize behavior independently of intentions, and we cannot characterize intentions independently of the settings which make those intentions intelligible both to agents themselves and to others … a setting has a history, a history within which the histories of individual agents not only are, but have to be, situated, just because without the setting and its changes through time the history of the individual agent and his changes through time will be unintelligible.[24]

Thus, for example, the American experience is far more pluralistic, experimental, open-ended, and individualistic than is more usually the case. Throughout human history, people have come to self-consciousness within the frame of a given cultural drama. Sometimes conflicting dramas may be at stake, though more often than not, such conflicts mark the challenge posed by a competing social group, which, if they were to conquer, would most likely impose their "stories" (and gods) upon the conquered. But even within a cultural drama, all is rarely harmony and light. Conflict is as pervasive among the Greek gods as with the ancient Hebrews. Why else do the Hebrews need prophets to warn of YHWH's wrath, rail against disobedience or injustice, and insist that "Thou shall not worship graven images?" These personified gods embody the active forces of nature. The world of the Hebrews is "peopled" with active spirits they believe effectively control their destiny, and to which they must make appeal—in the "appropriate" manner, as dictated by the prevailing worldview, interpreted and administered by the priests—if they are to preserve their life and advance their values and goals.

Their world is made meaningful by those divine beings, who embody its dramatic structure, sustaining values, and "salvific" consummation.

Similarly, few throughout human history would have thought it was "up to themselves" to stage their personal drama. The more pervasive experience is rather that of "playing one's part" in a cosmic drama authored by others, almost invariably by mythic, heroic, or divine beings living in sacred times. It was only for current priests and rulers to fulfill their divinely designed roles by ritually administering and often symbolically enacting that sacred drama. In such a world, individual originality is not only not valued or encouraged, it is usually viewed with suspicion and hostility, even as the vehicle of satanic evil.[25] With the cosmic drama viewed as sacred and eternal, and individuality completely subordinated to the dictates of social place, it is quite unlikely that the metaphor of drama—itself a rather recent and culturally limited invention—would emerge with which to interpret human existence. And yet, that metaphor well captures essential elements of the collectively created, historically developed, and interpersonally enacted staging of the ontologically free individual's personal effort at partial self-creation. Our self-consciousness grounds our freedom, requiring at least our complicity in the meaningful structures of social life within which the uncertain drama of our personal life unfolds.[26]

No wonder humans are so fascinated by stories. We tell them from early childhood. Communities celebrate them in sacred rituals at crucial stages throughout the year. Religions can be seen as cosmic stories that provide us with the stage setting within which to enact the drama of our personal meaningfulness and possible salvation. In the contemporary world, literature and the arts increasingly compete with religion in dramatizing our life. Often, subtly, many in the West have come in recent years to view their lives through the prism of the screen, imitating "matinee idols" and unconsciously enacting their lives in accordance with the dramatized patterns of the stage. How many have come to view marriage in the pattern of a screen performance? Or to subliminally reenact the style of celebrated professional coaches when coaching a little league team? How often do youngsters "reenact" the fighting behavior of their heroes during a street hockey game? Wiretaps by the FBI in the United States have even revealed members of the Mafia suggesting they model their behavior on that of the mobsters depicted in film. And a recent U.S. president was reported to have often confused actual historical occurrences with roles he enacted in the movies.[27] Even in more "intellectual" settings, as when listening to a speech, we are far more likely to remember any dramatized stories than the basic thematic message of the presentation—unless, of course, the story is used as the vehicle for communicating that message.

And who among us can resist "telling our own story" when invited to do so in a friendly and welcoming context? What better way for a shy person to relate to others when uncomfortable at a social function than to earnestly inquire about the other's "story," and to show real interest and attention? Few will refuse, or can't be drawn out—often in great detail—by sincere and persistent entreaties. That is rarely a problem. The more usual problem is that few are so interested in the stories of others, but are rather looking for any opportunity to tell their own story. In fact, all too often, such communication involves a subtle struggle between competing efforts to tell one's own story—interspersed monologues replacing engaged dialogue—with each participant not so much listening to the other as waiting for an appropriate opportunity to get their story in.

We want to tell our story, to dramatize and often reinvent it so as to increase both its significance and our importance. We even fight for communicative space, where historic male dominance can be seen by both the amount of time occupied by men talking and the lessened attention paid when women speak. Not only is this a matter of quantity, but also a struggle to determine what are the significant story lines, or dramatic scenarios. Are sports more significant than clothing and fashion? Politics more important than art and culture? Business more important than family and children? Or relations with neighbors and in-laws? Or vacations? Different cultural scenarios featuring different players, often differentiated by gender, class, race, and culture, compete across the dinner table, as well as for "market share." No wonder it is often said that one ought not to discuss politics or religion on social occasions. Too much is at stake—namely the meaningful structure of each of our worlds within which the personal meaning of our lives is worked out. These are literally matters of life and death, which it is often quite difficult to engage in objectively and dispassionately.

"Man is in his actions and practice, as well as in his fictions, essentially a story-telling animal," comments MacIntyre. "He is not essentially, but becomes through his history, a teller of stories that aspire to truth. But the key question for men is not about their own authorship; I can only answer the question 'What am I to do?' if I can answer the prior question 'Of what story or stories do I find myself a part?'"[28] Thus, "telling our story" is central to the inevitable crafting and enacting of that story. The historical reality of culture is rooted in the need to dramatically stage and individually express our personal and collective itinerary. We desperately need our stories, and we need them to be rooted in a socially integrated and collectively sustained cultural setting. Any effort to approximate an adequate understanding of this reality requires the use of categories of interpretation that are irreducibly hermeneutic. Even the categories and inquiries of the natural sciences only take meaning within the historical contours of the cultural drama. That was the point of Hegel's brilliant exposition of the dialectic of "Geist" or spirit—the historically developing totality of meaningful human experience. Self and world, subject and object, knowing and known, the "real" and the "true"—these are only meaningful concepts within a linguistically articulated and historically developed culture that constitutes an open-ended existential totality. What appears before us as the Truth of Reality can only be that which is made possible by the meaning-frame of the cultural mind (or "Geist") within which we find ourselves. The meaning of objective nature is far from adequately determined on its own terms. Similarly, the possibility of its "adequate" comprehension may be precluded or obfuscated by the culturally predominating metaphysical worldview. We tell our story—individually and collectively—and identify with those stories to which we have become used, and/or which speak most movingly to us. But those whom they gratify the most may be but a segment of the wider society—though no doubt a quite powerful one. They may in fact impose their interpretation, intentionally or not, upon us in their own self-interest.[29]

What, then, is the true story? In the most profound sense, Hegel was right when he observed that the only truly adequate story is the whole. Each perspective is inevitably limited and partial. When asserted by a subject, whether individual or cultural, it inevitably brings forth a series of counter assertions, giving expression to aspects of what it leaves out. Like the Sun, of which Heraclitus spoke, we must not overstep our limits or "moira," the god of "retribution," will make us pay for our cosmic "injustice." Similarly, we must give our due to the objectively irreducible nature of the cultural drama, without ever forgetting the biophysical setting within, and in terms of, which encompassing totality its dialectic development unfolds. Failure to do so inevitably confronts us with unexpected "externalities"—which are but testaments to the inadequacy of our initial perspective. In fact, there are no externalities. They are nothing but the "return of the repressed"—the objective antithesis to our cultural thesis—the inevitable expression of nature's revenge upon our cultural hubris.

6

Ecosense: Niches, Nodes, Networks, and Matrices

> Every single body of the universe stands in some definite relation with every other body in the universe.
>
> *(Mach's Principle)*

On Externalities

The claim that there are no externalities, with which I concluded the previous chapter, is equivalent to the claim that there are no isolated systems in the universe. Everything is connected to something else—and hence, in some sense, to everything else. Otherwise, we would not be speaking of a "universe," but of multiverses, though it is not at all clear how we could then even speak or know of them.[1] But this is not to say there are not relatively coherent and autonomous systems that pursue a more or less coherent systemic logic of their own. In fact, they are pervasive—and it is one of the central theses of this work to argue not only *that* they exist, but also that many of them are *not reducible* to their ontologically necessary constituent and boundary conditions. At the same time, however, it must be emphasized that no system functions in complete isolation and self-subsistence. It thus becomes patently clear that every field of endeavor, whether theoretical or practical, exists both in relative autonomy and in ongoing transaction with its environs.[2] Often it becomes crucial to be able to grasp and express the nature, extent, significance, and consequences of the connections that link a system with its environs, both local and pervasive.

Theoretical and practical undertakings, therefore, need to be concerned with, and alert to, both the inner coherence of their relatively autonomous undertakings and their "ecological" grounding in a world that gives them place, import, and sustenance. When you change the "external" context of any system, you almost certainly, over time, transform its "internal" structure, invariably in ways most of which are likely to be unexpected and unanticipated. At the same time, the ongoing action of a system's inner logic is bound to have objective effects on its surroundings. This is precisely what Hegel meant by the dialectic of totality—the historically developed irreducibly patterned field of essentially interdependent and conflicting relations that bind together semiautonomous elements into a complex and evolving system. Each element both pursues its intrinsic logic and generates a pattern of responses that transform the meaning and consequence of its behavior in ways that neither it nor any other participant could have totally prefigured. Only a transcendent perspective could aspire to grasping the whole—but only by claiming to occupy a stance outside of that whole, viewing it as it were, in the beautiful words of Spinoza, "*sub specie aeternitatis.*" Such an omniscient view is, however, ultimately denied to us, since we are not gods, while relativity and quantum mechanics have made patently clear that all "embodied" interpretations are both perspectival and interactive—with only the scope and degree of influence relative to the framework and purpose being at issue.

The prior discussion can lead us, therefore, in one of two opposed, though interrelated, directions. On the one hand, we can move from a concern with each individual's effort to develop a dramatically sustaining life story to a consideration of the historical and evolutionary development of his or her enabling cultural dramas, or, on the other, to an exploration of the existential requirements of psychic and physical health and personal satisfaction. Both of these, however, can only find their programmatic integration in a comprehensive theory that roots human personal and cultural development in the evolutionary ecology of sustaining communities. I have thus outlined the remaining tasks before us, to be taken up in that order in this and in the succeeding chapters. The only exception being a detour in the penultimate chapter into a reflection on the American Drama, offered as a brief case study in the application of a field-theoretic perspective to cultural interpretation.

Evolutionary Ecology

I may well be belaboring the obvious, and yet it seems so often overlooked or neglected by economic and social theorists. Human life is a series of historically developing, socially organized transactions with the biosphere. These (socially mediated) transactions are literally the air we breathe and the water we drink, interpenetrating the most intimate fibers of our being. Such historically organized social organisms interacting with their environment constitute an ecological system. That system is continually selecting "favorable" variations from among the indefinite number of random variations that are genetically produced, thus continually recasting each "species" and the environment of which it is a constituent.

Even more, the biological organism is not itself simply an individual, but rather a historically developed and closely integrated community of individual cells. Each cell is capable of surviving on its own, independent of the "corporate" organism, and depending upon when it is separated from its biological community, it will follow a distinctive developmental path. Thus, while the individual human being is in one very important sense a completely unique individual—separated from its surroundings by the permeable membrane that is human skin through which it transacts with its environs—in another, it is itself a society of societies of diverse and distinctive types of individual cells, performing distinct functions required for the continuing existence of the communally constituted individual self. At the same time, that communally constituted individual self is itself only a center of action and reaction within the environs that constitute and sustain it, and is constituted and sustained by it. Apart from its environing field, it will quickly wither and die. We thus have a nested system of living systems. The individual is *both* a relatively autonomous center of activity and an immersed participant whose being is sustained by, as it sustains, the ecological field of which it is a part. The autonomous individual is a fiction. Individuality is always partial, embedded, historical, and transactional.[3]

Incessant Variations and Individual Uniqueness

Evolution thus refers to the complex historically developing ecofield process of "descent with variation" in which such relatively autonomous individuals are continually producing slightly modified variations of themselves. These variations interact with their surroundings in unexpected manners that "select" those variations that are more "adapted" to the environment within which they happen to find themselves, thus leading imperceptibly to the transformation of their "type" so that it begins to become a different "variety," and slowly becomes a distinct new "species."[4] At what level of organizational complexity and relative organismic autonomy does selectivity operate? Which differences constitute purely individual variations within a population, which a new "variety," and which a distinctive "species"? To what extent is that determination a matter of empirical fact? To what extent is it only a conceptual construct determined by our practical need to organize our transactions with our "confreres" or simply to chart the world around us in the need of conceptual order and/or psychic familiarity and "at homeness"?

The simple answer to these questions is that evolution is primarily a matter of the selection of individuals, not of genes or species. Natural selection takes place essentially at the level of the phenotype—that is, with respect to the selective fit between the developing organism and its surroundings.[5] Since variation is pervasive and continual, and greatly enhanced among sexually reproducing organisms, it inevitably produces a range of organisms within any specified population, each one of which is to some extent different from all others.[6] In their interaction with their fellows and with their surroundings, such slight variations will give individuals who are even ever so slightly better adapted to their surroundings a marginally better chance of being "naturally selected" to survive and produce offspring. Over time, the norm of variation within any population will thus move in the direction of those "preferred" variations, thus modifying the "species"—which is nothing other than a "reproductive community."[7]

Populations, Not Essences or "Natural Kinds"

A point of vital logical—and ultimately, metaphysical—significance (to which I will have occasion to return later) should be underscored here. The species is a biologically reproducing community of distinct and unique individuals. It is not a distinct type, with a fixed essence or nature that is to be found in each of its member individuals. As Mayr observes:

> The assumptions of population thinking are diametrically opposed to those of the typologist. The populationist stresses the uniqueness of everything in the organic world. What is true for the human species—that no two individuals are alike—is equally true for all other species of animals and plants. Indeed, even the same individual changes continuously throughout its lifetime and when placed into different environments.[8] All organisms and organic phenomena are composed of unique features and can be described collectively only in statistical terms. Individuals, or any kind of organic entities, form populations of which we can determine the arithmetic mean and the statistics of variation. Averages are merely statistical abstractions, only the individuals of which the populations are composed have reality. The ultimate conclusions of the population thinker and of the typologist are precisely the opposite. For the typologist, the type (*eidos*) is real and the variation an illusion, while for the populationist the type (average) is an abstraction and only the variation is real. No two ways of looking at nature could be more different.[9]

Niches and Phenotypic Adaptation

As the environment "selects" those individuals that are best adapted to it, the average population of the group changes ever so slightly—until, over time, the successful individuals either enhance the adaptiveness of their structure or find themselves transformed into a different structure. While the environment is thus "selecting" favorable individual variations, the selected individuals are themselves continually selecting (and thus modifying in their favored direction) those aspects of the environment that best suit their needs. Thus, each successful "phenotype is the result of the interaction between the genotype and the environment."[10] This process of mutual adaptation of individual and environment is best seen as an interactive and "coevolutionary" process.[11]

"It used to be believed," observes Mayr, "that bipedal locomotion and tool use were the most important steps in hominization." More recent evidence, on the other hand, has added that "the rapid growth of the brain seems to have been correlated with ... the emancipation of hominids from the safety of the trees and the development of speech, the human system of communication."[12] "Homo sapiens is the result of two major ecological shifts [habit preference]," writes Mayr,[13] from rain forest to tree savanna to bush savanna. These ecological transformations threatened the survival of tree-dwelling primates while opening up ecological niches for more upright, bipedal, social, and ultimately intelligent hominids. It was this adaptation of individuals to a changing environment, thus slowly occupying an emerging ecological niche, that led to the emergence of *Homo sapiens*. Little need be added here on the extent to which that emerging species has modified in turn its biotic and abiotic environs.

Further, even though "it is the phenotype that is exposed to natural selection"—the "gene can never be the object of selection" nor the species, only the "individual as a whole"[14]—"a group can also be the target of selection if it is a social group and cooperation within this group enhances its survival."[15] An enlarged brain seems to have been vital for the development of the language, communication, and social cooperation required to adapt successfully to this new ecological niche. In order for a bipedal primate to develop the needed brain size, it had to be born prematurely, with its brain continuing to grow through a period of extended infancy that required sustained nurturing and the development of family life.[16] Thus emerged a social group with language and the communication skills needed for cooperation and mutual support, out of which culture developed. In this process of ecologically pressured adaptation, the human species evolved, increasingly revolutionizing its relation to its environs, and over the last few tens of thousands of years increasingly transforming the Earth's biosphere.

Economic Ecology

Clearly, therefore, evolutionary theory is a complex, historically developing, ecofield discipline without fixed and definitive boundaries demarcating species, or individuals. It points to an incessant process of patterned transformations through time without purpose, guidance, or direction. Human intervention often seeks to "correct" that process—to redesign it, and (re)produce organisms that meet designed objectives, realizing desired values and obtaining preferred and perfected types. Often, that is the most economically efficient and profitable mode of production for a corporation. Unfortunately, however, species need diversity, experimental variations, even genetic "failures," to expand, diversify, test alternative developmental pathways, adapt to changing environmental circumstances, or ward off invasive challenges, if they are to survive. Efforts to impose our will on nature, such as through bioengineering, however immediately useful, may well lead to a dangerous thinning out of organismic diversity, placing organic survival on more tenuous grounds. It certainly constitutes a radical ecological transformation, most certainly leading to unexpected evolutionary variations, thus further underscoring our ontological nesting in planetary ecology. This is *not* an argument against intentional interventions, which, in any case, are practically inevitable. Our very existence constitutes an ongoing intervention in the evolutionary process, with the only important questions being whether that intervention is purposeful or random, farsighted or nearsighted, intelligent or foolish. Our remarks here are simply meant to underscore an objective fact that suggests a procedural caution, to further consideration of which we will return later.

Our social life is thus clearly rooted in, and nurtured by, nature. It is further shaped and sustained by the organized economic activity that produces and reproduces our means of subsistence, offering us the possibility of enhancing the material and spiritual conditions of existence. Economic growth and development inevitably require the extraction and depletion of natural resources and the production of waste in the process of providing human service. Economic activity is thus an increasingly significant constituent in the evolution of biospheric ecology. That activity is no doubt guided in part by what we think and desire—thus requiring careful consideration of the intentional complexities of the human psyche—but it is literally fueled by what we physically extract and consume. Economic activity thus provides the material sustenance and institutionalized backbone of social living, and it no doubt follows a relatively autonomous systemic logic that is the subject of a highly technical theoretical and practical discipline. But that logic cannot be treated as autonomous and self-contained.

In a further series of nested systems, each relatively autonomous, yet dialectically interrelated, the individual psyche, socially produced and educated, is fed by economic production and distribution through regular transactions with the biosphere that inevitably impact the evolution of natural ecology. We know that human work is both vital to human personal development and necessary for material survival. Thus, personal activity cannot be separated from the life of the economy. Similarly, economic activity cannot be carried on as if the Earth were an inexhaustible source of materials and useable energy and an infinite sink for disposable waste, or as if human activity did not involve radical transformations in the conditions of existence of the entire biosphere. This requires us both to place economic theory and practice clearly within the confines of an encompassing natural ecology and to qualify its operative principles by careful attention to the existential demands of meaningful individual and social living. It further requires an appreciation of the inevitable evolutionary transformations that such transactions necessarily engender.

No one has better understood the necessity of seeing the economy as a subsystem of natural ecology and the radical transformations of economic theory and practice occasioned by this conceptual relocation than Herman Daly. In *Beyond Growth,* he offered a series of major revisions of current economic theory occasioned by this reframing. Since they illuminate both the inadequacy of a reductionist approach and the dialectical integration of economics with ecology, evolution, and ethics, it is worth summarizing them in some detail, even though much abbreviated:

(1) The first thing to change [in economics textbooks] would be the ... diagram that [treats the economy] ... as an isolated circular flow from firms to households and back again, with no inlets or outlets.... . It is exactly as if a biology textbook proposed to study an animal only in terms of its circulatory system, without ever mentioning its digestive tract! ... What concept in economics ties the economy to its environment? Circulation of blood is to circulation of money as the digestive tract is to ... (*what?*)... . To this concept ... (of "entropic flow"), [Kenneth Boulding] gave the name ... "throughput".

(2) Standard economics is mechanistic, it is "the mechanics of utility and self-interest"... . Mechanics studies reversible and quality-less phenomena. The circular flow of exchange is quality-less and reversible, ... but the entropic flow is irreversible and qualitative. Entropy is a measure of the qualitative difference between useful resources and useless waste.... . Therefore, mechanistic models cannot deal with the most basic facts of economic life.... . the presence of the entropic flow ... necessarily introduces qualitative change into the very environment on which it depends... . As the environment changes, the economy must re-adapt—a co-evolutionary process... .

(3) The circular flow can theoretically grow forever because abstract exchange value (debt, purchasing power) has no physical dimension. But growth in the entropic flow encounters the physical barriers of depletion, pollution, and ecological disruption... .

(4) In the circular flow paradigm we have an intergenerational invisible hand and harmony. In the entropic flow paradigm we have an intergenerational "invisible foot," and conflict of interest... .

(5) [Hence] the "miracle of compound interest" can no longer be appealed to as the way to "grow" everyone in the present generation out of poverty. Growth cannot forever substitute for redistribution and population control in fighting poverty... .

(6) [Nor can] national income accounting [continue to] ... write off the value of man-made assets against current production as they depreciate, but make no such deduction for the depreciation of natural assets... . [We cannot continue to deplete resources and count it as income.]

(7) Capital and labor ... [can be] conceived of as funds or agents that transform the flow of natural resources into a flow of products. [But] the dominant relation between funds and flows is complementary. Substitutability between fund and flow is strictly marginal, limited to reducing process waste. [You can't make as many houses with more saws and less wood.] ...

(8) [Finally,] the issue [sh]ould not be how many people, but how many people for how long, ... living at what level of per capita resource use? The relevant question would be how to maximize the cumulative person-years ever to be lived over time at a standard of per capita resource use that is sufficient for a good life... . We would have to emphasize the temporally parochial nature of prices ... [and recognize that] future generations cannot bid in present markets.[17]

In this extended excerpt, Daly has taken apart the systemic logic of current economic theory by explicitly locating the economy as a subsystem within the wider biosphere. What is in one sense patently obvious, our economic dependence on nature, by being placed within its natural environs suddenly becomes a revolutionary manifesto, necessitating the radical restructuring of the internal logic of economic theory. At its center, the notion of unending growth in consumption of resources and production of waste is revealed as an extensive centuries-long Ponzi scheme in which no attention has been paid to the "carrying capacity" of the Earth.

This point can be further underscored by a brief consideration of the significance of applying the discount rate to the evaluation of natural processes. Depending upon the rate of interest used for the calculations, the current value of future resources rapidly diminishes toward insignificance as one thinks beyond one or two generations. In effect, economic theory simply discounts the future. No wonder it is so eminently rational for whale-fishing nations to draw down the natural stock until all whales are extinct, so long as the current return on its investment is sufficiently lucrative to amortize current investment and earn a sufficiently high rate on the reinvestment of profits. Conventional economic theory has simply institutionalized and normalized Louis XV's famous slogan, "après moi, le déluge."

What we have here is a demonstration of the marginal value of marginal analysis. As Eric Davidson has so well noted, the last stock of timber to be cut down may well have a very high marginal utility due to its economic scarcity, but it no longer has any ecological value, because that value comes from its contribution to the life-sustaining cycles of nature that require large tracts of forest—for habitat preservation, soil conservation, water purification, air recirculation, and photosynthesis. Marginal utility does not value the entire stock, only the additional opportunity cost and expected benefit.[18]

Then again there is cost-benefit analysis, and the quantitative weighing of expenditures against returns. But what gets valued, and how, is problematic in the extreme. Certainly, the industrializing West has, in effect, taken nature and its resources for granted for the last 400 years. That is why it can simply overlook the uses of nature, treating resource depletion as income, and acting as if "Land" were simply one factor of production, interchangeable with Capital and Labor. And it can assume that The Market will assign an appropriate price to everything worth being considered, including "so-called" externalities. But nothing has here been said of the fundamental difference between localized "externalities" and those that are pervasive. Both have effects on the "public"—being those affected by the actions but all too often having no effective role in the decision-making process.[19] But, while localized effects can, at least in principle, be specified and their effects on particular people and structures to some extent quantified, the same is clearly not true for such pervasive externalities as global warming and ozone depletion. In fact, Davidson suggestively contrasts the economic pyramid with the ecological, showing how one is in effect the inverse of the other. Where the popular mind, trained by conventional economics, can treat soil as being "dirt cheap," ecologists recognize that the viability of the food cycle depends in large part on the painstaking and often time-consuming nurturing of a nutrient-rich soil.[20] Hence, the logic of economic rationality can be seen as the height of madness once relocated and reconceptualized.

It should be further noted that nothing has yet been said of the motivational assumptions and organizational objectives that undergird and direct conventional economic analysis. The former tends to treat humans as if they were solely motivated by the most narrow pecuniary self-interest, thus making a mockery of all social, ethical, religious, and philosophical concerns, while the latter reduces both the descriptive and normative logic of organizational behavior to "bottom-line" thinking. In both of these contexts, it is usually quite unclear whether we are supposed to be dealing with an empirical theory of personal and organizational behavior or a set of ethical and logical proposals as to the correct and proper way to act. The political usefulness of this essential ambiguity should be lost on no one.[21] We will return shortly to the philosophically muddled understanding of the so-called fact-value dichotomy by which these confusions are both theoretically obscured and implicitly justified.

Ultimately, we are led to the realization that the mythologized "Market" is an elaborate shell game, created by myriad human actions and policies. The popular injunction to "leave it to The Market" is usually little more than an ideological cover for the interests of the powerful. Markets are not natural, but constructed. They depend upon collective decisions with respect to "property rights, physical and social infrastructure, the distribution of income and wealth, (and) the myriad regulations that govern economic affairs,"[22] including laws dealing with incorporation, bankruptcy, and advertising.[23] Actual market decisions themselves are inevitably *private* transactions that generally do not value *public* consequences affecting those who are not direct parties to the transactions. Such nonmarket participants fall within the scope of so-called externalities, and are effectively unrepresented and thus systematically undervalued. This is precisely what Dewey meant by the "problem of the public." Traditional market solutions to ecological problems tend, at best, to be essentially patchwork efforts, dependent for their success upon the political will and organized power of those who can use the law to transform those "externalities" into corporate "internalities" of which their cost-benefit analysis will then have to take note. At worst, such solutions effectively discount long-term and pervasive environmental consequences while maximizing the private actor's short-term return on his/her investment. However useful "free" markets are, therefore, in determining allocation by setting prices that adjust supply and demand within the parameters of existing institutional structures, their operation is ultimately an instrument of social policy that is subordinated to the values and goals of those who dominate the social order.

Evolutionary Cultural Ecology

Hegel's conception of the dialectic of "Geist" beautifully captures the systemically complex network of historically developed transactions that constitute the social order, however much he and others falsified it through oversimplification. (For example, it is rarely the case of a single thesis generating a single antithesis, and even more, although the process is developmental and cumulative, there is no reason to think it is inevitably directional and ameliorative.) The dialectic demonstrates how a change in one part of the system reverberates throughout the entire system, with most of the consequences being unintended, unpredictable, and only retrospectively knowable.

The significance and continued relevance of the Hegelian analysis can be better grasped, however, by translating "Geist" not as "Mind" or "Spirit" as is usual, but rather as "Experience." By so doing, we focus attention on the ongoing complex and interconnected transactions between socialized subjects and their social and (socially mediated) natural environs. Those transactions are both similar in many ways to the complex ecological networks that drive evolution, and unique to the extent that they depend upon the subjective appropriation of meanings that mediate social interactions. Thus, the social field, whose existence depends upon the continual, though mostly unintentional, appropriation, reproduction, and transformation of social structures, develops by way of the mutual interpretations of each other's actions. In this process, the dialectical element refers to the way in which any assertion tends to generate a set of counterassertions that both reinterpret the initial assertion, and offer an alternative generated by a perspectivally distinct perception and grounded in differential interests. It is the process of reinterpretation through internalization that grounds the historical dialectic.

Evolution proceeds in a similarly comprehensive fashion, but does not generally depend upon the subjective processing of meanings. It is comprehensively networked, historically developing, pervasive, and unavoidable. Every action constitutes an intervention that interacts with its surroundings, changing them, and consequently transforming the role and function of everything within them, in an unending, unpredictable, and inescapable process. The Hegelian dialectic is itself a historically developing social process that radically transforms the natural ecology, lending its pervasive stamp to the evolutionary process. Many of the unintended consequences of social activity flow directly from its ecological impact upon the surrounding natural environment. Examples include the (positive) improvements in agriculture and horticulture and the (negative) consequences of global warming and reduction in biodiversity.[24]

The very existence of this volume itself constitutes an intervention that will transform the behavior and consciousness of its readers in untold ways. At a minimum, whether boring or amusing, it will simply occupy a portion of the readers' time, soon to be forgotten. (It has certainly impacted a significant portion of mine, effecting my interactions with family and friends, the consequences of which are better left to others to evaluate!) If more successful in its intended purpose, it will induce a change in the way thoughtful people approach, interpret, and act on a range of social meanings, institutions, and cultural practices, resulting in significant transformations of social institutions, accepted cultural understandings, and historical processes. But it cannot exist without exerting an influence on that with which it inevitably interacts, thus constituting, however minimally, a contribution to the evolutionary process. Experience and theory—beliefs and practices—are inextricably linked and essentially open-ended. Efforts to claim a definitive interpretation for this "ecosense" are but more assertive interventions that inevitably bring forth their own distinctive counterassertions, in an ongoing process that is as unpredictable as it seems to be never ending.

The essentially open-ended and recursive nature of social theory and philosophy, and thus its essential incompleteness, is underscored by the realization that, since social structure and cultural evolution are constituted by the action of purposeful human agents, any successful theory that occasions a rethinking of human beliefs, values, and actions itself becomes a constituent of the very cultural processes it is trying to understand, which process thus escapes, at least to some extent, the conceptual grasp that was sought by the theory. This work is no exception. The cultural totality can only be pointed at, it cannot be grasped—that was the truth of Hegel's concept of the dialectic of Totality—and is itself a constituent of a more encompassing biospheric evolutionary process. As for the impact of that process on the more encompassing evolution of the cosmos, little can be here said, except to offer the cautionary remark that all interventions seem to transform to some extent, however limited, and in ultimately unpredictable ways, their surroundings.

Therefore, every theoretical formulation, including this one, involves an actual intervention in the ongoing life of a culture, and thus an ecological modification with unanticipated evolutionary significance. "Social science is non-neutral in a double respect: it always consists in a *practical intervention* in social life and it sometimes *logically entails* value and practical judgments."[25] Even the assertion of an obvious factual truth, not to speak of a creative insight and theoretical breakthrough, has potentially unlimited normative consequences for human and sentient life, thus revealing the fundamental artificiality of any claim to the existence of an impassable gulf between facts and values.[26] This is said without any reference to the essentially recursive quality of social life, in which reflection on the structure of social reality inevitably becomes an aspect of the object under study.

Of Facts and Values

It is precisely that self-reflective and recursive aspect of social reality that fundamentally undercuts the force of the supposedly unbridgeable gap between facts and values. Of course, many have often allowed for the numerous and pervasive ways in which an inquirers' values tend to influence the selection of subject matter, the prioritization of theoretical alternatives, the degree of commitment and perseverance, as well as his/her differential sensitivity to the facts.[27] But few in modern times have credited the logical viability of the alternative movement, from facts to values. Yet, such movement is pervasive and practically unavoidable—and of particularly crucial importance when it comes to the understanding of society and culture.

Consider the following. Society has no distinct physical existence. As has already been noted, you cannot point to it as you can point to a natural object, such as a rock or a plant. Its existence consists rather in historically developed and institutionally structured patterns of thought and behavior. These are continually reproduced, and subtly transformed, by each new individual and generation that is socialized into the culture. These institutionalized patterns have a remarkably resilient structure that endures more or less consistently through time, constituting, structuring, and channeling the character, thought, and behavior of each new generation through its norms, institutions, and practices. These structures are themselves in turn continually, though subtly, modified in this process of socialization through which they regularly reproduce "normality."

This process of acculturation proceeds by way of the communication of values, beliefs, and practices. In order for socialized humans to act and interact within a cultural context, they must have some idea of who and where they are, with whom they are involved, what is expected of them, what is appropriate in different situations, what is worth pursuing, and how the world works such that some relatively reliable relation can be conceived to exist between specific actions and their likely consequences. All of this requires some theory of the nature of the "real" world, in both its natural and social dimensions.

Clearly, therefore, the very "objective" existence of the social world depends in an important sense upon the beliefs and values of its members. Each of us collectively constitute—reproduce and transform—the social world within which we find ourselves. What we believe *about* the world is a *constituent* of that world. That is what is meant by saying that social theory is essentially self-referential. Further, any theory about society is—recursively—itself an aspect of the society of which it is a theory.

Since consciousness essentially constitutes the social world—though not particularly mine or yours, and not usually as a matter of individual, or even collective, conscious choice or volition—its theories and factual claims (even natural scientific ones) are not simply comments about, or observations of, the world, but also constituent elements of that social world of which they are an integral part. (The Ptolemaic theory of the solar system had a profound effect on the beliefs and practices of the medieval Church.) Cultural institutions and practices cannot exist unless participating individuals share the beliefs and values that sustain them. In a sense, believing makes it real. If *we* believe this is money—a mutually agreed-upon and accepted medium of exchange backed up by the organized power of the state—then it *is* money, regardless of what *you* or *I* think or say. But you or I cannot simply decide to make this or that money, nor can we decide that it's not money. Rather we *find* ourselves in a society in which *people* in general (Heidegger's "*Das Man*") have already *decided* on the existence, nature, and function of money. In far more complex and interrelated ways, we have theories about the nature, importance, function, operation, and uses of money—as they operate within the structure of existing economic and social institutions. Thus, for example, every one of our "economic" undertakings, however trivial, presupposes theories about the nature of economic relations and the operation of money. These theories, whether correct or incorrect, both help to constitute social reality and have practical and moral consequences that flow from the reality so constituted. Were a sufficient majority of citizens to think and behave differently, the world would be different, and so would the values by which it operated. Consider, for example, how a generalized loss of confidence in the money supply can generate a financial panic, a "run on the banks," and a complete breakdown of social order.

Social theory must therefore take seriously the meanings that events have for social agents, precisely as they are understood and experienced by those agents. But there is no reason to assume that the agents' beliefs are adequate or correct. In fact, they may be systematically in error, and an adequate social scientific theory may require a complete reinterpretation of the meaning of those beliefs and actions in the light of a more comprehensive understanding of the reality in question. An interpretation of what the agents believe they are doing may well be a necessary condition of an adequate scientific theory of society, but it is neither sufficient to explain their behavior nor is its truth self-authenticating and beyond criticism.

It is important to further emphasize the dependence of social evolution on the interaction of these institutions, practices, and human agency with their natural environment. All of these presuppose the causal efficacy of conscious human purpose, itself grounded in personal beliefs. Further, if there are social structures, institutions, and practices whose existence depends upon the production of false beliefs either among those who continually reproduce those systems or among those who allow or support their continued existence, then a critical theory of the social causes of false beliefs can become a liberatory force for radical social change, and thus have a significant effect upon the development of social ecology and the long-term evolutionary impact of human culture on the biosphere.

Consider the following: Christians believe that Jesus was the Messiah, and many believe that by really consuming his blood and flesh during the Eucharist they are contributing to their personal salvation. As a function of such beliefs, historically developed institutions and practices have molded the behavior of billions of adherents, built churches, employed both religious and nonreligious personnel, ministered to human needs, consecrated marriages, mourned the dead, received confessions, provided absolution, condemned abortion, meaningfully structured our relation with the sentient and natural world, empowered monarchs, dethroned opponents, and literally mobilized millions in justified religious wars leading to the death of vast numbers of both believers and infidels. These are real events operating in accord with definite social structures that can be said to cause the behavior of human actors. As with the garbage man referred to in the previous chapter, the individual's reasons for acting—such as the desire to be married, or to obtain salvation—are rarely the same as the institution's reasons for the creation of the "positioned practices" that structured that action. But without the individual belief in the capacity of the practice to obtain the desired result, the practice and its corresponding institutional basis would eventually cease to exist. That belief and value system is thus a necessary constituent of its factual reality.

Let us take this one step further. The institutions and practices of The Church obtain the required beliefs and behaviors of their adherents by the development of an elaborate system of rituals and ceremonies, vestments and buildings, rewards and punishments, that are explained and justified by a historically developed complex of both simple and sophisticated theories often elaborated in a highly technical language in erudite and esoteric publications. These writings make claims about the nature of reality and the facts of history. They tell stories about what *really* happened and offer theories about the nature, structure, and mode of operation of *objective reality*. These histories and theories are constituent elements of the religious institutions and practices they seek to explain and justify.

If a scientific inquiry into the truth of these histories and theories then reveals that they are completely mistaken—that the facts are not as presented and the real world does not operate in accordance with the forces as claimed, and that, in fact, those purported forces do not even exist—what rational (and practical) effect does (and should) that "objective" inquiry have on the belief in the truth of those theories and in the efficacy of those practices and institutions? What kind of behavior is called for by those who understand the truths thus revealed? How can we separate the objective and "factual" truth of the world thus revealed from the "evaluative" judgment of its illusory nature and the consequent "moral" obligation to act on that truth? Were not those social facts constituted in part by both false beliefs and mistaken values? Would not the critical revelation of these errors call for moral judgment and practical action that corrected these mistaken cultural facts? If one were then able to show how the very existence of those institutions required the popular acceptance of those false beliefs, would one not have provided a remarkably compelling argument for radical systemic social change? Would not such science constitute a demythologization of an ideological mystification that would serve as a moral force for individual and collective liberation?

> To show that agents are systematically deluded about the nature of their activity is (logically) impossible without passing the judgment that [their belief] is false; and [observes Bhaskar, to say that] "[their belief] is false" is not a value-neutral statement... . If, then, one is in possession of a theory which explains why false consciousness is necessary, then one can pass immediately, without the addition of any extraneous value judgments, to a negative evaluation of the ... generative structure, [or] system of social relations ... that makes that consciousness necessary (and *ceteris paribus,* to a positive valuation of action rationally directed at the removal of the sources of false consciousness).[28]

We thus see how values can become facts, and how facts can entail values, and action. It should also be clear how the failure to see both the legitimate distinction between facts and values and their interconnections can have profoundly significant social consequences. Take, for example, the ambiguities associated with the idea of normality. To be overly simple about it, the normal can be that which is usual, expected, or appropriate, or that which is healthy, desirable, and ideal. In the former case, its opposite is the unusual, unexpected, or inappropriate; in the latter, it is the abnormal, sick, or unhealthy. The former use is essentially factual and descriptive; the latter, essentially moral and evaluative. By failing to clearly make this distinction, it often becomes easy for established authorities and institutions to treat those who behave in an unusual and unexpected manner as if, in not behaving normally, there must clearly be something wrong with them. What torments can wrack the minds of those who fear to behave, or to think, or even to be thought by others as thinking, non-normally. What an effective device for social control! And how effective can this intellectual confusion be in creating a social situation in which such thought or behavior is treated as mad—even to the extent of driving the nonconforming individual into madness, thus creating the reality envisaged, retroactively confirming and justifying the initial claims.

Joseph Heller tells the story of a young man who, during a basketball game, took pity on an opponent who was clearly quite dejected after missing a shot. In an act of thoughtfulness and consideration, the young man picked up the basketball and gave it to his opponent so that he might correct his failure. The coach immediately removed the abnormal youth from the game, and he was taken for psychological counseling as there was clearly something wrong with him. He had clearly failed to internalize and observe the unwritten rules, the norms by which the attitudes, values, and behaviors of the participants were not only to be guided but also by which they were to be constituted. Clearly these norms not only describe how people behave; they shape and mold the behavior thus described. To fail to recognize and respect such norms is to be mentally defective; to recognize but choose to violate them is to be subversive, either a criminal or revolutionary.

How similar is this, it might be asked, to the role and function of such previously mentioned economic notions as the primacy of economic self-interest as a theory of human motivation and of bottom-line thinking as the rationale for corporate decision-making? Are these scientific descriptions of the way in which individuals and corporations behave, or are they rather prescriptions of the supposed rational and appropriate way for them to behave? Is it not the case that individuals who wish to be taken seriously by those with power and influence within current economic institutions are obligated to act—and probably will have to think and value—in accord with the normative expectations of those "institutionalized" others? Will not those who act differently, not only condemn themselves to objective failure, but also leave themselves open to disrespect and moral condemnation? Even more, aren't the purported scientific theories describing economic rationality and organizational behavior really institutionally sanctioned exhortations as to how one ought to behave, backed up by the force of social convention, internalized belief, and institutionalized power? They have shaped social reality to their specifications, and then acted as if that is simply "the way things are."[29]

Rethinking Social Practice

Clearly, then, thought shapes not only action but also the meaningful structure of institutional life that makes culture possible. It is an *objective* constituent of cultural reality that carves out the evolutionary niche of civilizations. Human beliefs, values, and behaviors constitute and are constituted by social institutions, which themselves mediate our collective transactions with the biosphere.

Reductive, or atomistic, thinking misapprehends the ecological structure of our world. It inevitably constitutes an inadequately informed imposition of a biased perspective into an encompassing totality. As an effort to impose one's (individual or collective) will upon the world—usually seeking to subordinate the world to one's needs or values—it tends to create a series of unforeseen and often destructive counterfinalities that eventually undermine the initial objective. Perhaps no better example exists of the impossibility of such causal interventions in the evolutionary process than efforts to eradicate pests by the use of DDT. Unless *all* of the targeted pests are destroyed—probably an impossible objective, itself, no doubt, with unforeseeable consequences occasioned by the ecological niche thus evacuated and the activity of whatever will eventually come to occupy it—the few that remain, having developed a resistance to the pesticide, will rapidly reproduce, replacing those that were vulnerable, leaving us, within a fairly short time, with a probably more virulent and now pesticide-resistant population.[30]

This failure recapitulates the logic intrinsic to the Hegelian dialectic, pointing toward the necessity of rethinking human inquiry in a field-theoretic manner and restructuring intentional interventions in a way that locates an environmental niche for human cultural activity that is ecologically sustainable.[31] Given the expanding impact of human activity, this is becoming an ever-more important task. It would seem objectively to require the complete naturalization of human beliefs, values, character, and institutions in a way that is more respectful of natural process and cautious about human interventions. Subjectively, it would seem to require systematically addressing the experienced need of individuals to be personally more firmly rooted in their social and natural surroundings.

A field-theoretic metaphysic thus requires a transformed conception of theory and of human action. Theory must be seen as a historically embodied, socially constituting, ecological engagement with the natural processes of evolution. It must be ever humbly cognizant of the inevitably unforeseen consequences of its interventions and appreciative of its dialectical partiality and its ecological dependence. It must view itself not as an independent overseer and omnipotent architect, but as a participant helmsman steering the ship of human culture in the dark and oft-times torturous sees of a nighttime voyage, only partially illumined by the moon and stars. The environment in which we live and move and have our being has not been given to us as "our dominion." Rather than seek to rid the world of the pests that bother us, we must learn to till the soil that feeds us, and find a way to live in relative harmony with those creatures whose evolutionary development attests to their natural functions. That does not mean we must simply accept what is—all is not necessarily for the best in the best of all possible worlds. But our interventions must be cautious and prudent, not hubristic and complacent. They must proceed from the perspective of one who is implicated in, and an inescapable part of, the processes they seek to effect, not as one who is an all-powerful and all-entitled alien for whom the Earth is essentially only "raw materials" in need of development in the service of human interests.

7

The Webbed Self:
Deconstructing Individualism

I am because we are.
(Kenyan proverb)

The hardest disease to cure is the one that is caused by the medicine you're taking.[1]

Critiquing Individualism: Reductionism in the Social World

By now one thing should be totally clear: individualism is a theoretically untenable and socially destructive doctrine. It might well be called the social disease of modernity, completely mangling any capacity to understand the process by which society produces and nurtures individuals into adulthood. At its best, it is a well-meaning but failed attempt to shore up the value of individuality by asserting its ontological irreducibility, seeking to guarantee its success in advance by claiming that the individual's unique personal traits were there from the start. At its worst, it is a disintegrative attack on the pedagogical value and emotional sustenance of every collectivity, denying personal and collective moral responsibility for the quality of life of its members. It thus serves as a justification for a narrow self-seeking (often profit-maximizing) egoism.

We can now understand why individualism is such a completely misconceived effort. It is simply the atomism of the social world: an effort to reduce a complexly webbed relational world to the purported fundamental units encountered in direct perception out of which that world is supposed to have been constructed. Reducing society to individuals is thus all of a piece with the program of metaphysical reductionism, which at least implicitly serves as its theoretical justification. What it totally misses is the not directly perceivable relational structure that literally gives birth and substance to, and then sustains, the emerging individual—even providing those cultural inter-pretations that lead some to misconceive of themselves as "self-made men."

The attraction of individualism is clearly not limited to its apparent epistemological and ontological veracity, but is enhanced by the purported value it gives to the personal advancement of each individual. By asserting the ultimate social reality of the single self-determining free individual, it seems to be celebrating the values of human self-realization and individual achievement. But it does this only by failing to consider the social precon-ditions that make human development possible, thus implicitly sanctifying whatever is the existing structure of social benefits and burdens, no matter their source and moral justification. It further solidifies a social order that implicitly justifies a competitive struggle among individuals, ensuring that the success of some will inevitably be at the expense of the rest. Then it reflexively justifies that competitive order by appealing to the completely misconceived ontological foundation provided by the very doctrine itself. It thus constitutes a self-enclosed circle of self-fulfilling ideological justifi-cations for a destructive and unequal war of all against all in which those who are currently ahead are most likely to stay there, and can do so freed from any moral qualms concerning the fate of the less successful.

But none of this is meant to deny the ability of individualism to serve as a radical liberatory doctrine within the frame of essentially static, tra-ditional societies. These are rooted in fixed status and class positions in which the individual is completely submerged within the group, whether clan, tribe, village, manor, church, city, state, or nation. In the West, it clearly functioned as a dagger directed at the vitals of the medieval world, cutting the individual progressively free from the institutional constraints of a Church-dominated social order. Even in its incipient versions,[2] it provided a rallying cry for social, economic, and personal liberation that helped break through encrusted tradition to liberate creative energies and personal imagination. It was thus a vital propaganda tool justifying and helping to create alternative religious, economic, political, social, and esthetic institutions that became the Modern West. But we can appreciate its ideological role, however beneficially conceived, without mistaking that historical role for evidence of theoretical adequacy, or as a justification for continuing to defend that which is theoretically indefensible and increas-ingly socially disastrous.

John Dewey brilliantly addressed this situation by distinguishing be-tween the metaphysical doctrine of individualism and the moral value of individuality. By individualism, he understood the view of the individual as ontologically and morally prior to and constitutive of the social and political order—with society then seen as essentially the result of individ-ual activities and choices, the field within which essentially preconstituted individuals interact, and which they seek to use to realize their purposes. We might consider such classical examples as the Christian doctrine of the soul or its more recent secularization in modern social contract theory, most recently defended in opposed ways by Robert Nozick and John Rawls.[3] To this, Dewey clearly counterposed that naturalized post-Hegelian evolutionary perspective that we have developed previously. It sees the individual as essentially a social product whose development and flourishing (to use Martha Nussbaum's quite suggestive expression) ought to be the goal of society to nurture and facilitate. Individuality, rather than being the "given" that it is often assumed to be by those who promote versions of classical liberalism, is a highly prized goal of social policy for Dewey. The challenge is to create the social and cultural conditions that nurture individuality from the more or less inchoate and relatively amorphous and undeveloped biological individuals that are born into society.[4]

In their brilliant book on American society, *Habits of the Heart,* the authors quote Alexis de Tocqueville's observation that "'individualism is a calm and considerate feeling which disposes each citizen to isolate himself from the mass of his fellows and withdraw into the circle of family and friends; with this little society formed to his taste, he gladly leaves the greater society to look after itself.' As democratic individualism grows, [Tocqueville] wrote, 'there are more and more people who, though neither rich nor powerful enough to have much hold over others, have gained or kept enough wealth and enough understanding to look after their own needs. Such folk owe no man anything and hardly expect anything from anybody. They form the habit of thinking of themselves in isolation and imagine that their whole destiny is in their hands.... Each man is forever thrown back on himself alone, and there is danger that he may be shut up in the solitude of his own heart.'"[5] The authors then comment that, "immersion in private economic pursuits undermines the person as citizen. On the other hand, involvement in public affairs is the best antidote to the pernicious effects of individualistic isolation."[6]

But "'society does not consist of individuals (or, we might add, groups), but expresses the sum of the relations within which individuals (and groups) stand.' And the essential movement of scientific theory will be seen to consist in the movement from the manifest phenomena of social life, as conceptualized in the experience of the social agents concerned, to the essential relations that necessitate them. Of such relations the agents may or may not be aware."[7] "Sociology [the science of society]," therefore, "is not [primarily] concerned, as such, with large-scale, mass or group behavior (conceived as the behavior of large numbers, masses or groups of individuals). Rather it is concerned, at least paradigmatically, with the persistent *relations* between individuals (and groups), and with the relations between these relations (and between such relations and nature and the products of such relations). In the simplest case its subject matter may be exemplified by such relations as between capitalist and worker, [elected representative] and constituent, student and teacher, husband and wife. Such relations are general and relatively enduring, but they do not involve collective or mass behavior as such in the way in which a strike or a demonstration does.... . Mass behavior is an interesting social-psychological phenomenon, but it is not the [primary] subject matter of sociology."[8]

Theoretically conceived, therefore, "the real problem appears to be not so much that of how one could give an individualist explanation of social behavior, but that of how one could ever give a nonsocial (that is strictly individualistic) explanation of individual, at least characteristically human, behavior! For all the predicates designating properties special to persons all presuppose a social context for their employment. A tribesman implies a tribe, the cashing of a check a banking system. Explanation ... always involves irreducibly social predicates."[9] This irreducibly social constitution of the human self has been well understood by the best of the classical philosophers, from the "ancients" Plato and Aristotle to the "moderns" Rousseau, Hegel, Mill, and Dewey.

Competition: Individualism's Universal Elixir

The doctrine of individualism leads inexorably to both the theory of human competitiveness and its celebration, and this usually in tautologically circular fashion. The tendency is both to argue that humans are by nature competitive and, in praising the value of competition, to advocate its promotion in all fields of endeavor. Competition is thus the perfect compliment to the individualistic theory of human nature and one of its most fundamental social values. In one sense, humans are seen as being competitive by nature—the alternative, on this view, being boredom, passivity, ineffectiveness, and death. On the other, the value of competition becomes the unquestioned pole star of the social world, without which people are seen as adrift in a world devoid of interest, excitement, and purpose.

In one sense, competition is seen as necessitated by objective scarcity; on the other, innumerable artificial scarcities are generated in order to create contexts for competition. How often, for example, do Americans even organize their social and educational experiences around competition—from scrabble to spelling bees, from organized sports to grading and academic awards. I am reminded of a childhood birthday party to which my son was invited when he was in first grade. The child's mother, in order to ensure that everyone had a good time, had gone to great lengths to organize the party around a series of competitive games. She had even composed a scoreboard on which she had listed the name of each child down the side and the names of each game they were to play across the top. Even more, she had not only provided presents for the winners of each game, but in an effort to assuage the anticipated pain of all the rest who were destined to be its losers had provided presents for them, too. What better illustrates the pervasive hold that a competitive ethic has taken on our imagination, as well as the dim recognition that such competitions are not always the fun they are supposed to be, but rather are objective situations that inevitably create deep levels of sustaining anxiety, condemning the vast majority of people not only to experience loss, but to experience themselves as "losers."[10]

Thus are produced, as a kind of self-fulfilling prophecy, precisely those anxious self-preoccupied competitive characters that it was claimed it was our nature to be. Is it any wonder that people so brought up should tend to experience the continual need to "prove themselves," often finding it difficult to find enjoyment outside of competitive situations, even turning such completely noncompetitive experiences as skiing down a mountain into a competitive race, with poles symmetrically placed to increase the challenge? That they should even have their imagination so trained and channeled that they would often have difficulty in conceiving of interesting noncompetitive games and enjoyments. Still further, that they should have so identified achievement with competitive success that they would believe and feel that neither meaningful effort nor efficient work would or could be carried on outside of a competitive environment. No wonder such a culture should read evolution as a competitive struggle among individuals and species, and our appropriate relation to the natural environment as one of competition and the struggle for domination.

Individuals so nurtured are most likely to experience the world as a struggle between us and them, in which fear of failure or defeat is at least as motivating as the desire for victory, while the anxiety intrinsic to the combat, though it may well motivate greater attention and exertion, is as likely to be experienced as a continual strain, if not overwhelming burden, from which release into relaxation and leisure is not likely ever to be far from one's mind. In fact, the competitive situation is often on the verge of becoming overwhelming, such that the ever-present fear of failure may well be the most sustaining pressure that maintains involvement, with the lure of reward for success being the carrot before the donkey's nose that keeps the treadmill rolling. Numerous scientific studies have shown that regularly randomized rewards can keep both a rat and a gambler committed to pushing a lever.

No wonder the prevalence in such a culture of organized sports both for entertainment, leisure, character development, and business opportunities. The human need for dramatic significance is thus addressed by the organization of competitive spectacles, in which it is the reward for the winners that crowns the struggle and justifies the effort, while the fear of being a "loser" spurs one on, or drives one to dream of retirement and release from the competition.

At this point, it is clear that one will need release from the anxiety of such a pressure-packed world—of business, sports, education, even of amusement. We may fantasize a retreat from such a "heartless" public world into the "haven" provided by an idealized private world of love and family. Here we can better place the illusion of "romantic love" by which we may dream of "falling" in love with one who fulfills our every desire, and loves us for who we are, not what we do, or fail to do. Such infatuation is so different in feeling and behavior from the rationally calculating anxiety of the public world of business, politics, and organized sports. No wonder the celebration of privatization, fleeing from the public world in the hopes of finding peace and contentment "at home," only to find that world ultimately boring and uninteresting unless drama can be brought into it—and for characters so socialized, such drama must be competitive or "rewarding," that is, it must provide external fulfillment for characters not trained to integral self-development and constructive dialogue with one's surroundings. In the words of the Roman historian Livy, "We have reached the point where we cannot bear either our vices or their cure."[11]

The other side of the competitive ethos is the way it inevitably tends to devalue both the intrinsic satisfaction in the productive process and concern for the quality of the resultant product or service. If to win is to beat the other, how you do it tends initially to become of secondary importance, and then increasingly irrelevant. This speaks both to the objective quality of the process and product or performance as well as to the subjective quality of the experience undergone, the character expressed and developed, and the satisfaction obtained. One is not rewarded by others for, and probably less and less felt satisfied oneself by, the quality of one's effort and the product produced, but rather for the act of beating the others and the recognition and reward it obtains. Evidence in fact suggests that there is an inverse relationship between the value placed upon the result and that placed on the quality of the process: the more the result is prized, the less the intrinsic quality of the activity is valued.[12] In American society, the transformation to an increasingly encompassing competitive individualism can be seen in the pervasive replacement of Grantland Rice's motto that "it's not whether you win or lose, but how you play the game" with that of Vince Lombardi that "winning isn't everything, it's the only thing."

It should also be obvious that such an exclusive emphasis not only upon the result but also upon beating out the competition devalues the actual quality of the product, except instrumentally, while placing total emphasis upon the success in defeating the other, by whatever means necessary. This both severs any intrinsic relation between quality of product and criteria of success, reducing the connection to a matter of contingent relation, and reduces moral concerns essentially to matters of efficacy. It becomes increasingly problematic whether or not such a competitive system advances the quality or efficiency of production. It certainly does not promote mutual understanding and generosity of spirit.[13]

In such a world, the focus is inevitably on the others with whom you must contend, and on the strategy and tactics needed to defeat them. It is not, except secondarily and instrumentally, upon the intrinsic quality of your activity, the development of your character, or the human quality of your relations with others. What you are thus trained to attend to (and rewarded for) is not the activity, but its result, and the "payment" that others will provide to you for your competitive success. It is from them, with money, honors, and approval, that success and fulfillment is to come.[14]

Economics as the Rational Theory of an Instrumental Practice

From the doctrine of competitive individualism and its self-centered ethos, which is essentially dependent upon an extrinsic reward for its experienced satisfaction, it is a short step to the economic doctrine that self-seeking individuals engage in productive activity out of scarcity in order to obtain tangible rewards (to be paid with profit, goods, or power), the possession of which constitutes the justification of their activity. Why else would one "sweat and strain, body all aching and wracked with pain," if not because scarcity forces such behavior, and monetary or social payment rewards it— when, that is, punishments do not require it? Thus, social order is naturally seen to arise—as in Social Contract Theory—out of the needs that such individuals experience for the goods and services required to survive and prosper and the protection that such activity requires, while the attendant relations between individuals are seen to result from the formal and informal contracts into which people enter in order to use others to obtain the things they need—when, that is, they cannot simply overwhelm them and take them by force. The doctrine of "economic man" emerges naturally from the matrix of this metaphysico-social theory and practice.

Whether explicit or implicit, this conception grounds an often highly mathematical and technical theory of the structure of a social reality seen as composed of essentially autonomous self-interested rational goods purchasing or investing pleasure (and profit) maximizers. Such individuals are seen to operate essentially independently, relating to one another primarily in terms of commodity transactions in accord with utility maximization. Rationality can thus only be "getting the most for your money," or obtaining more while working less. In such a world, others are by definition "other" than the self, hence either competitors for scarce resources (who will bid up the price of what we need or want), potential instruments to employ in the production of commodities or the provision of services, abstract consumers who constitute a potential market for our goods or services, or actual purchasers of our products.

In this atomized world of isolated individuals, human beings are viewed as rational self-seekers and society as essentially a regulated series of competitive market transactions whose operative rule is "buyer beware." But what happened to the complexities and ambiguities of human values, feelings, commitments, and motivations? Into what realm did social relations evaporate, human loyalty and benevolence get reduced to marketing strategies, and shared history and group identification disappear? What makes it rational, for example, to destroy the whales in order to increase your stock portfolio, or to deplete the rain forest in order to produce hamburgers for overweight consumers and houses for suburban sprawl? In *You Can't Eat GNP*, Eric Davidson reports on farmers in nineteenth-century America who regularly boasted of "wearing out" several farms as they depleted its nutrient content in the accumulation of profits. He observes that "economists would argue that these farmers were acting rationally in terms of doing what provided them the greatest profit for their investment of capital and labor. Ecologists, on the other hand, see a sad irrational legacy of abuse of the land by previous generations, which limits the potential use of the land today and for several generations to come. Clearly, ecologists and economists think differently about the value of soils and other natural resources."[15]

There is actually little that is truly scientific about this economic theory of human behavior, except, that is, for the fascinatingly circular manner in which it operates, which is certainly worthy of note. Let me explain. Once a society has been organized in accord with the (mistaken) theory of competitive individualism, it creates a moral fabric, pedagogical and media infrastructure, and institutional complex of production, distribution, consumption, celebration, and reward that produces and nurtures precisely that character structure and ideology that predisposes its members to think and behave—and even to feel it "natural" to so act—in accord with the "objective" structure, "scientific" theory, and moral imperatives of its institutional order. At that point, an empirical sociology that samples societal behavior will obtain the "objective" evidence that confirms the motivational picture, while the economic theory will elaborate the complexities by which such individuals can and do succeed. That theory will describe how people behave, provide theoretical explanation of such behavior grounded in a theory of human nature and motivation, and it will then elaborate sophisticated theories of strategies for succeeding within the world thus encountered that has been "unintentionally constructed."

This economic reality has itself been socially constructed, with its consequent theoretical description then providing an implicit rationale and justification that both reinforces its operation and provides a practically successful strategy for operating in a world so constructed. What, in principle, began as an effort to improve the conditions of human life becomes a self-justifying closed circle in which increased consumption of those who "have"—to a large extent at the expense both of those who do not have and of environmental sustainability—is required to sustain economic vitality. Even more, this reversal of perspective has become enshrined in that theoretical frame in which the very notion of rationality has been inverted, so that the future can be effectively discounted by the interest rate, and the extinction of species can express an economically rational investment decision.

It Takes a Village

But then, all society is in a fundamental sense socially constructed—usually, mostly unintentionally, through individual and collective action over time. "Social Structures, unlike natural structures, do not exist independently of the activities they govern; … [they] do not exist independently of the agents' conceptions of what they are doing in their activity; … [and] may be only relatively enduring (so that the tendencies they ground may not be universal in the sense of space-time invariant)." Thus, "society, as an object of inquiry, is necessarily 'theoretical', in the sense that, like a magnetic field, it is necessarily unperceivable. As such, it cannot be empirically identified independently of its effects; so that it can only be known, not shown, to exist. However in this respect it is no different from many objects of natural scientific inquiry. What does distinguish it [from such objects] is that not only can society not be identified independently of its effects, it does not *exist* independently of them either."[16]

What makes the specific social structure I have been describing nefarious is the fact that it is dependent for its existence on the ideologically useful systematic misrepresentation of human nature and motivation that serves as its own self-fulfilling project. It is constructed and maintained by a socially dominant theory that completely misrepresents reality in order to serve the interests of a very powerful but limited group or class at the expense of the vast majority. That was the import of our previous discussion of ideology and the interrelation of means and ends (see Chapter 5).

A classic example of the power of such self-fulfilling social conceptions to shape social reality in accord with its initial preconceptions is provided by the study of "white flight." This often occurs in the United States when a few whites begin to fear that the price of their homes is going to go down because blacks are moving into the neighborhood. Their fear need not be—though often is—motivated by racism on their part; it can simply be the result of their (rational) expectation that other whites, similarly fearful, will leave before them. Thus, they may (rationally) seek to sell their own house before its value depreciates, unintentionally helping to create the conditions they had anticipated and others also feared. By selling early they may be able to beat the exodus and still obtain a fairly good price for their house, while unintentionally contributing to depressing the housing market for those who remain, thus increasing the pressure for those others to flee before prices drop further, poorer and less powerful people move in, the quality of services is reduced, and the infrastructure and quality of community life continue to deteriorate. Thus, white flight is often the unintentional consequence of a series of uncoordinated rational acts by isolated individuals seeking to maximize their personal utility faced with a perceived social reality that their very acts serve to create.

Not only does this phenomenon well illustrate the power of expectations in shaping a social reality that may not be the explicit choice of any of the actors, but it also suggests the structural inadequacy of relying on the isolated decisions of individuals to address such systemic problems and the often crucial importance of rational social intervention to create and sustain the public conditions that make possible productive individual initiative.

It should therefore be clear, in sum, that the autonomous self is clearly an abstraction that is empty of substantial content. Its very emptiness is the source of a pervasive anxiety, uncertainty, a dis-ease, that may be taken as driving the autonomous self into the world of competitive action, always seeking to do, obtain, win, conquer, own, possess, and thus finally to "be somebody." (Consider the Sartrean vision of freedom expressed by Orestes, for example, who, in "*The Flies,*" seeks to assume the burdens of the people of Argos to liberate them from their self-imposed crushing guilt, but also and more fundamentally to give himself an identity, a weight in the world, a substance his empty critical freedom so far lacks.) But lacking any substantive self other than its reflective capacity to criticize and choose, it can only prove its significance by the materials it can amass or possess, and the social approval that it can garner. It must look to others to set the criteria for its own success, requiring that it conform to the rules of the social game if it is to obtain from others the recognition that alone would seem to confirm its ontological significance—while always having to be wary of their reciprocal effort to "return the favor" precisely by stealing for themselves their own recognition and significance. Their basic ontological anxiety is therefore reinforced by an emerging and highly competitive interpersonal anxiety that is, no doubt, the root meaning of Sartre's famous phrase that "Hell is other people."

The Failure of Liberal Individualism

The theory of ontological individualism is also the basis for absolutist theories of individual rights—as with the American Declaration of Independence's claim that "all men are endowed by their Creator with certain inalienable rights." Such rights are claimed to belong to individuals independent of, and prior to, their "entrance" into society, whose responsibility it then is to preserve those rights (to the extent to which they have not been compromised by the agreed "compact" upon which the social and political order was founded) from infringements by others. To defend those rights, "governments were instituted among men, deriving their just powers from the consent of the governed." Thus, they can never be justified in taking away our "inalienable" rights, whether it be to private property, the freedom of speech, or the right to bear arms.

Precisely such an absolutist theory has formed the basis of the often admirable work of the American Civil Liberties Union (ACLU). Given the fact that governments have an almost unavoidable tendency to expand their power—whether from the need to address obvious social ills, to actively right injustice and to "promote the general welfare," to preserve society from threats to "national security" both internal and external, or simply by the natural tendency of bureaucracies to expand the scope of, while limiting knowledge of and responsibility for, their activities—every society would seem to be in continuing need of the work of an organization such as the ACLU: to protect the speech, free association, and social space for active citizen participation that are the preconditions of a vibrant culture that nurtures human dignity.

But that is, as it were, only part of the story. Such a vibrant and democratically participatory society requires collective integrity, social cohesion, and the capacity for group self-definition and self-determination. Democracy is a social process of collective self-determination, and it requires that the group be recognized as self-determining as to both its policies and its membership. Any group that cannot control who can enter (but *not* who can leave) has lost control over its identity, and potentially over its goals, directions, and policies. It would be like a household that could not keep others out—it could certainly be swamped by others; the better it was doing, the more likely such a result. Its success would be its downfall, like a Gresham's Law of social well-being: deprived or depleted groups overwhelm and destroy successful ones, with people fleeing depravation for prosperity, as "third world" peoples struggle for entrance into "developed" countries. It should therefore be clear that individuals cannot be seen as having an "inalienable" right to go wherever they choose, thus denying to communities the collective right to control their membership.

Further, individuals in the community obtain their rights from the community that has nurtured them into maturity. As our entire argument has sought to conclusively demonstrate, the notion of the ontological individual, the autonomous self, is completely incoherent. (In Classical times, Socrates made that point brilliantly in the *Crito*, while the classic modern expression of that seminal insight can be found in the writings of Jean-Jacques Rousseau.)[17] This being so, any notion that depends upon it, such as that of the "inalienable rights" of such an individual, must itself also be incoherent, and without theoretical or moral foundation. In actual fact, the insistence upon such purported rights can often have a highly destructive effect on the capacity of a self-determining collectivity to democratically determine its destiny and to advance collective well-being. Several examples should make this point quite clear.

In the late twentieth century, the ACLU actively intervened both to oppose legislative efforts to limit campaign expenditures and to stymie communities that sought to promote racial equality by using quotas to limit the number of members of a specific race that could move in. In the former case, the ACLU argued that efforts to limit campaign contributions were an indefensible infringement on the free speech of those with large amounts of money—who should be allowed to spend their money however they wished. They did not recognize the collective rights of the self-governing community to determine the groundrules for democratically electing their representatives. The purported inalienable rights of the individual trumped the collective rights of the community—essentially because that community was conceived not as an objective social reality so much as an instrumentality used by the autonomous individuals to advance their private freedom and well-being.

In the latter case, the reasoning was similarly flawed—and socially counterproductive. By insisting upon the free mobility of each person, and denying to a local community the right to determine conditions of membership on the basis of race or religion, they effectively destroyed the community's ability to maintain ethnic and racial balance—almost always resulting in that aforementioned "white flight" and re-ghettoization.

None of this is meant either to denigrate the noble intentions of the ACLU or to minimize the complexity of the issues with which we are here dealing. It is, of course, much easier to assert and insist upon absolute and inviolable standards—which may even tend in the long run more often than not to produce morally desirable results—than to enter into the far more complex, confused, and uncertain terrain of democratic realism and moral pragmatism.[18] What are the relevant criteria that should be brought to bear? How does one rank those different criteria? And do so differentially in each of the specific circumstances with which one has to deal? What are the claims that are legitimately denied, or subordinated? For example, if a community can exclude others—on what bases? To what extent? How does such a decision get reviewed? How do we insure that such power is not used "prejudicially?" Are we not entering onto very dangerous terrain when we let the government play any role in limiting the free expression of its members? How can we insure that such limitations will not be used to impede criticism of government officials? To stifle dissent? Ultimately, to suppress democratic self-government? Of course, we cannot! But the reverse process is at least as potentially perverse: allowing those with the most wealth or power to monopolize the means of communication such that they can in effect, if not in form, undermine the collective capacity of the citizenry to get a free flow of information, to have access to all forms of criticism and dissent, and to participate in relative equality in the decision-making processes. We cannot resolve these problems in advance or in the abstract—whether raised by the "Left" in defending people's "freedom of speech" or mobility, or by the "Right" in defending the right of an individual to amass property and engage in enterprise free from government interference—but we cannot even begin to seriously and constructively address them until we have disabused ourselves of the illusions of metaphysical individualism.

A further troubling expression of the conflict between individual and collective rights emerges with the issue of immigration. Abstract individualism often argues for the right of individuals to move wherever they want, and claims that it is an unjust restriction on individual freedom to limit or impede immigration. (They often add, especially in the American context, that we, or our ancestors, were all immigrants once, and thus it is purely arbitrary and selfish to seek to deny to potential immigrants the opportunity from which we have already benefited.) This argument is clearly wrong on both counts. It grounds its rights claim on that abstract individualism that we have been criticizing, and it fails to adequately consider the cultural rooting and historical transformation of values and rights. The latter issue is quite a complex one, rooted in the historicized metaphysical frame that we have been developing, but requiring a more detailed discussion in its own right, to which we will return later.[19] In the former case, our arguments about the rights of communities to maintain their political and social integrity are once again relevant. In fact, it is often precisely those forces most interested in using such immigrants to undercut the rights and power of the "native" population that make up the most forceful proponents of relatively unlimited immigration. Immigrants (especially illegal ones) can provide an ample supply of cheap labor that can usually be relatively easily exploited, and can be used to set up a struggle between native and immigrant workers, thus dividing the "working class" and further driving down wages for all. While it is not at all surprising that such forces should support the free mobility of cheap labor, this position is given moral legitimacy by those more humane social and religious forces that promote such immigration on the humanitarian grounds of social justice and human rights. Similarly, of course, foxes might promote the unlimited immigration of rabbits, but no one would consider that they were thus being more "humane."[20] But it should be quite obvious simply from the numbers that we will not even begin to make a dent in third-world poverty by permitting relatively unlimited immigration.[21] We do not thereby even begin to address the underlying conditions of poverty and exploitation in those third-world countries, to much of which U.S. economic, political, and military policies have actually contributed.[22] At best, all we do is provide a social safety valve for those third-world countries—with the most energetic and enterprising people being the most likely to leave—while allowing them to avoid addressing their problems of equitable economic development and excessive population growth, with its consequent environmental damage. At the same time, we undermine our domestic labor force, as well as our collective capacity for democratic self-government. But those misguided humanitarian arguments do serve to create guilt among many potential opponents of such immigration, split the democratic forces, and thus, unintentionally, contribute to the further disempowerment of the population at large, while contributing to an increase in the domestic population that can sustain traditional strategies for quantitative economic growth.[23]

Consider a couple of additional examples where the doctrine of individualism proves its structural inadequacy. First, the issue of the regulation of sound. Sound travels long distances, especially when unimpeded by physical barriers. It takes only one person to fill the air with sound; it takes everyone to maintain peace and quiet. Thus, only one person has the power to destroy the peace of the entire community. Sounds cannot be blocked out the way sights can. You can't even "close your ears" or look away, as you can with sight. Thus, the doctrine of individual rights must be constrained by the equal right of others not to have to listen to that sound. This requires collective action. Some argue that to regulate the ability of people to play amplified sound on their own property would be an infringement of their property rights, but that is completely mistaken. This is not to suggest that we should tell people what, when, and how they can play music in the privacy of their homes. But it is reasonable for the public to claim the right to stop people from playing music in public spaces or in the privacy of other people's homes. It is not where the music originates that is the important question, but where it ends up. If you shoot a bullet, you are responsible for where it lands. The issue is quite similar to that with "second-hand smoke." No one should have the right to make me listen to their music, especially on my property or in my home, any more than they have the right to make me breathe their cigarette smoke.

Of course, this issue might be considered, mistakenly, as simply one that regulates competing claims of individual rights, with the government serving as an arbitrator. But the same can in no way be done with the issue of drug taking by athletes. Here it is clearly a matter of the need for collective policy if one is to preserve the quality of the game while protecting the health of the participants. If there are no collective decisions, then there will be an inevitable pressure for athletes to gain a competitive advantage by taking drug-enhancers, thus putting those athletes who do not wish to so subject themselves at a serious competitive disadvantage. They will simply not be able to compete as effectively. But we cannot adequately frame this issue as a matter of individual rights, unless you wish to argue that people have a right to compete in games without having to take drugs. But that would seem to press the doctrine of individual rights quite far indeed. It is far more appropriate to see this as a legitimate expression of the exercise of collective right in the service of two overriding values: protecting the health of the participants and preserving the integrity of the competition—without here further considering the value of competition in its own right.

A similar argument with more potentially egregious consequences is the argument for so-called free trade. By denying countries the capacity to control investment, trade, and tariffs, on the grounds that they would thus be undermining the legitimate rights of private property to use their own resources as they wish—to produce and distribute their goods however the market will bear free from the imposition of governmental authority—you deny to them the capacity to protect the health, safety, labor standards, and environmental quality of their communities, while providing a differential advantage to those institutions and nations that systematically undermine such standards, thus resulting in an economic "race to the bottom."[24]

Deconstructing the Medical Model of Ill-Being

It should also be quite clear why the "medical model" of so-called mental illness is so dangerous, and that is for principally three reasons. It confuses a sociopsychological and existential behavior with the physiobiochemical processes that are its material condition; treats intrinsically meaningful human behavior as if it were nothing but the expression of an essentially foreign infection, chemical imbalance, or genetic disorder; and tends to assume a morally superior position from which it can subordinate those who are threateningly different.

Concerning the first issue, it is initially worth recalling the obvious. If there are no grounds for claiming existence for a separate and distinct mental or spiritual substance, a supernatural power that somehow enters into and takes control of our mind and action (as, for example, Descartes and the Western monotheistic religious have in essence claimed), then everything that transpires in the human mind, including all of our purposeful activity, must have a natural, physiobiochemical basis. For every human activity, there must be processes at work within the human brain and organism that make that activity possible. That is what I mean by naturalism. But it no more follows from this fact that those processes can completely explain human activity than it follows that neurons are conscious because consciousness depends for its existence on the activity of neurons. That has been precisely the point of our extensive prior discussions of emergent phenomena and systemic properties—even more, of the lack of any one-to-one correlation between brain physiology or neural chemistry and consciously expressed meanings.

Clearly, thinking, whether healthy or deranged, cannot take place without the existence of concomitant neurological processes. It should be obvious that any chemical or electrical intervention that impedes or short-circuits such processes is almost certain to have an impact on the subject's thinking activity.[25] We might well also reverse the process, and expect that any mental activity is most likely to influence the processes of brain activity, the production and dissemination of chemicals, the development of synaptic connections, the electrical stimulation of distinct sectors of the brain, the initiation of muscular activity, the triggering of gene expression, and even the secretion of hormones that stimulate emotions such as anger. One does not need to have any very sophisticated theory to appreciate that perceived threats can stimulate the production of chemicals that prepare the organism for flight, any more than we need such theory to appreciate the way that hallucinogenic chemicals can seriously derange one's capacity for rational thought. Since there are not two distinct realities within the human person, interactions between these functionally distinct levels are certainly to be expected, and are obviously pervasive. The challenge is to understand them, and to do so in a way that does justice to their manner of operation without forcing either one to be absorbed by the other in the service of some preexisting bias.[26]

I thus return to the issue. All good theorists know that correlation is not causation, that necessary conditions are not the same as sufficient conditions, and that systemic properties are not identical to those of their constituent elements. If we have shown how consciousness can be an emergent systemic property of individualized mentality, and how the mind is essentially a systemic quality of society, then it should be clear that human behavior is the expression of a meaningful social system that is constituted by the particular relational properties of socialized organisms. They cannot function without oxygen, but that doesn't mean that their behavior is "caused" by, or reducible to the processes of, respiration—any more than it can exist without, or is reducible to, the forces of gravity or electromagnetism. It is equally obvious that all such activities would be drastically altered, to say the least, by significant—usually, by even minor—modifications of these processes. (Consider the dramatic effect that can be obtained by the most miniscule medication, or poison, for that matter.) But these would be less likely to change the meaning and purposes of the behavior, than to impede or destroy it. For such behavior is at its core a meaningful activity, one that is usually motivated by values and desires, and intentionally directed toward goals or objectives. Human activity is not a property of the constituent elements or natural forces that are its necessary conditions.

We can see an example of this relation when we consider the processes generated by some "mind-altering" drugs. Clearly there is a physiobiochemical process that radically transforms brain activity, producing often bizarre hallucinations. These hallucinations often have many common properties, such as a tendency for ego loss or dissipation, which suggests the causal power of the drug. Further, the areas of the brain that are primarily affected by the activity of such drugs can be studied, as can the changes in brain wave patterns. But the actual meaningful content of the hallucinogenic experience cannot be predicted from the operations of the drug, while it can often at least be more reliably suggested by reflection on the psychic concerns and preoccupations of the concerned subject. It is better understood as an expression of the systemic world view and pattern of meaningful interpretations by which the person makes sense of his or her world. The drug does not constitute or cause that pattern of interpretation, nor the actions that emerge there from.

Neuroscientific explanations can typically explain how it is possible for creatures with such-and-such a brain to do the kinds of things they do. They can explain what neural connections must obtain and what neural activities must take place in order for it to be possible for the animal to possess and exercise the powers it naturally possesses. In the case of human beings in particular, neuroscience may aspire to explain the neural conditions for the possibility of the mastery of a language, the possession of which is itself a condition of the possibility of rationality in both thought and action. However, neuroscience cannot displace or undermine the explanatory force of the good reasons we sincerely give for our behaviour, or invalidate the justifications we give for rational behaviour. The rationality of behaviour that is motivated by good reasons is not given a deeper explanation by specifying the neural facts that make it possible for creatures such as us to act for such reasons. When we apprehend the propriety, adequacy or goodness of the reasons for which a person acted, then we fully understand why he did what he did.[27]

This leads directly to the second major problem with the "mental illness" model. Not only does it express a physiobiochemical reductionism, but it also treats the person as essentially the victim of an alien intrusion, and the disease as something that comes from without to infect the person. Such is the causality of the illness model. There are no doubt cases where it is appropriately applied, which only empirical investigation can determine. But for the vast majority of instances, we are dealing primarily with patterns of meaningfully interpreted behavior rather than biomedical "infection" or the like. That is not to say that different physiological or genetic constitutions may not be more or less susceptible to emotional disturbances, nor that, for example, such emotional disturbances may not be correlated with the appearances of certain chemical imbalances, as either predisposing factors or causal consequences. We know that anger can increase the level of acid in the stomach, while the heightened production of testosterone can predispose one to aggression. Yet anger and aggression also involve a conceptual element—a meaningful perception of a situation that, for example, one finds unjust, offensive, or threatening. Anger, for example, is an intentional response to a perceived insult or injustice—but it is only one such possible response. Youthful male aggression, for example, is more closely correlated with cultural conditions than with hormonal levels.[28]

One of the powers of Buddhist meditation, for example, lies precisely in its capacity to change the way we view an event or person, or the way we choose to respond to circumstances. By interpreting the situation differently, we can transform the nature of our emotional response, possibly removing any feeling of anger at the same insult or injury, even transforming it into sympathy or compassion. The fourteenth Dalai Lama has even gone so far as to thank the Chinese, who have occupied his homeland of Tibet since 1950, for giving him the opportunity of learning patience. Not the usual response, nor, to be sure, comprehensible as a biochemical reaction.[29]

Even more, such transformed emotional responses can change the level of chemical or neurological activity in the brain, as brain wave studies of meditation have well confirmed. But then again, that is to be expected once we realize that we are not dealing with two distinct entities, but rather with an integrated organism composed of functionally distinct though dynamically interrelated systems. All such systems involve the integration of elements whose operation makes possible the working of the totality, but whose elemental processes can be causally affected by the logic of the operation of the total system. Just because one finds a correlation between certain "mental disturbances" and the presence of certain chemical "imbalances" or unusual neurological patterns, it should not be assumed that the latter is the cause of the former.[30] Wherein one decides to locate the causal force may often depend practically upon the means available for intervention, but one must be wary of assuming that because one is most comfortable with using a hammer, everything must have been constructed with nails.[31]

There is then the further problem with the designation of behavioral problems as mental illness. It invariably assumes (an often hidden) standard of "mental health" that is "value-laden," and usually ideological. To judge a pattern of behavior as "ill" means that it is defective as far as the standard of health is concerned. But is that standard nonproblematic? Does it not involve judgments as to what is desired, appropriate, preferred, or even "healthy" behavior? But when are anger, annoyance, pity, sympathy, fear, even outrage, aggression, and violence appropriate, and when not? May not people rationally, or morally, disagree on such issues? Does not the appellation of "illness" tend to assert the morally nonproblematic character of the judgment, placing the expert on a moral pedestal beyond criticism and imputing quasi-paternalistic and well-meaning intent to the "medical" intervention? In fact, some of the most apparently "divinely" inspired religious leaders were often thought to be mentally unbalanced by those around them. Wasn't even Jesus' family embarrassed by his behavior and did they not claim not to know him? Was it not Matthew who commented that a prophet is usually not honored in his hometown?[32]

In sum, human activity is pervasively purposeful, framed by a perception of reality, motivated by an interpretation of its significance, and directed toward a result to be realized. The human organism is both the physical embodiment of this interpretation and the vehicle for its practical expression. But the evaluation of the moral value, practical significance, and psychic quality of the undertaking cannot be addressed from any impartial and morally noncontroversial medical pedestal. It requires that the activity be placed within the interpretive perspective that provides it with a meaning that is intelligible and defensible—in short, with a story that makes coherent sense, toward a consideration of which we will turn shortly.

What the Community Owes the Individual

Consider further the manner in which this metaphysical individualism can so subtly insinuate itself into one's worldview so as to undermine otherwise humane analyses of social rights and liberties. In Ronald Dworkin's discussion of the U.S. Supreme Court's 2003 decision on college affirmative action admission programs, he asks: "Do racially sensitive admission plans serve a compelling goal?"[33] After observing that "the briefs supporting the University of Michigan cite two different goals as compelling.... . The first is the social goal that ... emphasize(s) equipping more minority students for leadership in order to attack damaging racial stratification in politics, business, the professions, and the military. The second is the educational goal of classroom diversity."

Then, after noting that "opponents of the Michigan plan challenge both of these goals," he focuses on their claim "that past Supreme Court decisions rule out the first, social, goal because the Court has repeatedly declared that remedying past socioeconomic injustice cannot count as a compelling goal justifying racial classifications. But this objection," Dworkin claims, "confuses two different ideas: the backward-looking claim that affirmative action is justified in order to compensate minority students for past injustice to their race which the Court has rejected, and the forward-looking claim that it is justified in order to improve society in ways that benefit practically everyone."

He then gets to the heart of his response. "Several Justices have declared, in past cases, that though an institution may use racial classifications to compensate for its own past discrimination, it may not do so to compensate for discrimination by others or in the community as a whole." Dworkin agrees that "it is, in fact, doubtful that affirmative action can ever be justified as compensation, because compensation is a matter of individual, not group, entitlements, and allowing black applicants to have preference now cannot compensate generations of blacks who suffered injustice in the past."

While it is certainly true that compensation to the current generation cannot remedy ills committed to past generations, the argument proceeds as if each living individual is a metaphysically distinct and autonomous being, whose rights and powers are identical at birth, regardless of his or her group's "prior condition of servitude." It is, in fact, to speak as if one's group identity, origin, native affiliation, and social location do not have existence in a real social sense, but are at best a conceptual construct. The question of whether systematic historical disadvantages can effectively impede the capacity of a group's current members from having equal opportunities—why, that is, the current members of a historically disadvantaged group cannot personally suffer in the present in such a manner as to justify affirmative action on their behalf even though they were not themselves the direct target of such past treatment—that question is not even raised, I suggest, because of the unquestioned underlying assumption of metaphysical individualism. The self is treated as coming into being and being socially constituted completely ahistorically, so that not having been personally the direct object of past discrimination means that an individual has not suffered from it and thus cannot, in principle, claim compensatory treatment. At the same time, to grant such compensation would be at the expense of the rights of other individuals who themselves, however much they may have objectively benefited from their membership in a historically favored group, not being responsible for these past injustices, do not deserve such discrimination and have no personal obligation to make such compensation at their expense.[34]

Consequences of an Ideological Divide

It should be clear by now how the nonreductive naturalism that has been developed here seeks to address serious—and I believe, fatal—flaws in the traditional metaphysics. Those flaws seriously undermine the capacity of theoretical and practical inquiries to make coherent sense, and often tend to lead practical applications into diverse dead ends or socially and humanly destructive directions. Let me explain.

On the reductive side, in which mind is simply reduced to brain, and that is understood as nothing but an organ in the neurophysiology of the organism operating in accord with causally deterministic chemical principles, the possibility of human freedom as consciously determined and morally responsible choices among a range of imagined alternatives clearly becomes impossible—nothing but an illusion, a figment of the inadequately informed and ultimately confused brain. What Spinozistic determinism classically referred to as "inadequate ideas," and Daniel Dennett more recently calls "folk psychology." But I think I have already paid adequate attention to this point, and need not further dwell upon it here.

Let me now address in far greater detail the alternative problem: that created by dualism of one sort or another, namely the belief in a mind, whether functionally or ontologically, seen as essentially independent of the brain or body. This position, while having relatively little support among theoretical scientists, is probably the position almost universally held by most people worldwide and is presupposed by almost every major religion, with the possible exceptions of original Buddhism, Zen Buddhism, Confucianism, Taoism, and Ethical Culture. Being so widespread and more or less "taken for granted," it presents two very significant problems. On the one hand, it tends to frame almost all discussions of public policy and moral evaluation as solely matters of personal decision and individual responsibility. On the other, when seriously confronted with its essential scientific incoherence, it tends to rapidly collapse into what is usually viewed as the only other available alternative position, namely that reductive scientific materialistic determinism that makes moral discussion and talk of human dignity otiose. That was the challenge posed by my extensive quote from Daly with which I began Chapter 4, and the primary objective of that extensive discussion and defense of a nonreductive naturalism that constituted the major task of Part I of this book.

Turning, therefore, to a consideration of some of the most significant operative consequences of the prevalent belief in the autonomy of the mental will help to further underscore the practical importance of the inquiry I have undertaken in this work. Belief in the autonomy of mind from body very easily leads to the conclusion that humans are completely free and totally responsible for their choices and behavior, regardless of the circumstances and constraints under which they operate. One may consider such constraints as "mitigating" factors, thus limiting the punishment, but the moral guilt is clear. Moral choice is seen as solely a matter of conscious choice—an inner determination of the mind, self, or soul—and one is always ultimately free (and hence responsible for failing) to reject that which another is seeking to impose. It is precisely that ultimate moral purity that is to be prized above all else—it is holding to that which marks the saint or holy person, and which was so prized and praised by the Stoics in their heroic celebration of the Sage, or Wise Man.

We see numerous philosophers build moral systems around this, often presupposed and unselfconscious, dualism. Consider the great Immanuel Kant arguing that truly moral choices must be completely autonomous determinations of the pure will, that such a will must be motivated solely by the rational decision to act in accord with the Categorical Imperative, whose very nature was to command categorically, that is, without regard to the objective circumstances under and within which the act was to be done. Anything short of that compromised the morality of the act, and of the actor. Thus, the truly "good will"—"the only thing in this world or without" that was good without qualification—could not take into consideration in its willing anything that "came from without," from the world at large or even from the needs, wants, desires, or values of the concerned individual—all of which would fatally contaminate the purity of the moral action. (The Holy Will, that which is truly God-like for Kant, is the Will that not only does act solely from the demands of the Categorical Imperative, but also does not even experience any conflicting desires or inclinations, so that it is completely at one with the "demands of Pure Practical Reason.") It is thus clear how the moral theory of one of the greatest of Western philosophers is completely enthralled by that dualistic perspective, and this in spite of, or probably even more so, because of his deeply ingrained acceptance of, and belief in, Newtonian science and its view of the natural world. Kant thus found it necessary, in order to preserve the possibility of human dignity and the efficacy of "the moral law," to "deny reason in order to make room for faith" by providing for an autonomous realm for free rational choice and thus moral action.

It is a quite similar imperative that is at work in the thought of Sartre, who is so deeply a Kantian in his moral theory. His discussion of freedom, authenticity, and self-deception is completely grounded in an "Existential Ontology" that explicitly argues for the complete and irreducible autonomy of human consciousness, and explicitly eschews any inquiry into either the ground of its possibility or its historical causality. In *Being and Nothingness,* he rejects the latter inquiry as being "metaphysical," and outside of the scope of his work and asserts that consciousness is ultimately an unintelligible "surd." It is the indubitable fact of our existential being with which we are confronted, and the sole task of his work is to provide a "phenomenological" description of the mode of being of this undeniable metaphysical surd. One of the practical consequences of this perspective is his later claim that "we were never as free as under German occupation." The more theoretical conclusion is his often brilliant, incisive, and damning exploration of the numerous facets of "self-deception" by which humans, in flight from the fundamental and unavoidable anxiety that is the subjective experience of their ontological freedom, are ever "in flight" from that freedom, even when they seem to most sincerely accept it.[35]

It is only in such a dualistic context, which places a premium on moral purity, that one can adequately understand that pervasive distaste for actions which are said to "compromise" our "principles." In a normal social world in which one has to live and get along with others, you would think that people would value compromise. For what in fact is compromise but a result of the normal and unavoidable give and take of social living. How can one live with others without "compromising," that is, modifying one's goals, objectives, strategies, tactics, and tasks so as to take into consideration the views of others? What is the alternative, other than either the forceful imposition of one's own objectives or the withdrawal from the human community into the self-enclosed isolation of the hermit? Social living *at its best* is a continuing series of mutually engaged "compromises" that involve listening attentively and responding with respect, care, and concern to the interests of others. In fact, democracy can be seen as nothing other than a social structure that seeks to institutionalize this process in order to provide an equitable means for the determination of group policy. To denigrate compromise is to attack the very basis not only of democratic politics, but even more of sociability and the very possibility of cultural compatibility and human group survival. Is it any wonder that deeply Protestant America seems to experience such a profound ambivalence about democracy, highly contemptuous of the "compromises" essential to that democracy it celebrates, and is ever drawn to the puritanical asociality of "the loner" and "The Super Hero"? But of this, more will be discussed in the following chapter.

Of course, all of this, once stated, is quite obvious. *That*, the exponents of principles would certainly reply, is certainly *not* what we mean or are really saying. It is rather the "selling out" of one's moral principles for narrow and self-interested goals that they are criticizing. But what does that *really* mean? There is no theoretical problem in understanding most concrete cases of immoral behavior. Here we usually mean that people are acting under false pretenses, that they claim to do one thing, while "behind the scenes" they are doing something else, or that they are doing something that is only possible because most people do not know what they are doing, would not approve of it if they knew, and do not themselves generally act in a similar manner. Most of the time, we have little problem in understanding specific acts of wrong-doing: these are violations of generally accepted values, standards, and procedures that one usually seeks to hide from the public at large, either because one is not proud of them oneself or because one fears the negative judgment and possibly punitive action of others.[36] So much for the particulars of wrongdoing.

We usually know what are the generally accepted values, standards, and procedures of a society, and we know when we or others have violated them. But what sense does it make to speak in general or universal terms about "compromising one's principles"? Principles are standards for behavior. There are an almost infinite set of such standards, varying in degrees of specificity and generality, depending upon the circumstances.[37] They are reflective statements about how to behave in specific contexts with respect to assumed goals. By moral principles are usually meant the most generalized ways of behaving toward other human beings in certain types of situations, regardless of the specifics of the particular situation. But there are no completely "generalized" situations. Every situation is in some sense unique, however similar it may be to other situations. Even the "same" encounter done a second time bears the mark of its being a repetition. Of course, one can choose to neglect the uniqueness of the situation, and only focus on its common elements. Often that is desirable, even necessary. How else could any large organization function if it could not generalize procedures and pay little or no attention to situational and personal variations—at least most of the time! That is precisely the value of "principles," namely as historically generated and practically generalized standards for behavior and guides to conduct. As such, they are very useful. But they should be seen for what they are, that is, empirical generalizations, hypothetical formulations of the best way to proceed in these "types" of situations given the desirability of "these" types of objectives. Principles should be seen, and used, as experientially determined guides to action, not transfigured into eternal, unalterable, definitive rules of how one *must* behave. They should not be hypostatized into quasi-divine principles of behavior, the violation of which constitutes moral sin. The latter can only be done by taking principles out of the historical contexts that gave birth to them and placing them in a self-enclosed realm of their own, one that is accessible to, and makes a categorical claim upon, the purity of moral choice of the individual subject. It is only the presupposed (often taken for granted, if not explicitly asserted) autonomy of the moral self that can sustain this categorical imperative of principles. And it is this (assumed) dualistic framework that undergirds the demand for moral purity, which sees compromise as compromising, thus contaminating public debate and undermining the possibilities of constructive collective and democratic action.[38]

It is but a short step from here to the claim that people are morally responsible not only for their individual choices but also for their character and upbringing. Thus, social circumstances become ultimately irrelevant to human growth and development, and it is only "fuzzy-headed" liberals, socialists, or humanists who would excuse the poor and deprived for their moral and developmental failures. Can't we always—or at least usually—point to someone who emerged from impoverishment to become successful? Doesn't this prove that these "bleeding heart liberals" are simply making excuses for the failings of the poor? They are "blaming the society" instead of holding the poor responsible for their failures. Wouldn't one soon be led inevitably to ask, if the poor—or the criminal—are not "personally" responsible for their unfortunate situation? Since the society certainly is not, does it not stand to reason that there must be something about the poor or criminal, internal to their nature, which accounts for their deplorable condition? They probably deserve what they are getting. We should not coddle them. And we, the successful, should certainly not feel the least responsible or guilty. Had they the will, and made the effort, they could have succeeded as we did—even if they were at some disadvantage, it was not an unbridgeable impediment. It is their character that creates, and recreates the conditions of their own desperation, and not ultimately the responsibility of the society.

From this perspective, therefore, it is a short step to the conclusion that one should not look primarily to social policy for moral development and social improvement. Rather, we should look to spiritual transformation, to a change in values and attitudes on the part of individuals and their families. Social change in the final analysis will then be seen to depend upon spiritual transformation, for a spiritual "rebirth," for the politics of conversion. Hence, the strategy of religious preaching, of moral instruction, of personal "bearing witness" follows so clearly from, or leads most directly to, the vision of a spiritually autonomous Self or Soul.

In *John Dewey: An Intellectual Portrait*, Sidney Hook well sums up the pernicious effects of this dualistic line of argument in its tendency to celebrate spiritual change from within:

> By locating "the essential personality" in a mind or consciousness, discontinuous with the world of matter or nature, the consoling doctrine has been fostered that human beings in their "innermost selves" can never be compelled except by forces to which they voluntarily submit and which are therefore not really compelling; that human beings are "free" not in virtue of a power to do or to refrain from doing, but in virtue of mere assent or intention... .
>
> Even more fateful is the use to which this dualistic theory of mind-body has been put in urging that significant social change can only come from change within the individual soul or self. Down to our own day, eloquent spokesmen for powerful cultural and religious groups have counterposed "the revolution within" to fundamental institutional reforms... .
>
> Not all who hold the dualistic view are aware of it. But wherever knowledge is divorced from action or theory from practice, wherever action and practice are regarded as something which compromises the purity, the objectivity, the perfection of knowledge and theory, wherever the exigencies of living in a material world are deplored as a trial imposed on "the spirit," wherever faith is separated from works and ends from means, the dualistic theory of mind-body will be found lurking among the unexamined assumptions.[39]

I Am Born with a Past

Contrast this idealized individualism with Rousseau's more insightful conception of the natural and social constitution of the self—and thus of the substantive, mutual, and constitutive obligations of the individual and society. In that recently discovered, "*A Letter from Jean-Jacques Rousseau*," previously referenced,[40] Rousseau observes that:

anyone can see that it is quite impossible for a man to be born, live, and maintain himself in a society without depending on it for anything... . *It is not as individuals that we are all in each other's debt, but as members of society, to which each of us owes everything. Indeed, the price we pay for the help we receive is itself a gift of society. Can a man possess anything without the help and consent of others? Without this tacit contract,*[41] *neither profit nor property nor true industry would exist.* In the state of nature nothing exists but what is necessary, and *the superfluity we see all around us is not the sum total of individual efforts but the product of general industry, which with a hundred hands working in concert makes more than a hundred men could make separately... .* (Italics added.)

Such are the indissoluble bonds that unite us all and make our existence, our survival, our reason [lumières], our fortune, our happiness, and, in general, all our goods and evils dependent on our social relations... .

This sacred duty, which reason obliges me to recognize, is not strictly speaking a duty of one individual toward another but a general and common duty, just as the right that imposes it on me is also general and common ... . My benefactors may die, yet as long as human beings remain, I shall be obliged to repay mankind for all the benefits it has bestowed on me.

But our debt to our culture is more than simply factual and historical; it is also imaginative, dramatic, and ideological. Our lives take shape within the frame of an ongoing cultural drama that provides the script and the rationale for human action. We take our place within a setting that has been laid out for us, in the first instance by our parents, but more encompassingly by the self-understanding of our race, religion, nationality, and cultural history, of which they are but the primary and very particular transmitters. They live the story of "their people" and seek to inculcate us with the values, beliefs, habits, skills, and perspectives appropriate for our place in that ongoing dramatic undertaking. The very meaning of our lives, its obligations and possibilities, and its factual realities and imaginative illusions are inextricably linked within the vitals of our most intimate self, in mind and nerve and muscle. I *am* the person my culture has given birth to and nurtured into adulthood.

MacIntyre elucidates quite well the contrast between individualism and this "narrative" perspective:

From the standpoint of individualism I am what I myself choose to be. I can always, if I wish to, put in question what are taken to be the merely contingent social features of my existence. I may biologically be my father's son; but I cannot be held responsible for what he did unless I choose implicitly or explicitly to assume such responsibility. I may legally be a citizen of a certain country; but I cannot be held responsible for what my country does or has done unless I choose implicitly or explicitly to assume such responsibility. Such individualism is expressed by those modern Americans who deny any responsibility for the effects of slavery upon black Americans, saying "I never owned any slaves". It is more subtly the standpoint of those other modern Americans who accept a nicely calculated responsibility for such effects measured precisely by the benefits they themselves as individuals have indirectly received from slavery. In both cases "being an American" is not in itself taken to be part of the moral identity of the individual. And of course there is nothing peculiar to modern Americans in this attitude: the Englishman who says, "I never did any wrong to Ireland; why bring up that old history as though it had something to do with me?" or the young German who believes that being born after 1945 means that what Nazis did to Jews has no moral relevance to his relationship to his Jewish contemporaries, exhibit the same attitude, that according to which the self is detachable from its social and historical roles and statuses. And the self so detached is of course … a self that can have no history. The contrast with the narrative view of the self is clear. For the story of my life is always embedded in the story of those communities from which I derive my identity. I am born with a past; and to try to cut myself off from that past, in the individualist mode, is to deform my present relationships. The possession of an historical identity and the possession of a social identity coincide…. What I am, therefore, is in key part what I inherit, a specific past that is present to some degree in my present.[42]

That past within which I am born is that of a historically developed and institutionally rooted social narrative. It is the story (or, better, the somewhat discordant set of related stories) that constitutes the culture within which I take my place, assume my identity, and seek to carve out my future. To the extent that the embodied self is socially constructed, historically developed, institutionally located, practically engaged, and narratively experienced, my culture and its collective self-understanding are essential constituents of the person I am. My story is a part of its story, whether congruent or antagonistic, just as my mind is essentially an aspect of my society, and to miss that interpretive dimension is to phenomenologically amputate the human being.

Thus, our stories are rooted in and fed by our culture's dramatic narratives. These involve a complexly interrelated series of historically generated and collectively shared stories that are institutionally rooted in sustaining communities. These

communities … have a history—in an important sense they are constituted by their past—… a real community [is] a "community of memory," one that does not forget its past. In order not to forget that past, a community is involved in retelling its story, its constitutive narrative, and in so doing, it offers examples of the men and women who have embodied and exemplified the meaning of the community.... . The communities of memory that ties us to the past also turn us toward the future as communities of hope. These stories of collective history and exemplary individuals are an important part of the tradition that is so central to a community of memory.[43]

But memory is not so reliable and unproblematic, even when it is not distorted by explicit biases. How much of what we remember of our own life is what we want to remember. What puts us in the best possible light. Which, perhaps ever so slightly, "enhances" the story of our life. And how much that is embarrassing is quickly forgotten. Of course, our interpretation of events can only emerge, in the first instance, from our personal perspective. It is, after all, *our* interpretation, from our point of view, with our beliefs, values, and preferences. It is we who are telling our story, a story that defines who we have been, and thus in an important sense who we are, what we are responsible for, can hope for, and can claim as our rightful due. Our dignity, self-respect, and personal significance are being thus dramatically presented, and our future possibilities thus framed and justified. We are to ourselves, and urgently presented to others, as the person who has played *that* role (or roles) in the ongoing social drama(s) of our culture. Often, the very possibility of our "carrying on" with our life is dependent upon our being able to tell a convincingly ennobling personal story to ourselves and to our significant others. (An inability to do so is often the direct cause of deep depression, destructive outrage, or personal suicide.)

Is it the least surprising, therefore, that we usually have difficulty telling personal stories that shine an unfavorable light upon our past activities or motives? Or that we may be moved, either consciously or unconsciously, to fabricate a past that enhances our dignity and downplays, when it does not actually falsify, our misdeeds. There would be far less need for psychotherapy if it were easy to distinguish the conscious from the unconscious fabrications. To a significant extent, we are who we think we are—the person who has come to believe the complex, and often idealized and partially fabricated, story we tell of our life—and it is *that* person whose actions contribute to the unfolding of the person in question. Thus, our illusions as much or more than the past data and our factual self-knowledge contribute to the unfolding of our life.

But we do not act in a vacuum. "Aye, there's the rub." As social beings, we are inextricably involved with an expanding net of human connections within an encompassing social and cultural order. That order and each of its participants have their own stories to tell, which stories have a more or less (in)significant place for us. But it is one that we have only a limited capacity to influence. As they are characters in the dramatic unfolding of our life, so are we in theirs. The stories they tell—drawn from their distinct perspectives—invariably offer a quite different, and often far less flattering, description of who we are and what we have done. As we struggle in thought and deed to compose and enact a script for our life, designing an important if not starring role for ourselves and appropriate supporting roles for our significant others, they are doing likewise for themselves. We may not like the narrative casting of their drama. Depending upon our shared values and the quality of our relations with others, these interrelated but competing scenarios may be either mutually enhancing or personally destructive. It is the latter that Sartre had in mind, given his conception of the ontological antagonism between individual consciousnesses, when he has Garcin comment, in "*No Exit*," that "Hell is other people." Thus, social conflict is often and more pervasively expressed in the struggle to control the stories people tell—the worldview expressed, the roles assigned, and the values promoted—than in the actual exercise of physical force. In fact, if success can be had, for individual or community, in getting one's story publicly accepted, the actual implementation of force may well become secondary if not actually irrelevant. In the social world, the publicly accepted story often becomes the reality, regardless of the facts. It even tends to create the facts.

In observing that "nations are primary and states secondary," Kwame Anthony Appiah recalls Ernest Renan's observation that "a nation is a soul, a spiritual principle... . Two things, which, in truth, are really just one, make up this soul, this spiritual principle. One is in the past, the other is in the present. One is the possession in common of a rich legacy of memories; the other is the current consent, the desire to live together, the willingness to continue to maintain the value of the heritage that one has received as a common possession."

Appiah then continues:

> Renan's answer ... was that it is our common history—and the contemporary commitments this history underwrites—that makes us one... . What Renan meant by a shared history, rather, was a *story* of the past held somehow in common, what he called a "rich legacy of memories." The nation for Renan is bound together not by the past itself—by what actually happened—but by stories of that past that we tell one another in the present. What we remember—and, Renan famously added, what we forget—makes us the nation we are... . "Forgetting," Renan wrote, "and I would even say historical error, is an essential factor in the creation of a nation and that is why progress in historical research is often a threat to nationality."[44]

To understand a people then—just as with understanding a person—you must know their stories. That requires knowing their *language,* its subtle range of intertwined meanings, associations, and illusions and its implicit metaphysics—that inarticulate background of assumed and presupposed meanings that frames the explicitly expressed content and developed conversations. It is practically impossible to remain simply an impartial objective value-free "observer," viewing the situation from without. To the extent you truly understand the lived meanings of their stories, you have had to "enter into" their world and to some extent "feel" their experiences, and thus "compromise" "pure" objectivity. If you come to the world "from without," bringing your own metaphysical frame with its associated perspectives and range of meanings and values, not only do you not avoid this problem, but you also suffer the further limitation intrinsic to all efforts at "translation."[45]

If our self is but a player in an historically unfolding and culturally conflicted set of interrelated dramas that are in large part constituted by the stories we tell and the projects we undertake, it becomes excruciatingly difficult if not ultimately impossible to separate reality from fancy, fact from interpretation. For the way we see ourselves and our history in large part constitutes who we are and what we do. So it was in the past. There is no "one" past, any more than there is one definitive interpretation of a complex social situation. Luigi Pirandello sought to dramatize this complex interpretive dynamic in his plays, as when he has a character observing that while there are physically only three people in the room, experientially there are actually many more, namely each person as he is to himself and as he is to each of the others separately and collectively, not to mention how each thinks he is for the other, and they for him.

We need to acknowledge the actual perspectives of the interrelated cultural stories that constitute the ongoing cultural drama. These constitute and justify the existing institutions and practices that make up the social order. These stories themselves make claims about objective reality, some of which concern the natural world, others the social world. The former are amenable to more or less objective empirical analysis and evaluation. The latter are more complexly layered, as they involve those manifold and complexly layered interpretations of the meanings ascribed to other social actors, who themselves formulate meanings based on their perceptions of your perspectives—and this is in principle subject to an infinite regress.[46] Thus, the actual social reality of the culture is constituted in part by the imaginative stories that its participants contrive, whether consciously or not. Some of these may make claims that are scientifically falsifiable, and can in fact be shown to be false—thus, in principle discrediting those beliefs and attendant practices. Others are themselves part of the imaginative landscape that are almost self-validating when not completely indeterminate. But the belief systems at work, whether factually grounded and empirically defensible or purely imaginative constructions and even obviously delusional, can themselves be effective contributors to the historically unfolding cultural story that makes up human history.

Thus, the imaginative construction of a historical and cultural identity can itself become a potent historical force creating an objective social reality to which the facts will conform, for good or ill: All too often "the hardest disease to cure is the one that is caused by the medicine you're taking." It is to an illustration of such a socially created cultural reality to which we now turn with our brief case study of the American Enterprise in order to: (a) illustrate the complex objective reality of the narrative form of social experience, as factual reality and imaginative creation; (b) explore the manner in which fabricated cultural illusions tend to determine and self-justify the direction of historical experience; and (c) suggest the ways in which independent realities may confront cultural stories with potentially serious challenges, to which they may be tragically ill-suited to comprehend and consequently encounter profound difficulty in constructively addressing.

8

The American Enterprise

The "acute millennial consciousness" of North American Protestants, gave the new nation a powerful sense of being God's instrument in the coming of his Kingdom.[1]

Individualism … has marched through our history destroying those social integuments that Tocqueville saw as moderating its more destructive potentialities, (so) that it may be threatening the survival of freedom itself.[2]

"Making It"

Americans have ever been on the make and on the move. Consequently, they have never truly felt at home. Lured by the myth of Eldorado and the Idyllic Garden, pushed by the spatial, material, and spiritual inadequacies of the Old World, justified by faith in their divine calling, and challenged by the demands of the frontier, the New World became the horizon for their unlimited aspirations. Restless and energetic individuals, often fueled by deep dissatisfaction and unbounded self-confidence, mobilized their personal initiative and collective effort to produce a cultural expansion that has been the motif of the journey into the New World. Expansion of land and people has made possible economic growth that has been essential to feed a deep personal need to "prove oneself." That effort has been largely measured by the growth of private material wealth, which has been so crucial to the Americans' sense of self-esteem that it well may be said that they measure themselves more by the direction of their movement than by their actual location on the proverbial ladder of success. "Some of us often feel, and most of us sometime feel," reports Bellah et al., in that incisive study of America character, *Habits of the Heart,* "that we are only someone if we have 'made it' and can look down on those who have not. The American dream is often a very private dream of being the star, the uniquely successful and admirable one, the one who stands out from the crowd of ordinary folk who don't know how. And since we have believed in that dream for a long time and worked very hard to make it come true, it is hard for us to give it up, even though it contradicts another dream that we have—that of living in a society that would really be worth living in."[3]

This rootlessness of Americans—often grounded in a deeply Puritan sense of original sin—was ever drawn forth and sustained by the often idyllic image of creating a new life and a new home,[4] establishing a more just and sustaining community, building a Reformed "city upon a hill," that could redeem the "fallen" and corrupt Old World and save humanity—by, for example, "making the world safe for democracy." Rootless energy and idyllic home—pervasive guilt and salvific work—mark two poles of the American adventure. This energy and ideal suggest an intrinsic tension between community and individual from the very outset of this journey into the New World. Though the initial undertakings were often, and by necessity, communal, the motivating energy and encountered opportunities ever pulled in the direction of individual (or family) aspirations, spurred on, no doubt, by the deep-rooted individualism of that Reformed Christianity which has so deeply marked the Enterprise of America.[5]

This "New World" tended to draw the most energetic, adventurous, visionary, or mercenary, as well as the oppressed, desperate, or criminal. In short, those who didn't fit in, and were driven or inspired to "make something of themselves" by "moving on," to "come unto themselves by relocation."[6] It offered a more or less open field for personal advancement and the (practical or imagined) working out of individual or collective salvation. While its resources offered practically unlimited opportunity, they also provided far less constraint on native impulses and aspirations. Many social constraints were made up "on the go," or quickly modified from inappropriate Old World models. No doubt, all of this was quite invigorating, contributing to that American "can do" attitude, in which most limitations are thought to result from inadequate determination, and in which the most energetic can realize the American Dream of "making it," going "from rags to riches" within one lifetime. Not only could Americans realistically expect to do better than their parents, but so could their children expect to do likewise.[7]

To adequately appreciate the dynamic threads that tie together the unfolding American Enterprise requires an appreciation of its unique natural environment, the specific characters and beliefs of the individuals who colonized the continent, and the institutional structures that were initially imported and then of necessity continually adapted, historically unfolding in dynamic interaction both with those environmental and individual structures and with alternative social orders. That means specific attention needs to be paid to the role of a vast and relatively under-populated continent with abundant natural resources. Spread mainly from east to west, the continent provided the general climatic continuity adequate for the horizontal spread of fruitful flora and fauna, and yet with its north-south spread and the diversity of its rivers, mountains, and deserts provided sufficiently wide climatic variations to offer environmental niches for a vast range of animal and plant species, and ultimately for significant cultural diversity. Moreover, this fruitful yet relatively humanly unpopulated continent, with a largely defenseless indigenous population—itself highly susceptible to the colonists' wide range of diseases[8]—provided an almost unlimited field for the exercise of individual initiative as well as for the play of the imagination that could not easily be contained by established social structures nor by traditional patterns of character, morality, thought, or behavior.

Into this "field of dreams" came the martial spirit of a feudal Europe whose Christianity was deeply marked by the hierarchical structures of a dogmatically authoritarian Catholic Church. Its pervasive sense of original sin and messianic vision of the "end of times" was then further radicalized by the Protestant Reformation, leading to a heightened need to individually experience personal salvation. Feeling thus divinely ordained tends to limit one's tolerance for opposition, especially from those who can be seen as either agents of the devil or outside of the pale of divine dispensation—as were the indigenous people, the natives of Africa, and, of course, the plants, animals, and "natural resources" of the New World, over which Judeo-Christian man had been given "dominion." Clearly, such an attitude can be quite invigorating, and threatening. "The 'acute millennial consciousness' of North American Protestants" carried to the New World by the original Puritan settlers and successively passed down to each new generation, gave the new nation a powerful sense of being God's instrument in the coming of his Kingdom."[9] This vision of a New World was framed by the bifurcated psyche of a Reformed Protestant Christianity, that experiences a deep, personally irremediable, sense of pervasive sin that can, in theory, only be remedied by a complete psychic transformation, understood as being "born again." The profound need to experience that rebirth—which in theory cannot be earned but can only result from the wholly undeserved reception of divine grace—in accordance with a remarkable psycho-logic, tended to mobilize practical human effort in order to provide the psychic assurance of personal election that could only come from worldly success. Hence, sinfulness fueled a deep discontent with oneself and the world that mobilized human effort and transformative activity. It thus framed the encounter with the New World as one in which transformed Christians could bring the Ideal into being—thus recreating the purity of a prelapsarian world. The vision of the world remade expressed the practical need to remake oneself and one's people.[10] The merging of the psychic sense of deep self-dissatisfaction that is our innate sinfulness with the religious ideal of a reformed world, brought down to earth by successful and determined effort that proves they are among God's elect, ultimately found expression in profit-oriented enterprise within a free market economy. That became the practical vehicle for unlimited striving and never consummated salvation, leading to the need to continually prove oneself, while justifying this expansionism as the campaign to redeem the world—with freedom and democracy for all.

Never far from the surface of this divinely inspired mission has been the tendency to project those repressed sinful desires on to any who resist American expansion. Seeing the Other as the embodiment of sin and evil allows one to feel justified in unleashing repressed desires in the service of a holy crusade, while symbolically purging that evil from oneself. (In this demonization of the Other, America is, of course, far from unique, as many peoples have seen fit to so treat their "enemies.") The New World thus allowed for playing out this inner drama while treating the continent both as an unpopulated wilderness and as the location of the crusade to either "save" the Indians or to demonize and destroy them. No wonder the "paranoid style" of American politics so incisively depicted by Richard Hofstadter.

As this idealized religious vision merges with, or appropriates the language of, the Enlightenment, it gives rise to the energizing secular ideal of the self-made man. America is a world open to opportunity; its justification is the promotion of human happiness, the celebration of individual freedom, and the defense of the innate rights of man. No one better expressed this vision than Thomas Jefferson, who, on his very death bed, wrote of America,

> may it be to the world, what I believe it will be, … the signal of arousing men to burst the chains under which monkish ignorance and superstition had persuaded them to bind themselves, and to assume the blessings and security of self-government. All eyes are opened or opening to the rights of man. The general spread of the light of science has already laid open to every view the palpable truth, that the mass of mankind has not been born with saddles on their backs, nor a favored few, booted and spurred, ready to ride them legitimately, by the grace of God.[11]

Here is a vision of "free soil, free labor, and free men," in which each person can aspire to better his conditions and expect his children to do better than himself—and in which a nation could be born that defined itself more by this mission and ideal, as a truly imagined community, than by its genesis, race, religion, or national origin. That inspiring ideal mobilized the oppressed and the disaffected, those huddled masses yearning to breathe free, of the cramped Old World—and sent off shock waves to the ruling classes across the globe.

Thus, Reformed Christianity and Enlightenment Rationality produced the dynamic psychic and communal energy in the service of an imagined and idealized view of freedom, self-determination, and ever-increasing happiness that was linked to a secularized vision of inevitable progress as the wealth of nations was to be amassed by the uncontrolled operation of innate human sinfulness. Human selfishness under the force of the Market's providential unseen hand nicely weds Reformed Christianity with free enterprise *laissez-faire* capitalism and Enlightenment rationality as the providential order is naturalized through the sanctification of utility and human happiness. Benjamin Franklin captured this very American "pragmatic … spiritual vision that emphasized the degree to which virtue and happiness were not only correlated but discernible and achievable," where one could expect to "do well by doing good."[12]

Not to be outdone, the Scientific Revolution followed hard-upon the Protestant Reformation and the occupation of the New World, providing increasingly powerful tools with which to pursue the exploitation of the New World's potential. And this, within the context of bourgeoning capitalist institutions that tended to reduce value to price within an increasingly unregulated market, legitimated by developing Enlightenment political theories that liberated the individual from feudal constraints, theorized the natural and inherent rights of all individuals, and increasingly legitimated utility—however divinely authorized in the providential natural order—as the ultimate criteria of moral action and social policy.

A heady mixture, indeed, was all of this, but certainly not without profound ambivalences and conflicts. For celebrating utility and natural happiness does not comport well with a deep sense of original sinfulness and the need for Salvation, nor does scientific reason comfortably coexist with biblical moralizing, nor with divine revelation. An untrammeled individualism tends to tear at necessary social bonds, while personal and material expansion squeezes out the less energetic populations and tends to run roughshod over the natural environment and settled community life. It is this complex and dynamic cultural drama that I seek to outline, if only to suggest the dimensions of a more adequate holistic theory of cultural development.

Thus convinced of their divine election and the sanctification of their cause, the Puritans referred to themselves as "saints," identified with the Exodus of the Israelites from bondage in Egypt, and envisaged the community they were building, in Winthrop's suggestive phrase, as a "city upon a hill"—a "New Jerusalem"—upon which the eyes of the world were focused, and upon which, by implication, the salvation of mankind depended. Such holy missions do not easily brook opposition. Feeling entitled, nay authorized and directed, to impose their will on nature and people, they undertook to tame the devil both in the soul and in that wild, demonic, and often seductive nature, of which the "native Americans" were an integral part. This theme of divine election, in many ambiguous and diverse forms, ever pervades the American Enterprise, whether by "civilizing the natives," realizing our "manifest destiny," "making the world safe for democracy," providing an "open door" for trade and enterprise, or bringing free markets and prosperity to the entire world. America's practical success—its material well-being and geographical expansion—was the proof of its divine election, its democracy and free enterprise the practical reasons for its success. Clearly, everyone dreams of being American, or so many Americans suppose, and how could they not—with only the devilish forces of resentment and reaction standing in opposition. And, clearly *they* have no moral standing.

This "American Dream" carried with it a powerful democratic message of the capacity and right of all to govern themselves—and to believe in the equal dignity of each. (Initially, of course, that only applied to white males, but the power of that "partially secularized" and egalitarian Enlightenment message has significantly contributed to eating away over time at the moral roots and institutionalization of such prejudice.) Embodied in the Declaration of Independence, for almost two centuries that vision has electrified the world, from the French revolutionaries of 1789 through Ho Chi Minh and the Vietnamese independence movement of 1946 to the tearing down of The Berlin Wall and the "liberation" of eastern Europe. It was one of the most powerful meanings that attached to the doctrine of the self-reliant individual articulated by the likes of Franklin, Jefferson, Jackson, Emerson, Whitman, Thoreau, Douglass, and Lincoln. Who better expressed that "can do" attitude of the "self-made" man than Franklin, or that spirit of equality that was exemplified so well during the Jacksonian era when waiters would reject tips as an insult to their dignity: what do you think we are, servants?!!

And who better expressed the evangelical faith in the divine mission of America to provide free men with the unprecedented opportunity to continuously improve their condition by free labor and hard work than Lincoln? Soon after taking the Presidential oath, he set forth the rationale for the coming civil conflict as "maintaining in the world, that form, and substance of government, whose leading object is to elevate the condition of men—to lift artificial weights from all shoulders—to clear the paths of laudable pursuits for all—to afford all, an unfettered start, and a fair chance, in the race of life."[13]

How much of this experience of the "new man" in the New World was an interiorization of the possibilities provided by the climate, geography, natural resources, and limited (and generally discounted, when not simply moved out of the way, dead from contagious infection or killed) population that the Europeans encountered? That was certainly claimed by many, of which Henri St. Jean de Crevecoeur was only the most fervent and explicit.[14] To what extent did this "virgin land" percolate in the fertile imagination of "Reformed Protestants," imbued as they were with a profound sense of their original sinfulness, and deeply needful of evidence of their divine election—thus driven into energetic activity whose very success attested to, or at least could be experienced as, evidence of their spiritual rebirth?

But that "can do" attitude of the "self-reliant" individual was ever ambivalent about whether he was building a new community or making it on his own. Often such individuals tended to resent efforts to limit their field of opportunity, to socially constrain what can be done in pursuit of their goals, while yet suffering from the solitude and loneliness that is its inevitable result. No wonder that so many dreamt of community, and with quasi-sentimental enthusiasm idealized the "neighborhood" and the "New England town meeting."

American individualism has long had a deeply ambivalent attitude toward community. "No one can tell me what to do," "I don't care what others think," "it's my life," and "it's my property": typical expressions of the individualism that Americans prize and celebrate. So much so that it has almost become the meaning of democracy for them. Yet that suggests a problem, for democracy is *collective* self-government. And that means deciding upon a social policy and then telling others what they can't do. The so-called conflict between "the individual" and "the community" runs deep throughout American history. At the same time that Americans value their individual freedom above all else, they continually express a deep aspiration, perhaps even craving, for an often idealized community. The New England town meeting, the local neighborhood, the church, the religious congregation, the college fraternity or sorority, the small town, the family—how many times can one hear that "it's not like it used to be," "the old neighborhood is gone," and "how much would I love to live in a community of caring individuals." How deep in the American psyche is the distrust of the "big city," of the crime and moral laxness that it represents, of the threat that its immoral lifestyles pose to "traditional family values." Yet we all know how stifling small towns can be, how neighbors pry into your personal affairs, and how we don't want others to tell us what we can and can't do. In fact, many have precisely fled from their small town in search of the freedom, opportunity, and anonymity of that big city.

There is a confluence between the predominant psychic structures of Americans, the operations of their social, cultural, economic, and political institutions, and the country's domestic and foreign policy. And that is to be expected. But such confluences are neither one-to-one causal connections, nor direct parallels. There are sufficient conflicting values and beliefs to create continual tension—and so it is with most all societies.

Most central to the expansion of American culture has been that deep and pervasive sense of possibility that marks the American psyche. I think it is reasonable to believe that that is in large part an interiorization of the actual experience of many that the land provided practically unlimited resources and opportunities. Further, the relatively undeveloped social structure, itself constantly being exported and reinvented as the frontier expanded, meant that in practice often the only limit on human activity was that set by the limits of human ingenuity—imagination, technical skill, and resourcefulness. No wonder Americans should have developed such a deep sense of possibility, an experimental attitude that was reluctant to accept limits on what could be accomplished before at least trying. Hence, the Old World experience of "limits," of that which couldn't, or shouldn't, be done was replaced by that "can do" sense, which views traditional limits as but one more challenge to be met and overcome. "We can do almost anything we set our minds to—and we won't know our limitations unless and until we try, push the boundaries, test our capacities." Americans refuse to be resigned to fate—but feel that the world is out there to be made, and it is up to them to participate in the making. How American is William James' notion of a universe in which human actions can make a difference in its ultimate fate, and in which God invites and requires people to join with Him in order to help make Good prevail!

That "can do" attitude placed within a context of relatively unlimited resources and opportunity fits quite well within a moral structure in which you are responsible for what you make of yourself. It invites and comfortably supports a competitive ethic that identifies success with moral worth and sees failure as proof of sin or moral inadequacy. It thus provides a comfortable theological cover for individual success and failure, and lays the groundwork for a public policy that links national aspiration with divine authorization, thus tending to justify in advance all of its undertakings.

Few, if any, nations have been more successful in accepting, when not actually welcoming, and integrating people of various ethnicities, nationalities, religions, and creeds into their daily life. No doubt, the very fact that America in its history and in its self-conception is essentially a "nation of immigrants" that defines "being American" more by creed and self-identification than by birth and national origin has made it possible for people from all across the globe to migrate to the United States and become accepted as "American."[15] Granted, this has certainly not always been problem-free, and on many occasions this process has taken a few generations to be completed. Yet, not only have no insuperable barriers stood in its way, but that very explicit historical self-understanding (in the context of economic and national demands for an ever-expanding supply of labor and markets), given ideological legitimacy and support by America's founding documents and articulated creed, has placed on the defensive all those who would put barriers before such assimilation. Thus, the American story is that of a remarkably open, welcoming, and success-fully diverse nation.

The only major continuing exceptions to that remarkable story are the systematic efforts continuing well into the last half of the twentieth century to wipe out the culture of the indigenous peoples, and the pervasiveness of the ongoing color divide, that has made it quite difficult to show adequate respect for, and fully integrate the peoples and cultures of, African descent. The so-called racial question has so far proved relatively intractable. And this in spite of scientific evidence that there is no adequate biological basis for such racial classifications.[16] Nevertheless, such classifications have proven profoundly significant in determining social relations, access to power, wealth, residence, life style, health, and longevity. Clearly, race remains a profoundly significant social category, rooted in the pervasive cultural per-ception (and individual perception of self and other) that regularly trans-mits and continually recreates its social and psychological reality.

The resilience of racial stereotyping is doubly remarkable, since it, too, must operate in an ideological climate that is in principle so inimical to it. For a "democratic" society that "holds these truths to be self-evident, that *all* men are created equal" must continue to experience a degree of (at least subterranean) guilt at the obvious discrepancy between its self-justifying creed and its prejudicial deed.[17] No doubt, the pervasive "ontological" guilt experienced by a Reformed Protestantism that takes "original sin" as given helps to spread out the burden, and makes it both more comprehensible and bearable—as bearable as all the rest of their sinful inclinations and behaviors. Then there are the numerous and ever-reappearing efforts to justify such pejorative discrimination with different variants of the position that in effect blames the victim, whether by bearing their specific infirmity as a descendant of Ham, or due to their inherent childishness that requires and benefits from the paternal care provided by a plantation aristocracy, or because their culture lacks strong family traditions and pays little attention to intellectual achievement, or more recently and "scientifically," because of their genetic inferiority as attested to by IQ scores. (Of course, black culture has itself tended to "normalize" and thus reproduce many of its "destructive" patterns of thought and behavior, which it then subtly inculcates in its members, thus tending to reproduce self-demeaning and destructive patterns of personal behavior, as is normal with long-standing oppressed populations.)

Whatever the rationale, the tension between American racial practice and its ideological self-justification grates on the national psyche and on its political dialogue—and the longevity, perseverance, and resilience of such prejudice can only attest to its powerful roots deep in the psyche and culture of Christian America. Many may well wonder to what profound needs this prejudice speaks and to what does it bear witness. It is my deep suspicion, to a further discussion of which I will turn later, that racial prejudice in American can only be understood by being placed within the depth psychology and social dramaturgy of a Reformed Christianity deeply marked by that bifurcated consciousness fixated on the struggle of Good with Evil, of God with the Devil. This same bifurcated consciousness feeds the American competitive ethos, its capitalist ethic, and its idealistic imperialism.

Privatized Expansionism

It has been, however, just such people, primarily white males, endowed with this rootless energetic character, with its insatiable drive to dominate the material and social world—riven with guilt and driven to achieve practical salvation—that have thus far been the sustaining force behind the expansion of the American enterprise. The focal point has been the personal ego, the active "I," whose self-esteem has depended upon its ability to exercise effective control. Central to Americans' evaluation of their social position, and hence of their self-esteem, has usually been the degree of their possession of, or control over, material wealth and other people.

The ever-expanding frontier was both the natural challenge and the ideological cover for this enterprise. Other human beings—Indians, Blacks, Spaniards, Orientals, then Irish, Italians, Poles, Germans, and Slavs—have been either destroyed or incorporated in order to be exploited. Eventually, many of these groups have been integrated into the decaying core of America that this expansion has tended to continually leave in its wake, slowly acclimating themselves to the American enterprise and coming to demand a "piece of the action."

This relentless expansionist surge pushed America across the continent in the eighteenth and nineteenth centuries. That was clearly its "manifest destiny." No sooner had the 1890 census announced the close of the frontier on this continent than Americans found themselves conquering

Hawaii in 1893, fighting in the Philippines in 1898 for Cuban emancipation, and in 1900 aiding the imperialist powers in China in the suppression of the Boxer rebellion. In fact, America's concern for the "well-being" of the people of Asia seems to date primarily from this period.[18] The Vietnam War can be seen as but one more stage in this journey of American westward expansion, as Americans have sought to keep open the sphere for unlimited growth. Vietnam in the 1950s and 1960s, Central America in the 1970s and 1980s, and south central Asia in the 1990s and beyond may not have been essential—but American penetration of world markets (with the concomitant control of natural resources and cheap labor) was and still is.

In 1855, Senator William Frye summed up the problem with noble simplicity: "We must have the market of China [or the oil of the Middle East, minerals of Africa, grain sales to the former "Soviet bloc"] or we shall have revolution." While this claim is no doubt overstated and simplistic, the question remains: What happens to the American enterprise as the *"open door" of (westward)* expansion is squeezed closed? Can Americans continue to satisfy their personal demands for spiritual rebirth and material advancement without the continually expanding frontiers (and economic growth) upon which their personal satisfaction in the past has seemed to depend? And what happens at home if the social space for the expression of their unlimited aspirations is to be closed, locking the neglected within the narrowing confines of the depressed rural and urban centers of America? In many ways, the suburbs have been an opportunity offered to those who were gaining a little wealth to separate themselves from the problems and people who were being left behind. Now the suburbs are becoming urbanized, their infrastructure decaying, their housing priced out of reach for the vast majority, and their jobs departing for "free enterprise zones" in a globalized economy, when, that is, they are not domestically undercut by uncontrolled immigration. The temptation to "move on," however, confronts the prospect of vanishing frontiers. Meanwhile, those left behind, both at home and abroad, increasing their pressure to move in, become the object of a growing anger generated by declining standards of living. Those in the suburbs who have "made it" feel threatened by "them." They can neither make way for them, nor finance the needed reconstruction of those decaying central cities, not to speak of the historically exploited third-world societies. Overburdened, and increasingly under-financed, they simply want "them" to do their jobs and/or go away.

Expansionists Americans have always been. Yet it is also true that they have been and remain isolationists. It might be wondered how Americans can be both isolationist and expansionist, but there really is no problem; they are complimentary in the deepest sense. For expansion has been a concern at the social and personal frontiers that has served to relieve pressures in the centers of America. Expansion has been a publicly supported process that has offered relatively free play for individual initiative and private accumulation to many. It has thus held out the lure and in part offered the reality of growing material wealth by which the energy of Americans has always been mobilized. And it has allowed the American enterprise generally to neglect the public arena and ride roughshod over settled community life. A glaring but hardly atypical example drawn from my locality was the attempt on Long Island in the 1970s and 1980s to build the Oyster Bay-Rye Bridge by driving major highways through the villages of Oyster Bay and Bayville. In the name of expansion of enterprise, the planners—spurred on by Robert Moses and Nelson Rockefeller—were seeking to destroy two well-established communities. Communities, it should be noted, with deep roots and long traditions that mark them as something special in comparison to the more or less transient residential areas that are the hallmark of suburbia. It is precisely this total lack of regard for the public sphere and settled community life when it conflicts with the demands of business enterprise—alias "progress"—that has been the driving force behind the continuing deterioration of America's core areas—a deterioration that long could be tolerated for basically two reasons. First, as a people Americans have been quite ambivalent, and tending to care less and less deeply, about the public sphere and social environment. They tend to be primarily concerned about the latter only to the extent that it not interfere with their individual initiative aimed at unlimited acquisition of private material wealth and personal prestige. Second, if the surroundings got bad enough, Americans could always move on: to the central cities from the decaying rural areas, then uptown and to the suburbs from the decaying cities, and then westward (and even southwestward) from the cramped and cold northeast and mid-west. Individualists that they are, Americans generally do not want to be bothered or constrained by others. They want to be left alone to pursue personal accumulation and to cultivate their private gardens—or enjoy their home entertainment centers. Others are either unwanted intrusions upon this private sphere or potentially useful material to be manipulated in the service of that personal advancement. Of course, this relation is mutual and self-sustaining. My attitude toward others is mirrored in their attitude toward me, which only serves to confirm me in my justified attitude toward them. Isn't everyone doing the same thing? Isn't this human nature?

The suburban home dependent as it is almost totally upon automobile transportation constitutes a perfect expression of this "privatizing" impetus that is the essence of American isolationism. The suburban home is usually set off from any deep involvement with ongoing community life.

It often expresses the American's demand to be left alone with his or her possessions through the construction of fences that clearly demarcate where my property ends and where you shall not trespass. Within that enclosed sphere the location of the "porch" or patio in the rear reinforces the rejection of unsolicited intrusions, while the manicured lawn serves as a remnant of the idyllic garden myth in this little Eden from which the problems of the world are to be excluded —and above all that means the cities and their "alien" minorities, especially "The Blacks." This ideal of privatization has, through the corporate domination of the media, increasingly been translated into a generalized rejection of "governmental interference," in the name of promoting "individual initiative."[19]

The automobile has, no doubt, been the ultimate symbol of this vision of America. It provides Americans with frontier mobility without any obvious dependence upon or personal interaction with others. They can have the world brought to them—or transport themselves directly to it—while the problems are kept away. Note, for example, how the Interstate Highway System allows Americans to avoid slum areas, even when its construction has often contributed to their development.[20] Automobile ads, on the other hand, have even gone so far as to extol the virtues of cars that are so noise-tight that with the windows closed the driver cannot hear the slightest sound from outside—including, no doubt, the sound of the horn of another motorist. Other ads proudly proclaimed the smoothness of the ride, free of the intrusion of bumps from pot-holed streets. The promotion of the digitized home, in which all of the business, home-making, and entertainment needs can be supposedly satisfied without leaving the privacy of the residence—or the emergence of personalized devices from "Walkman" headphones to IPods—simply reinforce the same privatizing impulse. So many Americans only seem to need and want others when their aid is required to further their own personal demands for achievement. Otherwise, the less they have to deal with them, the better. For what are these others but similarly motivated individuals who are continual threats to our personal prestige. Isn't the "law and order" movement essentially the conservative reflex of people who want to be left alone faced with the growing pressure of those who have been left behind?

There is little new here. What is new is the fact that the frontier is gone. The unlimited space for American expansion is fast disappearing, while the "new frontier" beyond the earth is in practical terms a valiant delusion. America is now faced with crucial limits to the continuance of its economic and political expansion. It is now obvious that the heroic resistance of the Vietnamese people was but the top of the iceberg of a pervasive opposition growing in the "third world"—and across the globe—to the exploitation and oppression that has been their lot since the advent of Western imperialism in the sixteenth century.[21] Americans simply inherited and developed this imperialism—usually under the rubric of promoting freedom and democracy—as the energizing fuel for the continued material growth that the frontier made possible and the American people demanded. As the third world struggles to take control of its destiny and claim its resources, America's "Western" allies, including the European Union, Japan, Korea, and Taiwan, and then India, China, and possibly Russia, are beginning to achieve levels of economic and political development that make them potential economic equals—and rivals—in the search for exploitable markets as well as for sources of raw materials and cheap labor in the third world.

In addition to these limits placed upon America's overseas expansion, it must increasingly face the challenge to economic growth and material expansion that is the practical meaning of the environmental crisis. Americans can no longer continue to randomly exploit the natural environment without paying an increasingly heavy cost—financial, medical, climatological, and esthetic. There are limits to the "carrying capacity" of the Earth, however difficult it may be to spell them out. In short, the American enterprise is being squeezed. These resistances to continued expansion challenge the basic postulates of American growth fueled by American initiative and material abundance, therefore threatening to close off the safety valves pressurizing the neglected and resentful American core. Americans can no longer simply respond to frustration and alienation at home by urging young Americans "to go West"—or its equivalent. For them, the "West" is no more.

The Withering of the Dream

Americans may have never been truly at home—but now they have no more places to go, and are rapidly becoming increasingly frustrated, scared, threatened, and rebellious. Their journey into the New World is being squeezed by the growing confrontation between their unlimited individual aspirations and the narrowing socioeconomic and political frontiers. It is clear that this squeeze will be increasingly felt throughout the social world. Since Americans predicate self-esteem upon continued advancement and since the social space for such movement is being cramped as a result of the twin rebellions of the "underexploited" humans of the third world and the overexploited natural environment at home and around the world, not to speak of the emergence of "Western" and then Asian economic competition, was it not inevitable that the outward push of the American enterprise would be forced back upon itself? Did not this inward turn have to lead to an intensification of domestic conflicts and a growing need for the reexamination of American institutions and basic values? How can Americans continue to predicate personal self-esteem upon successful advancement through an institutional hierarchy when that hierarchy is no longer expanding quickly enough to absorb even a reasonable amount of the "up and coming"? Is there any wonder that there has been increasing pressure for early retirement—until, that is, the economic cost of social security was considered? Without going into the disasters for personal self-esteem that are involved in putting aggressive Americans "out to pasture" at an early age—and one must not mistake these new "leisure villages" for anything but that—the coming end of the mystique of growth bodes ill for the advancement orientation of Americans.

Is it any wonder then that in the 1960s and early 1970s many youth were increasingly rejecting traditional values, even in their idealized "new frontier" expression, as in the Peace Corps and Spatial Exploration? It was rather the "inner frontiers" first suggested by the beat and psychedelic movements, and then institutionalized in hippie communes, encounter groups, transcendental meditation, as well as in demands for women's liberation, tax justice, and ecological balance that commanded increasing attention. Those movements took direct aim at the basic structures of American society, structures that could no longer be the subject of general neglect. They were the more hopeful and optimistic side of what Herbert Marcuse aptly called "The Great Refusal." The underside was, of course, the growing use of heroin, cocaine, barbiturates, amphetamines, and soporifics that, try as they might, stimulant-addicted, mainstream suburban America could not eradicate with Drug Education seminars. The problems simply go too deep into the psyche of "the American."

A fundamental confrontation was thus taking shape between those for whom growth is the solution for all social problems, led by the major corporations and unions, and those who challenge growth in the name of a fundamental reorientation of American priorities and the restructuring of America's centralized hierarchical institutions. A personal sense of resentment and a defensive-aggressive psychosis has been growing within the breast of the mainstream American, as the social space that his or her psychic demands require becomes ever more cramped. Objective inability to move up a narrowing hierarchical order has inevitably aggravated the pervasive competitive pressure for success, leading to a deepening sense of personal failure. But who is to blame? Having committed everything to the system, few are able to see their increasingly inevitable personal failures as due to the system's inadequacies. Quite the reverse: the system has been praised with increasing vociferousness and in inverse proportion to its ability to do the job of providing opportunities for advancement.

Americans are too much addicted to "rugged individualism," the Protestant ethic, and "Social Darwinism" not to feel that their frustrations may be testaments to their personal inadequacies. As a psychic defense, Americans are more likely to repress their sense of being cheated, wrap themselves more snugly in the flag of American opportunity, excoriate the devil in whatever form he may be packaged, and tell those others who have the temerity to question *the* system with which they identify "to love it or leave it."

Such at least is the "first language" of American individualism, in the insightful terminology of *Habits of the Heart*. This provides the central thematic pattern for the expansion of American enterprise, but, of course, it does not provide a simple, linear, unambiguous, or uncontested dramatic plot. Rather it emerges out of a Protestant Reformation themed by an Augustinian sense of individual sinfulness in which only divine election through freely given grace can save one from eternal damnation. To this anxiety-laden agitation about the possibilities of personal salvation, for which no works were theologically seen as adequate, was linked a practically unlimited field for human aspiration and self-creation through a burgeoning commercial market and a vastly expanding world of conquest and riches, both of which provided ample opportunity for that latent anxiety to experience a release of psychological energy and accompanying material rewards that were often felt as quasi-salvific.

Even more, from the middle of the nineteenth century onward, the United States became "the most thoroughly Reformed Protestant Christian Commonwealth the world has ever known."[22] To be an authentic Christian in America thus comes to require each individual to personally undergo a "rebirth" experience—to be "born again"—which, as time tends to institutionalize religious experience, seems to demand that every few generations need to carry out their own "revivalist" movement in order to challenge that inevitable sedimentation of religious practice through a "great awakening."[23]

Is it any wonder that such physical and psychic exuberance and material success were often experienced as practical signs of God's favor, and taken as evidence that the successful had been so blessed by God that they could feel confident they were among God's elect—that, in fact, God had shed his grace on them, literally crowning "thy (collective) good with brotherhood from sea to shining sea"?[24] Nor is it any wonder that this entire process was understood and found articulation through the language of the religious tradition out of which it emerged—thus seeing material accomplishments in trade, commerce, and conquest as divinely sanctioned.

The "divine election" that resulted from each individual's success in working out their personal salvation through dedication and hard work—the freedom of enterprise to choose one's life style and to bear the burden or reap the success of one's individual effort—increasingly becomes the operative meaning of freedom and democracy, with Harry Truman even replacing Roosevelt's "freedom from want and fear" with "freedom of enterprise."[25] Thus, private enterprise marginalizes Christianity's communal spirit as well as classical Republicanism's concern for the polity and civic well-being.

Tensions were ever present, however, between the collective nature of the initial undertakings, without which none of them could have succeeded, and both the unlimited and uncontrollable opportunities for individual initiative that were offered by a practically unlimited frontier and the overwhelming preoccupation of Reformed Christianity with the individual's sense of guilt for his/her own sinfulness and the deep need of each person to work out their own salvation. Thus, *Habits of the Heart* nicely contrasts the vision of collective and communal salvation of Winthrop's "city upon a hill" with the more individual and down-to-earth turn that Franklin gives to the moral program of Cotton Mather, what was then called the "Protestant ethic," rebaptized as the American "work ethic," however much now more honored "in the breach than in the observance thereof."

Although, by the mid-twentieth century, Americans had become far less enamored of the requirement of actually working to earn their wealth and power, they still felt the need to defend its possession in the name of its having been earned.[26] Americans both justify those who "have it made" as having earned their success by personal hard work and ability—developing those "God-given" talents to their fullest so as to excel in the competitive struggle that is the condition of human life—and hold those who have failed to realize the opportunities provided by the free market and democratic society as individually responsible and implicitly morally culpable. Such individuals can only be "saved" from the condemnation their failure justly sanctions by both assuming full personal responsibility for it and turning themselves over to the power of spiritual rebirth that will make them new individuals. It is but one more irony of American Protestant individualism, that not only is it given birth, sustained, and even nurtured by the collective culture, but the spiritual rebirth possible for the failed and fallen can only come to be within the context of a sustaining community, whose role is to both encourage self-abasement and to nurture individual responsibility.[27] But whoever said that cultures are thematically linear and dramatically unambivalent and coherent.

It is here that we must situate the emergence in the last quarter of the twentieth century of the "New Right," the "Moral Majority," and the election first of Ronald Reagan, and then of George W. Bush.[28] The "politics of nostalgia" bemoans the fading of "The American Dream." The psychic loss roots in the disintegration of local communities and traditional moral values, themselves the casualties of the unbounded faith of Americans in individual initiative and the "free market." Meanwhile, Corporate America, legitimized by a faith that it itself has in fact long given up, uses these movements as cover for its efforts to recapture the economic and political initiative at home and abroad. This revitalized imperial mission in the service of private accumulation calls for military expansion to protect the free world from the "threat" of the "demonized," first the Russians, and then the Chinese and the Arabs. Who knows what others will have to be (con-)scripted to play the role of the "Evil One."

But the contradictions are pervasive. As the unconstrained free market search for profitability undermines settled community life and traditional values, the latter gives expression to its attendant and increasing anxiety with more fervent support for expansion of the imperatives of corporate profitability. As the public sphere increasingly deteriorates under the push of unbridled corporate expansion, individuals retreat ever more into the privatized worlds of home and church, themselves ever more subject to the vagaries of a corporate power less and less understood and controllable. Meanwhile, the home becomes a bastion of security under continual threat from a public world, dominated by the corporations, but increasingly experienced as the locus of potential criminal assaults from *them*—themselves but the most pervasively exploited segments of a deteriorating social order in which it is every man or woman for him or herself. Thus, the home (or church) as refuge is felt to be under constant attack. Similarly with the psyche, in this marketing world of idealized individualism, where every one is encouraged to compete for success at the expense of others, and to market himself or herself in order to present the most attractive package. Americans can no longer know whether others are sincere, or simply more clever in the way they present themselves in order to seem so. Not only is the home and family disintegrating under the impact of competitive individualism, but personal relations cut loose from the ties of sustaining communities, and increasingly from settled, not to say extended, families, tend to be reduced to short-term contracts in which one must withhold one's deeper feelings for fear of their being used against one.[29] In any case, since moving is so pervasive, and human relations of such short duration, to get too involved risks a personal suffering to which only a masochist would look forward.

The home as refuge roots a "new feudalism" that is the social counter-part of the emerging "new colonialism" of the world of transnational corporations. In the contradiction between private accumulation and public decay—each feeding the other in a descending spiral—the "American Dream" withers, giving place to a resentful, revenge-prone, frightened psyche, seeking redress from *them* for what *they* are doing to it. At home, *they* are blacks, gays, women's libbers, radicals, druggies, and aliens of various sorts. Abroad, *they* are bandits, Commies, Russians, drug lords, Arabs, Ayatollahs, terrorists, and those who "front" for *them*.[30] All of this fits well with the economic imperatives of transnational corporations for a world free of political impediments to their search for profit, and free of those who would resist the lifestyle that bureaucratic organization imposes upon its workers. (Of course, there are imperatives of behavior different for the ruling elite than for the rest of us, but that is another story.) At the center of this dynamic resides the twin axes of privatization and growth, as the ideological and psychic poles of attraction that seem to draw forth the energies of all Americans.

Privatization and Growth: The Universal Elixir

America's psychic needs have been coordinated with its cultural and institutional dynamic. Privatization and growth have thus been dialectically linked. Privatization has nourished and been nourished by the continual growth of the American Enterprise. The "American Dream" is the idealized expression of an unfettered individualism riding the crest of the wave of enterprise as it flowed across the continent, and then washed onto alien shores, drowning under military arms and libratory rhetoric communities, nations, and peoples with the temerity to resist. Growth has made privatization possible, both by expanding the space for action and by providing the reduplicative commodities that might be individually possessed and privately used. Privatization, in turn, has fed growth through the creation of multiple needs, thus expanding the market for a practically unending series of "necessities." What better marketing possibilities than those provided by the proliferation of suburban residences whose ideal was to be the self-sufficient refuge from the storms of public life. From dish- and clothes-washer and dryer to swimming pool, tennis court, personal stereo, TV, games, toys, books, and, hopefully, cars—to each his own. In fact, middle-class suburban Americans tend to apologize if they are not able to provide each of their children with their own room. Of course, such privatization helps avoid the need to share, to learn to accommodate one's personal aspirations to the desires of others, and to develop the skills to constructively respond to conflictual interpersonal situations in an equalitarian fashion. The motto for group interaction has become "Lead, follow, or get out of the way," as one poster so aptly puts it. The nuclear family has been the paired down social infrastructure whose light baggage was well suited to follow the dictates of the market in the search for advancement, while promising to each member *both* emotional support *and* personal space. Whether it can deliver on either is another question, as are the related concerns of the extent to which a family needs wider community roots in which to flourish, and whether psychic health is sustainable in the long run when grounded in such a narrow range of personal relations, themselves without historical depth.

Behind the nuclear family, however, and the twin dynamics of privatization and growth that have vitalized it, reside the institutionalized requirements of capitalism, for both expanding markets and a fluid labor force. As transnational corporations have consolidated their competitive position—horizontally, through the conquest of producers of similar commodities; vertically, through control of the process of production from raw material to marketed final product; and through diversification of product line and range of profitable endeavors—they have become quasi-autonomous empires, operating across political boundaries. Owing allegiance to no community, nor, increasingly, to any country, they are less and less geographically locatable. They exist rather as a network of operations. Localities are reduced to sources of exploitable raw materials, sources of cheap or skilled labor, markets, or tax havens. Transnationals shift resources around to take maximum advantage not only of climate, geography, and natural and human resources, but also to maximize political, economic, and military leverage. The world-wide scale of their operations facilitates the subtle, and often not so subtle, blackmail that seeks to insure a "favorable climate for business investment."

Neighborhoods, localities, and even nations thus become but manipulable instrumentalities within the world-wide empires of transnational giants. The corporate network is replacing the nation state, instituting a New Colonialism, or, perhaps better, the recolonization of the New World and retro-colonization of the Old World. Of course, these new colonizers are no longer small expeditionary forces carrying the national flag, but transnational conglomerates controlling market forces and international movements of capital, backed up by the "legitimate" military might of the "home" country—as well as its not so legitimate secret police with their subterranean alliances with the secret services of the "client" states. Increasingly, their power is being given transnational legal expression through purported "free trade" agreements that guarantee the free movement of capital at the expense of local or national autonomy and democratic self-government.[31]

This New Colonialism can thus destroy jobs and relocate factories, or blackmail communities into accepting lower wages, granting extraordinary tax benefits, weakening environmental and health and safety regulations, and allowing the deterioration of social and human services; in short, the community is held hostage to the power of international capital.[32] A vicious spiral is set in motion, as the lack of effective local control furthers the process of neighborhood deterioration, which itself increases the individual's urge to withdraw from public involvement in community affairs. The retreat to the privacy of the home offers itself as a refuge from the impotence, disillusion, and social disintegration, of which rising crime rates and growing juvenile delinquency and drug use become the symbolic expressions. (With wages being driven down by corporate globalization, and the social wage being progressively undermined through competitive disadvantage, and more and more families needing to have more than one wage earner, and for each of them to work ever longer hours, the process of withdrawal from civic engagement is still further exacerbated.) Of course, the less one is attached to one's community, the easier it is to pack up and move on. Such mobility, while quite suitable to corporations, only serves to reinforce the same descending spiral. Thus, the world-wide market under corporate domination furthers the disintegration of communal bonds and collective morality.

As for the privatizing retreat of individuals into the refuge of their home—fleeing from an alien world felt to be out of their control—it is motivated by a growing resentment at the failure of personal expectations. The resultant anger tends to be directed *not* at the corporate forces responsible, but rather toward the major victims of exploitation. Those reduced to ghettos, poverty, and the violent struggle to keep their head above water—whether through disorganized crime or organized rebellion—tend to become targeted as the primary threats to the "American way of life." Thus, the legitimately engendered experience of vulnerability is easily and effectively translated at a conscious level into a preoccupation with *crime*. Merging with the *reality* of a disintegrating social world that tends to increase actual criminal activity, the public portrayal of domestic dangers conveniently focuses upon "alien" minorities, themselves the major victims of transnational capitalism, effectively directing public attention away from systemic corporate evils toward individual criminality where such criminals tend to be young, male, poor, and black or hispanic. Middle America is led to believe that the major internal threat to its health and well-being comes from "the black," "the poor," or the immigrant, those "below them" in the socioeconomic hierarchy, rather than from those above them, the wealthy and the corporate establishment. And why should they question those at the top? They are the ones who have made it, and deserve what they get. If we, on the other hand, have not made it as well, and if those below have not made it at all, well it's simply our or their fault. Perhaps we will make it yet. Such, at least, is the "conventional wisdom."

Thus, TV programs often treat one-on-one crime by such individuals as the major dramatic problem in life. Local TV news is generally little more than sensationalized reporting of crime and disasters, interspersed with sports, weather, and commercials. Discussions of work-place hazards, contamination of air and water, and deterioration of the "public sector" (except as an expression of "bureaucratic" indifference or union corruption) are covered at best in passing, with reference to individual failures without consideration of institutional factors—except, that is, for the occasional swipes at government bureaucrats, corrupt union officials, or greedy and lazy workers. While "bureaucrats" are fair game, "executives"— certainly as a class—seem to be almost beyond reproach, regardless of the few "rotten apples in the bunch."[33]

No wonder that the retreat into the private home is increasingly offered as an idyllic refuge from a "dog-eat-dog" public world. If the American's home is his or her castle, improved electronic security systems are rapidly becoming the moats by which they seek to protect themselves from unwanted intruders, not to speak of the increasing development of gated communities. This process of refeudalization constitutes a desperate attempt to avoid the inevitable effects of a world market, dominated by the profit requirements of transnational corporate empires, whose subtly disintegrative impact is completely undetectable by even the most sophisticated home burglary alarm systems.

A further and quite pervasive effect of these disintegrative forces that is almost invariably missed is their impact on youth. Members of the last two generations of the twentieth century were probably the first in American history that could not reasonably expect to achieve a better material standard of living than their parents. Sensing, though not yet clearly grasping, the closing door of material advancement, they had at the same time to confront a culture that no longer offered a believable sense of historical mission. Americans will not "make the world safe for democracy," however much its leaders proclaim that as their mission. The innocence and hope that was the meaning of the journey into the New World has given way first to a post-Vietnam, post-Watergate cynicism and disillusion, and then to a fear of terrorism and the alien other. Americans have turned inward in increasing preoccupation with narrow and short-range personal goals. This self-centeredness has been encouraged by corporate advertising that, driven insatiably to increase sales, has expanded needs—often through the generation of anxiety about personal inadequacy, as trivially as that with bad breath or the lack of white teeth—and then justified immediate satisfaction of them. The traditional Protestant work ethic has been an inevitable victim of advanced capitalism's "consumer society," as the ethic of "self-indulgence" replaces that of self-denial and constructive effort. (It has even been provided with an economic rationale in the need to continually expand consumer demand in order to sustain economic growth.) Youth are thus invited to partake in the "celebration of commodities" at a time when it is becoming increasingly difficult to obtain a satisfying job.

Meanwhile, as the future becomes shortened and narrowed, the demands of discipline and hard work are less impressive. Then there is *terrorism and the bomb,* as both symbol and reality—not to speak of "global warming" and the depletion of the ozone layer. Lurking on the horizon of our future, placing everything in doubt, is the sense that collectively we may have *no* future. What can long-term commitments mean in the face of this patent and uncontrollable reality? What can call youth to serious and sustained effort in such a world? Joined to the loss of history consequent upon the disintegration of extended family and settled community life, renewed each day by the narrowed vision and condensed time frame of commercial media, contemporary youth must make sense of their life and its possibilities confronting a world whose future is temporally shortened and culturally narrowed almost to the point of irrelevance. Cut loose from ties that can bind, sustain, and vitalize, many, with practically unlimited choices before them, drift purposelessly before the abyss, prey to each succeeding fad, caught up in an unending series of heightened moments leading nowhere.

If this analysis correctly portrays the dynamic forces currently tearing apart the "American Dream," an exploration of possible alternative responses is all the more urgently called for. The strategies of Corporate America are fairly clear. With "The American Enterprise" being so pervasively squeezed, corporate strategy vacillates between trying to placate, channel, or repress dissatisfaction on the home front, and efforts to buy out, intimidate, or destroy challenges to its world supremacy internationally. From the "benign" managed capitalism with some welfare emoluments of the "Eastern Establishment" to the militant, proto-fascistic urgings of the Far Right, Christian fundamentalism, and the Military-Industrial-Security apparatus, the logic of transnational ascendancy and corporate profitability remains the same. It is, however, beyond the scope of this chapter to explore these conflicting strategies, their institutional foundations, and ideological expressions. Whatever these may be, one thing remains clear: business as usual is no longer possible, and the powers that be know it well. We need only recall the 1975 report of their Trilateral Commission to the effect that the world is suffering from "an excess of democracy," not to speak of the "failure" of the Welfare State upon which the entire Reagan program was explicitly predicated.

On the other hand, this analysis suggests the need for an effective strategy to counter the growing imperial corporate offensive. It should be obvious that any such strategy requires both the development of an organized political opposition and the creation of an alternative worldview that would make such an opposition credible. Such an opposition would have to be rooted in those social groups and institutions whose essential interests conflict with the imperatives of the transnational conglomerates. Further, any such attempts to effectively mobilize a political alternative must also come to terms with the psychic dynamics of American character, which is so deeply wedded to the myth of personal success through aggressive domination of the alien other—whether it be nature or other human beings—that it experiences material accumulation and social domination as essential psychic needs, (Not to mention the way in which this dynamic tends to be glossed in terms of America's divine mission to bring freedom and democracy to the world.) If Americans are not "Number One," they tend to feel themselves to be failures. Without a concrete strategy to effect affect, to transform a concern with quantity into one for quality, a preoccupation with exclusive goods into a concern for inclusive goods, any such constructive strategy is bound to fail. And such a strategy must be rooted in a compelling narrative that makes sense of personal effort by placing it in a wider and ennobling worldview, which worldview must disabuse itself of any claims to a divine world mission or providential destiny for America.

The depth of the challenge now facing America should thus be clear. Torn between frontier and garden, between individual and community, the American psyche is easily whipped into action against mythological enemies at home and abroad. If we fail to combat the America of executive supremacy, national secrecy, capitalist audacity, and imperialist penetration—almost always in the name of promoting freedom and democracy—America will be unable to avoid the disaster of benign fascism toward which it has been more than creeping.

The revitalization of America thus requires both the breaking of the power of the large corporations and the remolding of the psyche of Americans. Unless the success orientation rooted in the competitive accumulation of material wealth and personal privilege is transformed into a more modest communal attitude, the growing hostilities now tearing at the fabric of America's personal and institutional life will not be able to be controlled. Save, that is, for the imposition from above of an increasingly repressive techno-bureaucratic order by those established bureaucracies of power and wealth. Such an order will protect the hierarchy of privilege of the controlling establishment while maintaining the class-based social antagonisms that permit the redirection of middle-class Americans' latent hostilities at the pressurized underclasses at home and the Evil Enemy overseas.

America's choices are at least relatively clear. Either it develops a moderately decentralized social system that, in coming to terms with its natural and social environment, revitalizes public life or it faces the growing institutionalization of a mass society rooted in hierarchical privilege and repressive social control, coming, no doubt, in the guise of "national security" and in order to protect "the American Way of Life." Having thus suggested some crucial issues toward which this analysis points our attention but which are beyond the scope of this work, there remains one very important matter bearing upon the diagnosis here undertaken that must be addressed. That concerns the theoretical possibility of a positive alternative to the social disintegration here portrayed. Diagnosis of a malady—even a psycho-cultural one—calls for the suggestion of a cure. Further, such a suggestion has practical consequences to the extent that it gives direction to the practical efforts to bring about the cure. Some remarks are thus called for which may suggest a perspective within which psychic needs and socioeconomic infrastructure may aspire to a concordance consonant with America's best insights.[34] The import of such remarks is *not* that they provide an easy answer to the present dilemma, nor that they offer a Utopian "solution," but rather that they may serve to reopen the conceptual field within which Americans may envision new horizons for critical analyses as well as for programmatic initiatives. The lack of such an expanded horizon all too often lobotomizes political thinking from the outset. Fortunately, there are alternative traditions within the American experience—what the authors of *Habits of the Heart* call the "second language of American individualism"—which draw upon the vision of a biblical commonwealth and of civic republicanism to give expression to a commitment to community integrity and democratic self-determination that offers a hopeful resource from which to counter the destructive effects of radical individualism.[35] It is to a discussion of that vision, suitably revised in the light of the analysis that I have sought to develop in the body of this work, which, to the extent that America has been a primary motor and model for globalization, may provide a suggestive framework for the development of a practical program for the reconstitution of sustainable human community that lies hidden within the emerging New World Order, to which I now turn.

9

Current Patterns and Future Prospects: Reflections for the Twenty-First Century

Democracy must begin at home, and its home is the neighborly community.

John Dewey

All my gods have feet of clay.
Albert Camus

Solitude

I will conclude with thoughts about, and proposals for, our current situation. It should now be clear that many of our traditional beliefs are increasingly at odds with the world they have helped to produce. Often their approaches are actually counterproductive, even potentially destructive. Science and technology have clearly increased the speed and scope of historical transformations. At the same time, they have tended to undermine traditional systems of belief without so far providing us with clear and coherent alternatives. A growing sense of uncertainty of purpose, loss of direction, and personal anxiety is tending to place in question the very future of the biosphere and life on this planet.

The problem is rooted in our self-consciousness. We are inescapably aware of our vulnerability, contingency, and mortality. We realize that the world is a threatening place, and that we may be struck down at any moment, often for no reason and without warning. Death is all around us—it is the very stuff of life and motor of evolution. It does not take long to realize that our own death is inevitable—and, throughout most of human history, and across much of the globe today, given the very short span of average human life, that death is not very far off indeed. And there hardly seems any rhyme or reason, other than (discredited) traditional beliefs, to sustain us. Even if we are surrounded by family, clan, or tribe of supportive and caring others—which certainly is not guaranteed—there exist many other humans and animals who are ever-present threats to our survival, not to speak of the often challenging world of inexplicable and unpredictable natural events. Thus, however beautiful may be our surroundings, they don't provide the physical safety or psychic assurance that can make us feel at home, that we belong, and can trust our environs to take care of us in a meaningful way. Individually or in our small group, we are alone in the world, with, at best, limited ability to make sense of it all.

This "primitive" experience of natural solitude has been given cosmic import by the "recent" discoveries of natural science.[1] Here we find ourselves and our "world" reduced to practical insignificance by the grandeur and scope of that cosmos, within which we seem, so far at least, to be the only living beings. That cosmic solitude only exacerbates our natural vulnerability and weakness, whatever may be our heroic pretensions. No wonder the somewhat desperate interest in finding life elsewhere in the universe. At least then we wouldn't be so terribly alone. In the last analysis, however, what difference would that make? We would simply find other life forms or conscious beings similarly fated as ourselves, with whom we might be able to commiserate. Yet, at present and for the foreseeable future that is at best a valiant hope, if not a vain delusion, which only detracts from the far more pressing problem of finding a way to honestly accept and live with our human condition. No doubt, that is what Nietzsche meant when he called man "the sick animal." For we do not seem able to accept our natural condition and honestly address, ameliorate, and cultivate it. We seem to need to deny our humanity—that is, our animality, vulnerability, contingency, and finitude—assume the garb of, or attach ourselves to, some divinely chosen being, and lord it over others, while often running roughshod over the natural world of plants and animals—treating them as only "raw materials" or "natural resources."[2] Even more, we seem all too often to need to deal with that usually repressed sense of vulnerability by feeling it to be bad or even evil, and then alleviating the distress it causes by projecting it onto others who may be seen as demonic, the embodiment of that weakness or evil that we have denied in ourselves. Having separated those others from ourselves and our "relatives," we are emotionally (and usually morally and religiously) free to reduce them to slavery when we do not actually seek to annihilate them. This act has the further, even if only temporary, psychological benefit of symbolically cleansing us of those nasty unconscious feelings of vulnerability and impotence by which we are inevitably plagued.[3]

Evolution

Contemporary experience has been further traumatized by the dawning realization—passionately rejected by so many, even though rarely well understood—that our actual existence is the result of a practically infinite number of purposeless historical accidents "naturally selected" for "reproductive success" over eons of time. Nothing is fixed, nothing is permanent, nothing lasts—in spite of our continual need to attach ourselves to that which is infinite, everlasting, and eternal. Energy is ceaselessly at work, only stopping for brief periods when confronted by equal and opposite energy in a state of temporary equilibrium; everything undergoes continual transformations in complex transactions with its ever-changing environs. Things come into being, undergo continual change, and go out of existence: "you cannot step into the same river twice," in fact, you are not even the same person the second time you step in. The Ancients had taken rest as the fundamental condition of existence[4]; the Moderns had replaced rest with motion, but had taken matter as basic and always conserved. But for post-Einsteinians energy has replaced matter as basic, with mass essentially the expression of the energy of fundamental "particles," themselves really only patterned clusters of bound energy left over from the "big bang."[5]

Not only are we not here for any transcendent purpose, nor is there any preordained path for us to follow, or any guarantee of "success," but the world literally won't sit still for us, and there is no fixed place to rest our weary self. We are in and of the natural world, not above it, can't control it, and can't get out of it alive. And it cares not for us, anymore than for anything else. This is not the kind of home we dream of, or long for—however beautiful and exhilarating it may often be. The tree of life has many and deep roots, and is profligate with its branches and shoots, but as a fruit of this tree we can only be nourished when rooted in the soil of life by way of its branches and stems. Thus, our life is fed (as it can be threatened) by its nurturing environs, whose ecological health or balance must be preserved if we are to preserve ourselves. And this cannot be, in any "long run," a matter of imposing our will on that world. Only a caring and common stewardship in which we tend to, but do not soil, our nest can provide the nurturance for life to flourish.

Emergence

But there is grandeur in this view of life in which "endless forms most beautiful and most wonderful have been, and are being, evolved."[6] The natural world proves to be far more interesting that any simplistic, or materialist, reduction can appreciate. Not only are the "things of the world" not ultimate, irreducible, or fixed in their nature, nor are they simply the result of the compounding of their elemental parts, but the processes at work take on different properties and operate in accord with distinct "logics" as their structures change, structures that cannot be completely separated from the environment within which they come to be and continue to act. In short, the natural world is webbed, networked, and continually full of surprises, however much they may come to be retrospectively explained and incorporated within a wider theory. Those surprises are not the result of magic, but the emergent result of new levels of reality, properties of the emerging structures. Thus, emergence is a pervasively real property of the natural world, in which levels build upon and incorporate other levels, though not in any linear hierarchical manner. Rather than conceiving of the "complex," at least in principle, as the logically deducible result of its elemental constituents, emergence requires us to see those more elemental levels as providing the enabling conditions for, and boundary conditions of, the emergence of distinct structures that operate in accord with distinct and nonreducible logics, that is, with a distinct set of nonreducible operable laws.

Thus, continuity and emergence mark the natural world, and novelty is empirically real and scientifically comprehensible. It is both prospectively unpredictable and retrospectively comprehensible. These are not contradictory aspects, once we get beyond the deductive logic that has been our conceptual straightjacket. Life is one of those emergents, as is sociality, consciousness, and self-consciousness. These are transformative realities that bring meaning and significance into a universe that was beforehand without them. The biosphere creates a natural setting within which complex life may flourish, and self-conscious beings emerge who may truly care for one another, as they appreciate and create beauty and dream of better worlds. But if such dreams are not to become nightmares, they need to cultivate values, practices, and institutions that enrich our common roots and shared home, and that develop from honest inquiry, involving solid practical and theoretical knowledge, mutual respect, and practical humility. Little can be more destructive than the failure, whether willful or inadvertent, malicious or poignant, to accept our natural condition and intelligently explore its contours, developing our strategies with humility, openness, and mutual respect. The immersion in associative and mythological thought, transcendent beliefs, and self-certain practice, that often grounds a delusional individual or collective self-promotion, is more than likely to lead to mutual demonization, incessant intercommunal strife, and ecological destruction. Intelligence may not be flashy, is usually more prosaic than dramatic, and tends not to be personally engrossing, but it is our only reliable guide to constructive action when employed in open-ended dialogic community development.

Sustainability

And we *are* all in this together. To speak of "spaceship Earth" is more than simply a metaphor. It is a statement of the relative self-containment of a planet that carries its biosphere with it as it hurtles incessantly through space, rotating on its axis, revolving around its Sun, circling around the distant center of its galaxy, speeding through inexhaustible space in no apparent direction without a specified destination or determined time frame. The Earth is a finite planet, whose resources can be mined, processed for more or less efficient use, and creatively recycled, but are neither infinitely malleable nor completely reusable. Each use carries a cost and excludes other possibilities. There are limits, however difficult to determine, to the "carrying capacity" of the Earth: there cannot be infinite growth on a finite planet.

In short, while qualitative development may be possible without foreseeable limits, quantitative growth is not. There must be limits to the size of population, the extent of materials extraction, the exploitation of flora and fauna, the human appropriation of photosynthetic activity, the deposition of industrial waste, the use of energy, and the release of heat. Humans must now transform an economy historically addicted to unlimited growth—in which the resources of nature were usually taken for granted—into one operating in a relatively steady-state equilibrium with the natural ecology, in which input and output, and thus throughput, are minimized while utility is maximized. Sustainability means that we fit in with the long-term carrying capacity of the Earth, leaving each generation at least not significantly less well off ecologically than was the previous one.

By now it should also be clear that there is no harmonious equilibrium that will naturally result from the unfettered operation of a "free market," any more than will there be an equitable distribution of the benefits and burdens of such economic activity. We can neither expect a tide of unending growth to "raise all ships," nor market corrections to operate in an efficient and timely manner to ensure a humane ecological equilibrium. The scale of economic activity and the equitable distribution of its production can only result from the intelligently managed collective planning of a coordinated world order that subordinates market operation to human needs and ultimately biospheric constraints. There cannot be ecologically sustainable economic and social development without foresight and intelligent global coordination. However painful to acknowledge and difficult to implement on a world scale, this is only to state the obvious. The challenge, rather, is in developing a coherent vision and an implementable plan of action, and in obtaining worldwide acceptance and effective institutional coordination.

Subsidiarity

In addressing the required vision, we need to draw upon our previous analysis of the human need to be "a locus of value in a world of meaning."[7] We have discussed the psychic as well as social and political importance of rooting human beings in effective face-to-face communities, pyramidally structured in accordance with the scope of activity and consequences. It should be evident that whatever power can be located at the level closest to the individual or nuclear unit should be so located, but that as the consequences of action radiate outward, so must the scope of responsibility and the effective power to make decisions. That is the notion of subsidiarity, long expounded—though "more often honored in the breech than in the observance thereof"—by the Roman Catholic Church, among others, namely, that power and authority should reside as close to home as possible. Further, such notions are not utopian but quite practical, as the following brief observations drawn primarily from, or proposals addressed to, American experience should make clear.

The development of miniaturized technology has made local control more possible than ever in the recent past. It facilitates both the production and distribution of information, providing an easily accessible informational resource base for the empowerment of localities. Even more, energy alternatives now facing humanity offer the possibility of multiple-sourced, small-scale, task-related, and decentralized solar technologies, suited to local needs, financing possibilities, and social and political requirements. Much of this was already well sketched out years ago by Barry Commoner, among others.[8] By moving away from capital-intensive, centralized energy production (which itself would inevitably be controlled by nondemocratic, transnational corporations, and/or central government bureaucracies, not to speak of the security forces required to protect them) toward decentralized solar sources scaled to meet energy needs, we would be preserving the environment as we free localities of the stranglehold presently exercised by transnational conglomerates. Obviously, local self-determination would be facilitated, as local planning would gain leverage against capital flight, and tax blackmail. Such localized power would seem to be a necessary precondition of any attempt to reconstitute relative local autonomy, without which the revitalization of neighborhoods and local communities would seem to be impossible.[9]

From energy to health, the watchword remains the same. Local control of the delivery of health care through the creation of health clinics and day-care centers, grounded in a universal health system, offers the possibility both for neighborhood revitalization and for improved public health. In the 1960s, U.S. representative Ronald Dellums presented the model of such an ideal program, in which democratically controlled local clinics are pyramidally integrated into a system of local, regional, and large experimental hospitals, drawing upon regional, national, and international research institutions.

Central to any such humane vision must be the reconstruction of walkable local communities and the concomitant reconstitution of neighborhood life, that is, of a relatively autonomous face-to-face public world. "In its deepest and richest sense a community must always remain a matter of face-to-face intercourse.... Democracy must begin at home, and its home is the neighborly community."[10] Drawing upon that residual American tradition of the town meeting, itself a casualty of the dynamic previously described,[11] the first priority of public policy must be the facilitation of the process by which individuals can be encouraged and supported to come together locally to plan and provide the general delivery of preventive medicine rather than rely upon cost-intensive sophisticated surgery. At a minimum, regardless of details, any community that cares about its members must address health care as a right, not as a marketable commodity access to which is dependent upon the ability to pay. Thus, it must find a way to provide affordable and accessible health care equitably to all at a level of quality determined by the society's available level of knowledge, expertise, and technological and financial resources.

Thus, energy and health must join with education as loci of community self-determination. In addition, neighborhood committees and crime patrols, in connection not only with local police, but also with neighborhood youth centers, offer the best possibility of reducing crime and reawakening concern for public welfare. No community can grow and obtain the respect and care of its youth if it does not show them that concern and offer them that public space in which spontaneous friendships can take root around common interests. Here, neighborhood youth centers can offer that indispensable service of providing quasi-supervised "hang-outs" for the development of face-to-face encounters, thus mitigating the tendencies to impersonality and manipulation fostered by the market and the media.

Further requirements of a revitalized public would involve: a sound public transport system—particularly crucial for youth and for the elderly; tax incentives for small- and medium-sized business; public oversight of investment decisions whose consequences would affect large areas or regions; credit allocation to facilitate productive investment; control over the possibility of capital or job flight; and efforts to facilitate the development of democratically controlled cooperatives and to encourage programs for worker participation in the management of business. People take more interest in, and show more care for, work in which they have a constructive role to play, as they show more respect for a community they experience as their own. These measures must seek to facilitate the development of programs and policies that provide a constructive place for the elderly. Only in this way can a people gain a deep sense of time and history, keeping active and involved those who are living embodiments of our collective past. Further, respect for family and the human person are deepened, as the skills of experience and the patience and perspective of age thicken cultural life, and soften the edges of our increasingly secularized and narrow focused world.

Finally, these strategies require the demystification of our present separation of public from private. In matters of large-scale public policy, exclusive emphasis upon the "private sphere" must be seen as the ideological protection of vested interests that it is. Strategies to further such privatization only contribute to the further deterioration of our public and social life, thus further driving us into the privacy of our increasingly vulnerable home. At the same time, they undermine the social supports for our personal psychic integrity, leaving us an increasingly isolated atom in a world of impersonal forces. Neither psychic health, social cohesion, environmental quality, nor our collective future are furthered by such a privatized collective vision and the greedy, self-seeking politics it inevitably spawns.[12]

Dignity and Self-Respect

But if the principle of subsidiarity is conceptually fairly clear, with a recognized history of significant institutional advocacy, however complicated and debatable may be the precise details of its implementation, its contribution to addressing the human demand for personal valuation by exercising some effective control over one's daily activities is even more powerful.[13] It is but a step from this recognition to the even more radical notion that such personal self-respect through individual empowerment and relative self-determination places in question all interpersonal situations in which the human being is treated primarily, even if not exclusively, as an instrument.

Of course, I am not the first to make that observation. At the center of Immanuel Kant's imposing philosophical edifice stands his "categorical imperative," the bedrock of his moral philosophy. In its most elemental form, it calls for respect for the dignity of each person as a rational self-legislating agent of The Moral Law. Kant insisted that we must treat each person "as an end in him(or her) self, and never solely as a means" to some other end. Certainly meaningful human activity has its uses, but these must never override respect for the dignity of the self-legislating human being whose activity is in question. The clear implication is that it is never morally legitimate to treat a human being as simply an employee, that is, as a human tool whose value is determined either by the quality of his or her work or by its price in the market. In fact, in spite of its almost universal spread, it remains essential to note the inevitable, even if hidden, moral degradation involved in treating people as marketable commodities, "hired hands," human tools who are to take orders from those who own the enterprise and thus have the supposed unquestionable right to dictate the nature and pace of production and the quality and extent of human interaction in the workplace.

In short, wage labor is a demeaning subjection of human freedom. It denies and negates human dignity, at least during the work day, and excludes the essential right of (relative) human self-determination. Such treatment is almost always felt as demeaning, even if one is brought up to believe that it is natural, unavoidable, necessary for effective operation, and completely unobjectionable. Being reduced to one who is only to "take orders," to "do as one is told to" by one's "superiors," cannot help but create, however unconscious it may be, an experience of degradation and probably incipient resentment that cannot fail to effect one's self-image, self-respect, and relations with others. In fact, the incipient resentment generated by being treated as simply an instrument of production can be expected over time, depending upon the extent and depth of the felt humiliation, to well up within and cry out for expression, often by finding others (at home or in the wider world) upon whom one can displace one's humiliation by treating them in a similarly demeaning manner—when, that is, it is not completely directed inward toward oneself.

Democratic citizenship is the precise opposite of a society of employees. Each tends to weaken the other, as they are polar opposites. One is built on the collective government of dignified and self-determining rational beings; the other, whether enlightened or not, is the organization of dependent human instruments of production, what Marx so telling referred to as "wage slaves," people who have learned to do what they are told or be fired. They are not participants in the decision-making process, are not valued for their human but for their productive capacities, have no say in the direction of the enterprise, and are usually dispensed with when they are no longer needed—"redundant," as the British so tellingly say.

Kant well understood the conditions of human dignity when he offered as one of his formulations of the categorical imperative—the basic rule of moral behavior—that we should so act so that we treat others (and ourselves) as if they were self-governing subjects in a kingdom of ends. It is worth noting here that American democracy was born in a land in which more than 90 percent of white males—who alone were allowed to vote—were self-employed, and hence relatively independent and self-determining individuals, and in which income disparities were relatively minor as compared with today. The situation was similar in the fifth century BCE at the height of Athenian democracy. When income disparities become great and most individuals are dependent on others whom they do not control for their livelihood, democracy is inevitably undermined, as Aristotle well understood.[14] In the words of the great American jurist and Supreme Court Justice Louis Brandeis, you can have great concentrations of wealth or you can have democratic self-government, but you cannot have both.

Community

Human dignity and democratic self-government therefore require a community that maintains respect for the capacity of each individual and nurtures that capacity into self-determining adulthood. Only in a community that values such individuality can democracy take root and grow. The earlier critical analysis of Individualism[15] was meant to underline the extent to which the human being is social to the core. That is to say that the most intimate and personal—even subconscious and unconscious aspects—of the individual self are socially constituted and sustained. Our apparent physical distinctness—itself largely an illusion resulting from our taking for granted the permeable membrane that is our skin, and our obvious dependence on the life support systems provided by the biosphere, nowhere more evident than when we seek to explore "outer space"—has obtained ideological precision, particularly in the Western world, in that doctrine of Individualism that undergirds almost all major theoretical formulations and practical strategies. In so doing, it has distorted human understanding, misguided social policy, and tended to undermine human psychic and even physical health.

It is not soft-hearted liberalism but hard-hearted social analysis that focuses on the extent to which human character development, personal values, and interpersonal behavior are primarily the individual's (mostly prereflective) appropriation of the prevailing norms. That, of course, was what George Herbert Mead meant by saying "that we become as we are addressed." But the implications of that truth are staggering, and go to the heart of an understanding of the historical clustering of such apparently random individual acts as assassination of leaders, development of "terrorism," and "suicide bombers" (or kamikaze pilots, for that matter). Can one believe, for example, that suicide bombers could exist outside of a religious culture that sustains and nurtures them both ideologically and socially, or kamikaze pilots outside of the quasi-religious nationalism that has been Imperial Japan?[16] Even more, consider the explanation for the flowering of creativity in Classical Greece or Renaissance Italy, for example, as compared with its almost complete absence for many centuries in both of those lands—clearly not explainable as the result of some radical alterations in genetic inheritance. Still more, and quite ironically, the very flowering of the doctrine of Individualism is a historical product that has fabricated a culture in the West, and even more, in Protestant America, that has socially produced, culturally sustained, and socially reinforced precisely that Individualism that itself has denied the cultural preconditions of its own existence. Have we yet adequately appreciated the irony of a culture that is so pervasively organized and ideologically orchestrated so as to produce, promote, and celebrate precisely that "self-made man" or woman whose existence is inconceivable without those cultural supports that are its living contradiction?

This is not an arid academic point that I am making, but one fraught with the most profound practical implications. We cannot understand human pathology or social disintegration, nor develop effective policies without correctly addressing this issue. We cannot deal effectively with criminality without understanding the conditions that foster and sustain it.[17] We cannot sustain positive values, counter the depressing effects of human contingency and the tragic nature of our natural condition, or contribute to the flowering of individuality, human creativity, and democratic self-determination without carefully attending to the cultural conditions that make these possible. Nor, for that matter, can we begin to seriously address the profound cultural impediments to constructive and humane social transformation.

Clearly, then, our individual health is inextricably linked to the "health"—the values, beliefs, practices, and support systems—of the community that has given birth and nourished us into adulthood. We are more adequately viewed as social plants rooted and nourished by the cultural soil than we are self-sustaining individuals. The quality of that community is the pervasive quality of our lives—to challenge which is bound to be profoundly wrenching intra- as well as interpsychically. It is to tear us apart from within as well as from without. It is to threaten to cut us off from that interpersonal support and social sustenance without which it would be difficult for us even to survive. Hence, it is not possible to address the conditions and provide for the maintenance of psychic health without considering the affective and practical character of our sustaining social environs.

Is there any evidence more simple, direct, and persuasive on the power of institutional authority to evoke hideous behavior from normal and well-meaning human beings than that provided by Stanley Milgrim's classic experiment on obedience to authority? There we see demonstrated the extent to which decent human beings will go in inflicting pain on their fellow humans when they are directed to do so by "legitimate" authorities, as well as their deep reluctance and often actual impotence to challenge such authorities. And this does not even begin to touch on the cultural processes by which far more insensitive, aggressive, angry, violent, xenophobic, and destructive or self-righteous and messianic characters may be produced, characters that take pleasure at the pain thus being inflicted. How else are we to understand the extent to which formerly normal decent people have been seen to descend into barbarism in the treatment of different ethnicities, races, and religions, in genocide, and in the infliction of excruciating torture on those "alien others" in their custody? Such treatment is rarely the act of isolated individuals, and almost always the encouraged and approved behavior of culturally sustained collectivities, often in conditions of extreme social tensions and psychic pressures.[18]

Consider a more recent, intimate, and positive (almost prosaic) example of the way in which personal health is socially rooted. In responding to a highly stressful situation, "researchers [have] found that people who had no friends increased their risk of death over a 6-month period, ... those who had the most friends over a 9-year period cut their risk of death by more than 60 percent... . The famed Nurses' Health Study from Harvard Medical School found that the more friends women had, the less likely they were to develop physical impairments as they aged, and the more likely they were to be leading a joyful life. In fact, the results were so significant, the researchers concluded, that not having close friends or confidants was as detrimental to your health as smoking or carrying extra weight!"[19]

That psychic health benefits from nurturing support groups, while those who function alone are more vulnerable to illness and depression has long been suspected.[20] It certainly fits in with our understanding of the origins and nourishing of the human self—as well as suggesting why humans are so needy of that social support and approval, and have such difficulty in confronting and opposing social pressures and legitimate authority. To be a social being is to be given birth by a family, and nourished into adulthood and sustained by the community of which one is a part. It is as if the individual self were umbilically tied to the community such that its psychic health is inextricably linked to its cultural sustenance. We are clearly misled by the physical independence of one body from the next into failing to recognize how intimately bound up the human self is with its social network.[21]

But this is only to repeat at the interpersonal level the field structure of reality we have repeatedly noted, from the subatomic through the ecological to the interpersonal and the intrapsychic. Reality is webbed and networked. Individuals operate in contexts that intimately shape their character and affect their behavior. We cannot adequately understand the world at any level by seeking to deduce its activity from the logic of its constituent elements any more than we can understand the elements from the behavior of the totality. We certainly cannot adequately address psychic or social reality by focusing solely, or even primarily, upon the character and behavior of the individual. To believe that crime is primarily caused by criminals, war by human aggressivity, or poverty by the lack of individual initiative is to fail to understand their structural conditions and to guarantee in advance that you will not be able to develop effective social solutions.[22]

Expanding the Perspective

Not only must we address the structural conditions that frame these problems, but an adequate understanding requires that we place them in a more comprehensive perspective, both within the context of the history of the particular culture and within the biosocial frame of the evolutionary development of the human species and its place in the biosphere. In one sense, we must understand the latter as the given genetic and ecological frame within which we have to design our practical strategies for adaptation and amelioration. This will help us devise strategies that are more likely to work. At the same time, we need to be cognizant of the potential long-term consequences of our shorter term solutions, because they will tend to influence the conditions and strategies that are likely to predominate in the future. It should be quite clear by now that relations between the human psyche, the social world, and its natural environs are continually changing, deeply interrelated, and mutually coordinated. Everything we do now affects what we are likely to be able to do later. If we wish to contribute to preserving and significantly enhancing the quality of life on this planet in the long run, we need to appreciate more profoundly still the likely evolutionary consequences of the institutions we create, the values we promote, and the human beings we celebrate, reward, and seek to reproduce.

We should remember that contemporary human social relations have emerged as a continuation yet profound modification of the behavior of our ancestors, from chimps and australopithecines to early hominids and beyond. With the development of pair-bonding and family relations, of language and religion, we see a continued expansion of the range and intensification of the quality of sociality. From patrilocality, narrow ethnicity, territoriality, and organized warfare with other members of the same species that predominates in chimp and early human societies have grown social institutions, perceptions, and expanded concerns that tend to mitigate the exclusivity of narrow kinship relations, widen the range of humane interactions, often by mythologizing our commonality, thus emotionally binding us to wider and even cosmic realities.

Evidence suggests that the evolutionary success of larger and more cohesive social units (than the band or tribe) has been facilitated by the partial replacement of "individual selection" and "kin selection" with "reciprocal altruism," particularly the "tit-for-tat" strategy, or "conditional altruism," in its several variations. This process has contributed to the relative deemphasizing of warfare along with an expansion of interpersonal contacts through trade, and the promotion of industry and culture, and even competitive games. This has been slowly transforming the conditions of success and the direction of evolutionary development, thus opening up a long-term perspective for the creation of a truly civilized and humane world order. Writing in *Before the Dawn,* Wade comments:

> The uniquely human blend of sociality was not easily attained. Its various elements evolved over many years. The most fundamental, a major shift from the ape brand of sociality was the human nuclear family, which gave all males a chance at procreation along with incentives to cooperate with others in foraging and defense. A second element, developed from an instinct shared with other primates, was a sense of fairness and reciprocity, extended in human societies to a propensity for exchange and trade with other groups. A third element was language. And the fourth, a defense against the snares of language, was religion. All these behaviors are built on the basic calculus of social animals, that cooperation holds more advantages than competition.... . [But] "Kinship-organized groups can only get so large before they begin falling apart," ... There appears to be an upper limit to the size of a group that can be cooperatively organized by the principles of kinship, descent and marriage.... . One principle that biologists think may help explain larger societies ... is that of reciprocal altruism.... . A tit-for-tat behavioral strategy, where you cooperate with a new acquaintance, and thereafter follow his strategy toward you ... turns out to be superior to all others in many circumstances.... . This set of behaviors, built around reciprocity, fair exchange and the detection of cheaters, has provided the foundation for the most sophisticated urban civilizations.[23]

Among the numerous examples of how such social transformations can develop in connection with genetic change, let me note the following. Gracilization of the human anatomy has tended to replace more robust features as humans have been developing more cooperative life styles while living in increasingly large social units, moving from band to clan, tribe, village, people, and nation. Lactose tolerance developed separately among cattle-rearing human beings in Northern Europe and in sub-Saharan Africa over the last 6,000 years. Wolves became domesticated barking animals (capable of serving as sentries) as humans adopted sedentary life styles and developed agriculture. How quickly significant adaptations are possible and what forces might work on them, especially when we are dealing with such complex issues as human nature, character, and social behavior for an increasingly integrated world population of more than 6 billion members is a highly complex question well beyond the scope of this work. These examples are only meant to be illustrative of the continued operation of evolution and its potential bearing on the long-term prospects of the enhancement and flourishing of human life. Clearly evolutionary processes can proceed far more quickly when there are clear and explicit environmental pressures, especially among populations limited in size and range of interaction, as is clear from such fairly recent examples as that of the English moths—changing from white to gray to white again as soot from coal first dirtied the urban environment and then was cleaned up—and the Galapagos birds, where beak size and shape changed within recent decades as climate first became drier and then changed again as the rains returned.

Adaptive pressures can set the context within which moral values emerge and develop. They frame human possibilities and shape our sensibilities to members of our own and other tribes as well as to animals. Debates over the sanctity of the life of the elderly look very different to Eskimos whose society is too precarious to expend precious scarce resources in maintaining the very infirm elderly. Or similarly, to the !Kung, with respect to care that mothers can provide to their children. In the latter case, !Kung mothers have the accepted right to kill their defective infants or even one of a pair of twins due to the excessive burden that such child-rearing would place on mothers in that society.[24] From their perspective, current debates on birth control, abortion, and euthanasia hardly make sense. Some of the very terms of the debate and values in question, such as what we mean by the sanctity of life, the dignity of the person, and the responsibility of the parents, would look quite different indeed.

Humility

But we can only work with what we have—creating positive conditions with the informed expectation that such conditions will tend within the foreseeable future to reinforce and reproduce themselves in the character and institutions of our society—while in the long run they will tend to selectively reinforce the evolutionary pressures for complementary genetic modifications and ecological transformations. We must remain ever mindful of, and appropriately humble about, the complexity of the biosphere within which our life unfolds. MacIntyre has incisively detailed several aspects of systemic unpredictability of which we must be continually mindful and which should generate a degree of humility about our ability to successfully impose any single vision upon the world.

> The first derives from the nature of radical conceptual innovation; ... the second ... from the way in which the unpredictability of certain of ... [each agent's] own future actions ... individually generates another element of unpredictability as such in the social world; ... a third ... from the game-theoretic character of social life; ... [and the fourth from] ... the necessarily open and indeterminate character of all situations as complex as the Vietnam war.[25]

After also noting four predictable aspects of human life,[26] MacIntyre comments on the inevitable continuing tension between the need for internal organizational predictability and that for continually flexible organizational responses necessitated by ongoing environmental pressures for adaptation to novelty. Thus, there is "the need to allow for individual initiative, a flexible response to changes in knowledge, [and] the multiplication of centers of problem-solving and decision-making."[27] Hence the need for valuing individuality within organizations and for promoting open and democratic interchange among perspectives.

This suggests the essential point of the previously discussed Hegelian dialectic, namely the fact that each individual (or collective) point of view is but a perspective within an encompassing whole the very existence of which transforms that whole. Any attempt to reflectively capture that self-reflective totality inevitably involves one in an infinite regress. The totality is always and essentially more and dialectically other than the perspective that seeks to articulate and transform it. It's a little like the essential unpredictability of quantum mechanics in the sense that the very observation constitutes a partially unpredictable intervention in the situation under study. The humility being suggested is itself rooted in an essential limitation of any human intervention.[28]

Practical Ethics

Thus, the multifold challenge confronting humanity is that of: first, developing a comprehensive naturalistic field theory; second, applying that framework to the task of the coordinated transformation of the values, beliefs, practices, social institutions, and personal character that constitute the current social world; and, finally, locating this process within the long-term evolutionary codevelopment of human nature, social institutions, and natural ecology. This would seem to call for, as its social foundation, the building of those viable neighborhood-based, face-to-face democratically self-empowered local communities pyramidally structured into more encompassing representative bodies in accord with the principal of subsidiarity that we previously discussed.

Further, such development will require the widest institutionally coordinated distribution of individual empowerment possible, consistent with available technologies, as well as the provision of universally available social and health services as a right. Economic activity should always remain subservient to the provision of collective human well-being. These institutions will need to operate, therefore, in accord with respect for ecological sustainability and the carrying capacity of the biosphere, as well as for human dignity, community integrity, equity in the provision of basic necessities, and racial and gender equality. They will need to find expression in social and cosmic narratives that celebrate our life on Earth, provide for shared joy and sorrow, and be consistent with rational inquiry and the best available science. And all will need to be done in a manner that tends in the long run to promote the values, practices, and individuals who can thrive in such a transformed natural and social world.

But if the technical and social outlines of a constructive strategy are fairly clear, the paths that lead there could hardly be more opaque. In the most obvious sense, current individuals are most often the product of partially dysfunctional character development, having largely been socialized into magical (religious and/or chauvinistic) belief systems, and authoritarian, hierarchical, repressive and/or competitive, and usually socially exclusive group relations and institutional practices. These are the consequences of an evolutionary process that has long tended to favor the narrowly tribal and excessively militant over the more open, inclusive, cooperative, and peaceful. In short, they are the natural and evolutionary products of the societies that have produced them, and that in their beliefs and practices they tend to reproduce. This is the natural cultural closed circle—or better, slowly evolving cultural spiral, aspects of which we have previously noted. Thus, culture and character tend to mutually produce and reinforce each other, as Plato so insightfully observed in seeking to address the need for systemic social change in his *Republic*. So where is the handle by which one can get a hold of this situation at present and constructively transform it? Unless, that is, one thinks it is essentially intractable, due perhaps to the intractability of human nature, as, for example, Machiavelli or Freud believed. Or that our "fallen" nature makes us incapable of self-transformation without the aid of divine grace, which is essentially inscrutable and about which we can do little or nothing on our own, as the likes of Augustine, Luther, and Calvin seem to have believed. Plato, on the other hand, was probably not the first, and certainly not the last (just consider Robespierre and St. Just, for example, or more recently, B. F. Skinner, and perhaps Mao Tse-Tung), to advocate the complete removal of human impediments to the comprehensive and coordinated refashioning of individual moral character and social institutions in the service of their revolutionary ideals.

Of course, the challenge is not only a matter of vision, technology, character development, and institutional practices, but also one of habits, inheritance, uncertainty, and "vested interests." Every change is bound to advantage some and disadvantage others, at least in the foreseeable future—which is, of course, the practical realm of our daily lives. We know what we have, and however inadequate, for most of us it is preferable to the uncertainty of the future and the distrust we, in our effective political impotence, have for those who would likely make the decisions. Clearly, those with the most power to make the changes are most likely not the ones to benefit most immediately from a more equitable distribution of resources and decision-making. Thus, institutionally vested interests, with their vast resources and control of information, communication, and the levers of power, inevitably conspire with the embedded traditions and social and personal habits to entrench current practices and to make progressive change appear fearful. It is certainly true that what exists, with all its inadequacies, is at least a known reality, while basic change is clearly an unknown quantity and quite disastrous things have been known to happen under the guise of social improvement.

Even more, such institutional power inevitably controls not only official policy, but, for the most part, also the official and popular means of communication and the "legitimate" sources of research and information that effectively shape public understanding. What the public knows about "the facts" and how it comes to understand and "frame" those facts into a coherent narrative is ever highly problematic. What could be more astounding in a relatively open and free society such as the United States than the public's continued belief in the so-called "democratic" goals of U.S. foreign policy?[29] Given the extensive evidence that exists on the U.S. role in overthrowing legitimate governments, as recently documented, for example, by Stephen Kinzer,[30] or in the manipulation of financial transactions, covert assassinations, and military interventions to protect and promote corporate interests, as detailed by John Perkins,[31] among numerous others—all of it publicly and easily available, especially with the emergence of the World Wide Web—the prevailing belief in America's benign and "democratic" overseas intentions is a testament to the propaganda power of the "powers that be" to frame and control public understanding, even in "a free society."[32] Such vested, and invested, concentrated institutional power presents an almost impenetrable barrier to an honest presentation of the facts, open public discussion, and intelligent engagement in the development of sustainable policy alternatives.

Our Tragic Condition and Mythological Fantasies

It is here that we can perhaps best situate the ambiguous place of religion in the modern world. Religions have clearly served many positive functions throughout human history: building and maintaining community;[33] facilitating life's passages, whether celebratory, mournful, or tragic; ministering to human sufferings and needs; regulating, adjudicating, mediating, and placating communal tensions and conflicts; and providing a moral framework and grounding for institutional practices, almost invariably rooted in a cosmic worldview that provides an overarching perspective on the meaning of life, the appropriate direction for human endeavor, and the bases for human hope. These address natural, inevitable, and vital human needs, and are the most culturally pervasive ways for addressing that basic human need to be "a locus of value in a world of meaning." By so doing, they motivate and invigorate their adherents, providing meaning, direction, and purpose to their lives.[34]

At the same time, however, they point us toward one of the most fundamental challenges confronting our species, if we are to find a way to survive and flourish on this planet without destroying ourselves and laying waste to the biosphere. That challenge is the need to think clearly and coherently on the basis of the facts of the world, using the best informed intelligence to address our most profound problems. While religions clearly are expressions of some of humanity's most fundamental needs and modes of thought, they also have been and continue to be profound impediments to intelligent appraisal and effective action. While our pervasive human needs can be addressed in secular and humane manners, religion's traditional modes of thought are deeply problematic, being almost universally anthropomorphic if not animistic, infused with mythology and fantasy, pervaded by wish fulfillment, and easily susceptible to illusion and demagoguery. How often have religions promoted magical thinking, superstitious rituals, the "true" path, cultural antagonisms, social exclusion, and even torture in the name of ritual purification, holy wars, and demonization of the different and other? The respected historian, William McNeill, has suggested the "primitive" roots of this conceptual problem with a brief description of the origins of religion from animism. He writes:

> Animism was universal among human beings in every part of the earth before complex, hierarchical societies began to develop diverse theologies and rituals of worship as they became civilized... . It was the first world view capable of explaining life and death, dreams and illness, and a myriad of everyday surprises and disappointments—by attributing them to the intervention of spirits, some benign, some hostile, and all endowed with a will of their own to help or hinder human hopes and purposes.
>
> Indeed human purposes were themselves often seen as the work of individual spirits that inhabit each of us for as long as we live, departing at death; and when we are asleep they may wander away into the strange places we know from our dreams.[35]

Religious thought is a remnant of the imaginative perplexities of primitive humans, overawed by the mystifying, incomprehensible, uncertain, and tragic world that their developing consciousness revealed. Not being able to understand or predict events, secure their daily lives, or control their destiny, early humans fantasized about spirits to which they were subject and which they might propitiate. Religion is but the contemporary expression of that deep human desire to feel "at home" in the world, overcoming our tragic destiny by placing ourselves "on the side of the angels," even if, as is quite often, we have to demonize others to convince ourselves that we are on the right path. Little is more destructive of our common future on this planet than the rooting of our need to belong to a sustaining community within the conceptual framework of mythological religious thought and institutions.[36]

Some have said that we need to adopt religious language, if only for the purpose of practical success, if we are to successfully engage vast numbers of humans almost all of whom are members of religious communities, living and seeing the world from within religious frames of meaning.[37] But the religious frame is not something from which one can simply take the pieces one likes while leaving the rest of the package. It is a total worldview, always with its own particular texts and/or stories that dramatically undergird its particular values, practices, and programs. To use its language is to invoke its worldview. It is usually to operate within a mythological and associative-emotive frame of reference, and thus to become more or less a prisoner of that discourse, addressing issues on its terms, and arguing about its problems. That is a devil's bargain. And it is not necessary. We can seek to find common ground on values, positions, and programs while coming to them from a secular perspective, expressing values in our terms and for our reasons. We do not need to argue about first principles when addressing practical problems and political realities. If we cannot find common values and make common cause around shared programs, then we are truly in different worlds, and there is very little cooperatively that can be done about that. There is no guarantee that all people are reachable through rational dialogue, scientific attention to reality, and a common concern for human dignity. But almost all religious traditions share values that can be accessed on rational and secular grounds. And we must never lose sight of the fact that how we address our immediate problems tends to contribute to, and reinforce, the patterns and structures of thought and action that will frame our inquiries and tend to predominate over the long term. In the broadest sense, means and ends are inextricably interwoven, and how we operate now cannot but affect the reality that emerges over time.

At the same time, if we are to effectively contribute to the progressive amelioration of human living, to "reknit the public," in the felicitous phrase of Dewey, we must respect and address those profound needs that have been the historical purview of religion. We need a secular vision of a religious ideal that can inspire human activity and sustain communal life. We must develop publicly accessible modes of ethical reflection grounded in scientific intelligence that do not make appeal to the supernatural, but offer the moral vision and provide and undergird the social institutions that can sustain and nourish community life and minister to urgent human needs. Unfortunately, there has been a general abdication of a public moral ideal on the part of the secular community, and unless we address those legitimate and profound human needs—and provide new religious institutions that give them expression—traditional religions have been and will continue to be quite eager and willing to fill that moral vacuum.[38]

We must always be cognizant of the likely long-term effects of current strategies at the same time as we seek to address current problems and propose short- and medium-term solutions. Most policy discussions tend to proceed more or less within the taken-for-granted condition of current evolutionary development. In a similar fashion, in drawing forth some of the visionary and strategic possibilities from the present analysis, I have generally taken the present constitution of human nature, social structure, and evolutionary development as given, as is appropriate for the short and medium term. But if I am to seriously address the possibilities for humanity's long-term future possibilities, I need to consider the fact that human nature, like everything else, is malleable and subject to evolutionary change. So are human social organization and its sustaining biosphere. If anything is now clear, the individual human being is through and through a social product, rooted in an ongoing cultural tradition that has tended to shape its biological endowment as it has coevolved with its flora and fauna in continual adaptation and response to climatic changes, which humans have increasingly become able to significantly influence by their collective behavior.

Thus, we must appreciate the inevitable, though highly uncertain, evolutionary consequences of our behavior, as we consider the kind of cultural values and genetic characteristics that our proposed institutional transformations are likely to promote. Clearly this can lead us down a dangerous path, as the sad history of modern eugenics makes abundantly clear. Yet the reality cannot be avoided, and ought to be directly addressed. If we are to seriously entertain the possibility of significant long-term improvements in human society, we need to address those aspects of our culture and psyche that promote and reward racist, violent, antagonistic, tribal, chauvinistic, irrational, mythological, and demonological behavior and thought. We must directly confront our violent tribal past as well as its obvious contribution to our current genetic endowment.

It would clearly be a hubristic danger in the extreme to think that we could, or should, seek to directly intervene with eugenic breeding programs as advocated by Plato, the Nazis, or Francis Galton, among others. For we know far too little about the complex and largely unintended ecological consequences that are likely to flow from any particular genetic modifications. Even more, it is a highly dubious and quite oppressive undertaking to seek to directly impose one's values on others. Further, any proposals for change need to express the values and vision we are seeking to bring into being—and if that vision is one that involves respect for the integrity of the human being as well as its capacities for individuality and self-realization, and that seeks to create the conditions that facilitate human flourishing, it must not engage in behavior that undermines that vision. But it would be naïve to think that our institutions and values do not contribute to the production of "socially appropriate" human character and behaviors, and that over time those "socially appropriate" characters and behaviors tend to be celebrated, reinforced, and most "successful" in selectively reproducing themselves and their conditions of existence. It is thus crucial for the long-term improvement of human life to currently advance preferred cultural practices, thus facilitating their expansion and intergenerational reproduction. We thus promote the gradual psychological development of individuals and the cultural institutionalization of practices that have the natural evolutionary consequences of tending to facilitate the evolutionary selection of those genetic traits and tendencies that make the desired long-term enhancement of human nature and its biospheric coevolution more likely.

It is fairly clear, for example, that significant social and moral improvements can and have taken place within modern times. The once warlike Scandinavians, who were the terrors of Western Europe about 1,000 years ago, when the Vikings ravaged what is now the British Isles, France, and the Low Countries, or more recently, when the forces of Gustavus Adolphus were the scourge of northern Europe during the devastating thirty years war of the early 1600s, have more recently produced among the most decent of modern societies and have become one of the major forces for cooperative international relations and humanitarian assistance.

More subtly, but certainly not less significant, radical changes have taken place, particularly in the West, in child-rearing, and in our attitude toward animals. With respect to the latter, for example, Luc Ferry documents the growing movement on behalf of the rights of animals. This has coincided with the proliferation of societies for the prevention of cruelty to animals, an expansion in the ownership of pets, and even quite recently a significant increase in the West in the number of vegetarians.[39] As for child-rearing, it is only in the last few centuries that people have "discovered" infancy, recognized its unique and formative influence, and promoted greater attention to the needs and emotions of children, with respect for their feelings and the specific requirements of human development. Such changes cannot but have positive effect in enhancing human sensitivity, cooperativeness, and the capacity for empathy, which themselves should improve the quality of social institutions and practices. One need only compare modern popular Western manuals on child-rearing with the established European practice of even the eighteenth and nineteenth centuries, as dramatized, for example, in the novels of Charles Dickens.

An important example of these changes in attitude and, perhaps to a lesser extent, in practice concerns the tragic field of warfare. Brutality that was normal and legitimate for the Ancient Greeks or Hebrews—as when Homeric heroes ravaged settlements, slaughtered the males, and raped and/or enslaved the women, or in the Jewish Bible, where Yahweh blessed the genocidal destruction of adversarial peoples such as the Ammonites or the kingdom of Og[40]—would now be labeled crimes against humanity and outlawed under the Geneva Conventions.

None of this is meant to suggest that such behavior does not still happen. Who could say as much after a century that has seen the mass murders of the Nazis and Soviets, the brutality of the Khmer Rouge, ethnic cleansing in the former Yugoslavia or in Rwanda, the firebombing of Dresden, the atomic destruction of Hiroshima and Nagasaki, and most recently the abomination of Abu Ghraib and Guantanamo and its "legitimation" by the American Congress? But these actions have been widely condemned across the globe, and been the object of extensive and continual opposition. The fact that their legitimacy can no longer be taken for granted, but inevitably generates significant moral condemnation and political opposition, thus placing the perpetrators on the ideological defensive is a matter of historic significance. It must not be dismissed or overlooked simply because it is not immediately effective in putting an end to the moral outrage and subjecting their perpetrators to effective sanctions and even individual punishment. In fact, the organization of an International Court of Justice, however limited in scope and effectiveness, its ability to try criminals such as Milosevic, as well as the willingness and ability of legal systems to go after state terrorists such as Pinochet, creating the conditions that facilitated his legal condemnation in Chile—all of this attest to significant improvements in the moral climate of international affairs—however far we still remain from the institution of a morally effective world order.

There are, of course, no guarantees that such improvements, however slow and partial, will continue. There is clearly no providential order overseeing our destiny. Major, even definitive, reversals are always possible. We must pay careful attention and assume collective responsibility for the development of conditions that make progress most likely. But these changes in the moral character of culture point the direction that we ought to commit ourselves to facilitating. They suggest the need to work at each level of human development, from changes in child-rearing and community revitalization to democratic and cooperative transformations in national and international values and institutions. For it is the structure of the culture, the way in which it frames the world in which we live, in the terms of our collective understanding, and in the structure of its institutions and daily practices, that condition the possibilities of human development. The proclamation of the "Four Freedoms" by Roosevelt and Churchill energized and mobilized people because it set forth a truly ennobling vision. Human beings need to be free from fear, exploitation, and humiliation, and secure in their access to the basic necessities of food, clothing, shelter, family, and community. They also need to experience the possibility of actively contributing to the preservation and enhancement of their daily life. When these basic human needs are met, people are not as susceptible to demagoguery and to being whipped into a frenzy of antagonism toward others no matter how different.

Clearly, then, profound changes in the patterns of societies' rewards and punishments can be expected to have an effect in the long run in the very constitution and evolutionary transformation of human nature and its social institutions and ecological adaptations. Most social and political theorists have acted as if nature and culture are biologically fixed, and that change can only work with what we are given. In the West, for example, some believe humans to be by nature sinful or selfish, as with Machiavelli, Hobbes, and Freud, for example; others take a more benign view such as Rousseau or Maslow. Christians such as Paul, Augustine, Luther, or Calvin, each in their own way, believe that humans are innately sinful, but can be changed by divine intervention, with limited or no human contribution possible to that end. Some messianic secularists such as St. Just, Robespierre, or Mao Tse-Tung (and possibly Plato) speak of the possibility of the creation of a "new man" by direct imposition of a transformed social order. But none of them place the issue of fundamental change in nature and society within the long-term perspective of evolutionary transformation while appreciating the ecological complexity that a holistic and ecologically nuanced perspective requires. And none of these link their vision with a systematic respect for the capacity of humans to participate in this process while being able to cultivate their current situation and its possibilities.

Conclusion

It is the possibilities of human freedom, as an emergent trait of biological evolution, which allow us to envisage a transformed future while recognizing our social rooting in a historicized present. That present provides both the resources for and limitations to transformative action. That personal freedom—rooted in our self-consciousness—allows us to stand partially outside of the moment and to envision what might become. It also makes possible our more or less adequate understanding of the present, which sets the frame for current action. Our life unfolds within the space established by that dialogue between where we are and where we want to go, between the real and the ideal. The terms of that dialogue constitute the existential meaning of our world, framing our self-understanding, practical projects, and future possibilities.

I have argued that emergence is a pervasive property of the natural world that, properly understood, can account for the complexity of objects, events, and processes, including the emergence of self-conscious free beings. Further, that emerging levels of complexity operate in accordance with laws that are made possible by, but not reducible to, their necessary conditions. Sentience gives rise to preferences, which are valued by reflective creatures who can evaluate the likely short- and long-term consequences of their preferences, and make choices on that basis. But such choices take place within wider contexts not of their choosing, and are always limited by the scope of their understanding. Imaginative beings can project ideal fulfillments that motivate, energize, and direct present energies, but have a tendency to overreach themselves.

At the same time, human self-consciousness grounds a deep sense of the tragic nature of the human condition, a pervasive however much repressed sense of human contingency, finitude, vulnerability, and mortality. Lacking complete confidence in our capacity to assure the success of our efforts, we seem inevitably drawn toward fantasizing a preexisting supernatural power that under appropriate conditions can guarantee the ultimate success of our hopes and ideals. Who would not be attracted by the vision of a life free from the "slings and arrows of outrageous fortune," whether by return to a mythological golden age or through the guarantee of a salvific future in which "all will be well." Human history is replete with examples of this urge to purity, idealized goodness, holiness, or utopia, whether secular or otherworldly. All of these constitute modes of flight from the tragic finitude of our natural condition. They are grounded in a completely mistaken understanding of the nature and function of our imaginative capacity to project ideals. Instead of the imaginative projection of current tendencies that can energize and give direction to present action, these mythological fantasies undermine our capacity for intelligent thought and constructive practical action. They invite messianic visions, divine campaigns, and imperial actions that seek to impose "revealed" solutions upon "recalcitrant," if not evil, others, by "divinely" authorized and inspired force if necessary.

But there is no utopia, and never was a golden age. There is no providential process, no "hidden hand" guiding human history to an idyllic conclusion. America has no "manifest destiny," and God did not "shed his Grace on thee." We need to recognize and sympathize with the fundamental human anxieties that have generated these fantasies, while recognizing them for the often quite destructive illusions they are. "Whatever religion we adopt must be consistent with the truth with which we have been enriched at the hands of science."[41] We need to reappropriate legitimate religious attitudes from the transcendent illusions that have sought to give them comfort and assurance, and to provide secular institutions and naturalized ideals consistent with scientific intelligence that can minister to human needs and energize human action, thus contributing to the progressive amelioration of human living. This is not a counsel of despair, but an invitation to assume our collective responsibility for stewardship of the Earth consistent with natural humanity's ideal possibilities. We must finally replace those mythologized "heavens" with relativized utopias, continually revised practical ideals that can provide constructive direction for present action, thus celebrating our common life on this Earth in which, in the words of Camus, "all (our) gods have feet of clay."

Notes

Chapter 1

1. James (1), *What Pragmatism Means,* 45.
2. And this is without considering the implications of the theory of inflationary expansion as developed by Alan Guth in the early 1980s, and now, however improbable, generally accepted by the physics community as the basic framework for understanding cosmic development. According to that theory, the universe underwent an almost instantaneous expansion on the order of 100 doublings in size at 10^{-35} seconds after the Big Bang. From that perspective, the entire known universe is but a spec of the totality.
3. Freud, 21.
4. Cf. *Collapse,* by Jared Diamond.
5. Note Lord Kelvin's famous comment that all the laws of nature are now (1890s) known; only a few details need to be worked out.
6. Let me use this footnote to be a little more technically precise. Metaphysics refers to the most fundamental categories of the World as we know it. It refers both to that which is fundamentally Real for us and to the basic concepts with which we interpret and understand that Real. The latter may be called the root metaphors, conceptual matrices, or basic paradigms that constitute our "preanalytic vision" of the way things really are. This vision then preselects the nature of the interpretive field, the kind of "objects" that make it up, the dramatic structure of our experience, the essential patterns and nature of their interaction, the manner of interpreting encountered problems, or anomalies, the range of "legitimate" possible interpretations, research programs, and envisaged solutions.

    We may sum up this discussion by saying that metaphysics is the reflective inquiry into the most fundamental structure of the Real. That Real is a regulative ideal behind inquiry into the World as we experience it, a World that is our personal perspective on that historically developed preanalytic cultural vision that has emerged out of our encounter with what is. Experientially, the World—our World—is given to us as the way things really are. What is "out there" for us and how we think about what is out there are given together, and usually taken more or less unselfconsciously as obviously and self-evidently true. It constitutes for most of us most of the time simply *what is,* within the reality of which we encounter problems that need interpretation and solution. If we speak of a person's or culture's metaphysics, we mean both what they think is the nature of the Real and the basic ideas or categories in terms of which they understand the Real. The fact that the word metaphysics may be used interchangeably to refer to both the "objective" and "subjective" sides of the experienced World—to the existent "out there," and to the concepts "in here" in terms of which we think the existent—simply highlights the existentially given unity of these two poles of the World as experientially given.

By World then, I mean that which is existentially given as Real. By metaphysics, I mean the inquiry into the presuppositions of that World. This inquiry may focus on either its "objective" or "subjective" poles. When I speak of another's metaphysics, I mean both that which they take to be fundamentally Real and that in terms of which they interpret that existent—since each is the experienced pole of the other, bound together in one unitary experience.

Another way of thinking about the metaphysical is as providing myths by which we live. Such myths are dramatizations of the thematic patterns that energize and pervade our more mundane concerns. Caught up in the events of daily life, we tend to lose perspective. Potentially revelatory patterns suggesting more pervasive concerns escape us. How often do similar themes reappear in different guises—what the Hindus no doubt intend by the notion of avatars, different embodiments of a single divine being. Our lives have an enduring structure, and a set of sustaining concerns that tends to motivate and vitalize daily events. These more pervasive themes and structures are the terrain of the metaphysical. Albert Camus spoke of "bringing myths to life," stripping events to their fundamentals, shorn of the diverse particularities of specific times, places, and people. We may speak of the pervasive themes of a culture, a nation, an era, a civilization, or a species. At every level of generality, there are abiding structural forces, vitalizing themes and concerns, and distinguishing problems and hopes. These tend to be the dynamic shapers of the more mundane affairs of daily life. They tend to express themselves in pervasive modes of thinking and generative root metaphors.

The mythic dimension thus refers to these dynamic and vitalizing themes and ideas that give shape and pattern to the pervasive concerns of daily life. Camus' literary success is but one of the many that suggest that, when dramatized, such myths are sure to find a receptive and responsive audience, speaking as they do to our most important concerns, even—or most particularly—when they are not explicitly recognized. So also, at a more mundane level, are the recurrent patterns in the story lines of popular television and movies. Such drama grabs us where it hurts, bringing us into direct and vital connection with our most profound hopes, fears, and anxieties, thus offering an opportunity to live out, and perhaps work out, those deeper unaddressed and so far unresolved concerns. At its visionary best, such art opens up an existentially transformed space in which these concerns can appear in new light.

Whether viewed as paradigms, conceptual matrices, or dramatizing myths, the metaphysical determines the contours and parameters of our World. It constitutes the meaningful context within which action and thought take place. It both guides our inquiry and constrains our choices. It preselects both our problematic focus and our envisaged range of possible solutions. It may—and I will try to show how in fact it often and crucially does—rule out in advance ways of understanding, relating to, and even reconstituting our World that might be both theoretically more adequate and practically more fruitful.

7. An example of John Maynard Keynes' statement about the role of visionary theorists in creating the common sense of future generations.

8. Sprintzen.

9. "Every action is the bearer and expression of more or less theory-laden beliefs and concepts; every piece of theorizing and every expression of belief is a political and moral action." MacIntyre, 61.

10. We will address this in some detail in chapters 5 and 7.

11. In *Collapse*, Diamond, after a detailed study of societies that destroyed themselves and others that have survived and prospered, concludes that their relative success or failure traces in part to their "willingness to re-examine long-held core values."

Chapter 2

1. Kaufman, 95–96.

2. Ibid., 447.

3. John Dewey insightfully observed that "The proper contrast is no longer between experience and reason, but rather between experience that is irrational or nonrational and rational experience that is funded by intelligence. The issue has now become one of finding ways of making experience, whether it is scientific, moral, esthetic, or political experience, more reasonable and intelligent" (quoted in Bernstein, 55).

4. Campbell, 2–3.

5. Kaufman, 515–16.

6. Becker, 134.

7. More recent scientific studies have raised the possibility that Neanderthals may have been the first to bury their dead.

8. Marx, 53–54.

9. This point is well developed by Martha Nussbaum in her suggestive work *Hiding from Humanity*, as well as by Sartre, particularly in *Saint Genet*, of which more will be explained later.

10. Cf., the *United States' Catholic Bishops' Pastoral Letter on the Economy*, particularly the first draft.

Chapter 3

1. Rorty, 9.

2. As was attested to by René Descartes' need to develop a metaphysical dualism of thought and extension.

3. It is difficult to conceive how Johannes Kepler could have persevered in his grueling decades-long effort to find a simple mathematical equation that would give expression to the cosmic centrality of the Sun as the expression

of the divine order were it not for his profound commitment to a mystical neo-Pythagoreanism that required the cosmos to be mathematically ordered. In addition, Newton was convinced that his theory of universal gravitation provided empirical evidence of divine providence, and that God's intervention was regularly required to correct for systemic anomalies. He even devoted a major portion of his last twenty-five years to detailed studies of astrology and biblical genealogy.

4. The "definitive" proof of the existence of atoms was only established by Einstein in his 1905 paper on Brownian motion, about 100 years after Dalton set it forth as the explanation of the simple numerical ratios at work in the chemical constitution of basic molecules.

5. I have in mind both Jefferson's substitution of the "pursuit of happiness" for Locke's assertion of the natural right to property as a human being's "inalienable right" and his far more democratic view of political structure. (Compare, for example, Locke's Constitution for South Carolina with Jefferson's vision of local government for Virginia, or Locke's defense of economic inequality with Jefferson's proposals for the equalization of property.)

6. In the words of Alasdair MacIntyre: "For liberal individualism a community is simply an arena in which individuals each pursue their own self-chosen conception of the good life, and political institutions exist to provide that degree of order which makes such self-determined activity possible. Government and law are, or ought to be, neutral between rival concepts of the good life for man, and hence, although it is the task of government to promote law abidingness, it is on the liberal view no part of the legitimate function of government to inculcate any one moral outlook" (MacIntyre, 195).

7. Among the greatest of the nineteenth-century countercultural figures were Kierkegaard, Dostoevsky, and Nietzsche.

8. MacEwan, 137.

9. MacEwan, 100.

Chapter 4

1. Laughlin, 20.

2. Quoting Donella Meadows, in Wheatley, 10.

3. Daly, 20–22.

4. To give but a few examples, randomly selected, in a series of lectures for The Teaching Company on *The Neurophysiology of the Brain*, Professor Robert Sapolsky says that depression involves "faking out" the hypothalamus, and the use of a "singulotomy"—"a single bundle cut"—to cut the signals from cortex to hypothalamus "proves" that this "disease" is neuroanatomically caused. Patricia Churchland made essentially the same reductionist point in a talk given at the State University of New York at Stony Brook on March 10, 2008. In *Wider than the Sky*, Gerald Edelman makes precisely this same reductionist assumption, of which more will be explained in the following note.

5. One of the more influential contemporary versions of this position is that offered in exquisite detail by Daniel Dennett. With his discussion of "sky hooks and cranes" and his strategy for "discharging the homonculii" he claims to have provided a program for the complete explanatory reduction of consciousness to brain states, of "folk psychology" to neuroscience. While he claims to have "explained" consciousness, I believe that it would be far more correct to see him as offering a reductionist research program that itself is rooted in some overstated and often highly dubious factual and theoretical claims—more an expression of desire than of scientific fact.

Perhaps even more illuminating is the approach of the distinguished Nobel Laureate for physiology or medicine, Gerard Edelman. Presenting an evolutionary theory of consciousness that he calls "neural Darwinism or the theory of neuronal group selection" (Edelman, p. 33), he asserts that "a theory of consciousness ... must accept the fact that the physical world is causally closed—only forces and energies can be causally effective. Consciousness is a property of neural processes and cannot itself act causally in the world. As a process and an entailed property, consciousness arose during evolution of complex neural networks with a specific kind of structure and dynamics. Before consciousness could emerge, certain neural arrangements must have evolved. These arrangements lead to reentrant interactions, and it is the dynamics of reentrant networks that provide the causal bases that entail conscious properties. Such networks were chosen during evolution because they provided animals with the ability to make high-level discriminations, an ability that afforded adaptive advantages in dealing with novelty and planning" (Edelman, 140). But this assertion just rules out emergent properties by definition. He simply assumes that there are only two possible alternatives, a reductionist physicalism or what I might call a dualistic "mentalism." He argues that "neuronal variability" is crucial to provide the basis for evolutionary selection. He asserts that consciousness is not an epiphenomenon of the brain, but was selected by evolution—and yet he claims it is entirely reducible to the deterministic properties of the closed system of neuronal chemistry and "cannot itself act causally in the world." But there seems to be an evident incoherence here, since if emergent properties are ruled out in advance, it is not clear why and how it would have been evolutionarily selected if it were not able to act causally in the world. It would seem that he can't have it both ways. Either consciousness can act in the natural world, and thus can be "selected" by evolution, or it can't so act, and then it must be an irrelevant epiphenomenon. It would seem that Edelman is boxed in by the metaphysical framework within which he is unselfconsciously trapped.

6. Rorty, 9.

7. Bhaskar, 130. "The very statement of the eliminativist's [that is, material reductionist's] claim presupposes the non-vacuous use of the concepts which the eliminativist contends are vacuous. For the mere use of language in making assertions and asking questions presupposes the applicability of such concepts as intention, meaning something by what one says, knowledge and belief, having reasons and being able to give reasons, understanding and explaining.

Does the eliminativist believe what he says—or does he not believe what he says, as the cooling of water in a jug does not involve the transfer of caloric? Or does he neither believe nor not believe? Does he intend to convince his readers of the truth of his words? Or does he not so intend, as the oxidation of iron does not involve any phlogiston? Is his utterance intentional? Or unintentional! If it is not intentional, nor yet unintentional, neither accidental nor inadvertent, is it an utterance at all? If he neither means what he says nor means anything by what he says, has he actually said anything at all? Does he expect us to be persuaded by his arguments? Does he have reasons for saying what he says, or is he speaking without reason? Does he have reasons for what he says, or are his contentions unfounded dogmatism? Obviously, he claims to be offering many different reasons for his strange theory. But can a being have reasons for certain claims, and yet neither believe nor fail to believe that these reasons support the claims? And so on. The eliminativist saws off the branch upon which he is perched. For if what he claims were true, his utterances could not be taken to be assertions, or claims, and his supporting arguments could not be taken to be reasons for believing what he says" (Hacker, 377).

8. In a quite different idiom, English analytical philosophy, largely under the influence of the later works of Ludwig Wittgenstein, pursues a quite similar path in its discussion of the irreducibility of the "logical grammar" of everyday speech. See, for example, the quite recent, highly technical, and often insightful *Philosophical Foundations of Neuroscience,* by M. R. Bennett and P. M. S. Hacker (Malden, MA: Blackwell, 2003), throughout referred to as "Hacker," since he is the primary philosopher among the authors of the text, excerpts from which were cited in the previous endnote, of which more will be explained later.

9. It would actually be more precise to speak of "physicalism" rather than materialism because, as will be emphasized later, the "material" world is made up of energy as well as matter. But, with this point clarified, we will let normal parlance dictate our mode of expression.

10. One further possibility, which is probably also Whitehead's, is that in some way spirit is pervasively present in all matter from the beginning. But that hardly seems credible to me based on the facts as we know them.

11. Silver, 234. Laplace's actual statement was: "We may regard the present state of the universe as the effect of its past and the cause of its future. An intellect which at any given moment knew all the forces that animate nature and the mutual positions of the beings that compose it, if this intellect were vast enough to submit the data to analysis, could condense into a single formula the movement of the great bodies of the universe and that of the lightest atom; for such an intellect nothing could be uncertain and the future just like the past would be present before its eyes" (quoted in Lindley [1], 22).

12. Silver, 239.

13. Ibid.

14. Ibid., 240, 244, 250.

15. Ibid., 238.

16. "Kurt Gödel revealed that any mathematical system is always incomplete ... that is, there are always questions that can be posed in any mathematical

structure that cannot be proved true or false. This, at some point, must also carry implications for the enterprise of theoretical physics in any quest to finally reduce all of nature into a basic set of defining equations … Mathematics itself defies a complete mathematical analysis … No logical proof exists of all the theorems one can pose in a mathematical system" (Lederman, 75). "Any mathematical system containing a finite number of axioma is therefore 'incomplete'—the content of Gödel's theorem" (Lederman, 325). In addition to Gödel's "undecidability" proof of the essential incompleteness of any system at least as complicated as arithmetic, Alan Turing demonstrated that there is no effective decision procedure, or algorithm, for arithmetic. Of course, he also laid the foundation for the computer industry by showing how one could design a system—a "Turing machine"—that could decide any question for which an algorithm could be written.

17. This is made clear by Stephen Hawking in his discussion of the "big bang singularity," to which he counterposes his conception of negative time, an explanation of which will not be attempted here. Nor will I consider alternative theories of colliding brane worlds, none of which would seem to affect the point being made here.

18. A classic statement of mechanistic reductionism is that of C. D. Broad in *The Mind and its Place in Nature:* "[There] is one and only one kind of material. Each particle of this obeys one elementary law of behaviour, and continues to do so no matter how complex may be the collection of particles of which it is a constituent. There is one uniform law of composition, connecting the behaviour of groups of these particles as wholes with the behaviour which each would show in isolation and with the structure of the group. All the apparently different kinds of stuff are just differently arranged groups of different numbers of the one kind of elementary particle; and all the apparently peculiar laws of behaviour are simply special cases which could be deduced in theory from the structure of the whole under consideration, the one elementary law of behaviour for isolated particles, and the one universal law of composition. On such a view the external world has the greatest amount of unity which is conceivable. There is really only one science, and the various "special sciences" are just particular cases of it" (quoted in the article on "*Emergent Properties*" in the *Stanford Encyclopedia of Philosophy,* 3).

19. See my further discussion of Aristotelian logic in the section "The Nature of Emergence."

20. Silver, 223.

21. Ibid., 221–22, 224.

22. Ibid., 220.

23. Ibid., 219.

24. By which I mean the different quarks, electrons, and neutrinos.

25. Lindley, 14. In classical situations, uncertainty and probability are simply matters of our lack of information, inadequate theories, or processing power— they are "technical" problems—while in quantum mechanics they seem to be intrinsic properties of reality itself. "Predictions in quantum mechanics are probabilistic not because of insufficient information or understanding, but because the theory itself has nothing to say" (Lindley, 25).

"The Copenhagen interpretation is, fundamentally, the uncertainty principle writ large. In its simplest form, the uncertainty principle puts limits on what we can know: you can't know both the speed and position of an electron; you can't measure its spin in both an up-down and a left-right sense at the same time. More elaborately, you can't ask to see an interference pattern and also know which way the photon went. And finally, you can't infer what's "really" going on in one kind of experiment and expect it to be consistent with what's "really" going on in a modified, and therefore different, version of that experiment. That's the Copenhagen interpretation, more or less" (Lindley, 71). Decoherence essentially resolves the measurement problem and explains how quantum weirdness and uncertainty can be compatible with classical determinism. "At every step, as we say, decoherence erases quantum superpositions but does not and cannot choose between different possible outcomes of a quantum measurement ... We can choose to measure different things. We can measure the polarization state of a photon with respect to this angle or that; we can measure the spin of an electron in an up-down or left-right sense, or anything in between; we can measure the position or the momentum of a particle, or some limited combination of the two. And once we have made such a measurement, we set in motion a chain of events that becomes irrevocable. Depending on the outcome of an experiment, a memorable paper might get published in a scientific journal, or a cat may die. The paper can't later be unpublished; the cat can't be restored to life.

Any quantum measurement, or series of measurements, can set in motion a chain of classical events, one thing following another in familiar manner. But once one chain of events happens, other possible chains of events cannot. Decoherence guarantees that a chain of events rather than a continuously ill-defined stream of quantum possibilities actually takes place. But it doesn't tell us which chain of events is going to happen. Probability has not been erased; measurements can have several different outcomes, and we cannot predict which" (Lindley, 219–20).

26. "For example, two photons, by definition, traveling at the speed of light (which it seems is the fastest possible speed; certainly nothing traveling at a lesser speed can be accelerated up to that speed, according to General Relativity) moving in opposite directions from an atom that has emitted them, retain an immediate nonlocal connection, such that if polarization of one is measured, the other will instantly have the opposite polarization, even though the polarization of each particle was not determined until the moment the measurement was taken. This is known as *quantum entanglement*" (Sheldrake, 307).

27. Ibid. Thus, while the quantum world whenever it is tested always appears to be constituted by discrete elements, the manner of its appearance reveals logical patterns of interconnection that suggests a networked and relational field out of which these discrete quanta emerge and return—as with the virtual particles that emerge from the vacuum of "empty space." This is the apparent reality of the Schrodinger wave equations that describe the probability of the appearance of the quanta when the wave function is "collapsed" upon its interaction with an "observer." This relational reality that seems to describe the behavior

of the most fundamental subatomic world may explain the fundamental and pervasive reality of conservation laws, as more basic than the particles of which the Newtonian world was supposed to be constituted. It is this fact that David Böhm was trying to express with his conception of an "implicative order."

28. "In other words, to reinforce the point we already made, an electron by itself is not described by one unique wave function; the way you describe it, the wave function you use, depends on what you plan to measure. And although the wave function obviously depends on the state of the electron, and on what you know about it, it can be misleading to think that the wave function somehow 'is' the electron. It's better to say that a wave function describes a system—the thing being measured and the measurement being made—rather than being an independent description only of the thing being measured" (Lindley, 47).

29. Laughlin, 18. Errol Harris quotes Louis De Broglie: "The particle truly has a well-defined individuality only when it is isolated. As soon as it enters into an interaction with other particles, its individuality is diminished … In the cases contemplated by the new mechanics, where particles of the same nature occupy, somehow simultaneously, the same region of space, the individuality of these particles is dissipated to the vanishing point. In going progressively from cases of isolated particles without interactions to the cases just cited, the notion of the individuality of the particles is seen to grow more and more dim as the individuality of the system more strongly asserts itself. It therefore seems that the individual and the system are somewhat complementary idealizations. This, perhaps, is an idea which merits a more thorough study" (Harris, 136–137). Harris then continues: "The chemical valency of any element depends on the number of 'unpaired' electrons in the outer shell—that is, those unmatched by electrons with opposite spin but otherwise identical quantum numbers. The resulting physical and chemical properties are, therefore, the characteristics of wholes, which their parts do not separately possess, but which arise in consequence of their ordered combination, and the exclusion principle proves to be one of organization and structural pattern governing the arrangement of particles upon which these new properties depend. A striking example of this is given by Margenau. Two hydrogen atoms may attract one another, combine and form a molecule, but any third atom which may now approach is repelled. The mutual attraction (or, when it occurs, repulsion) between single atoms may be accounted for by ordinary dynamic laws, but the repulsion of the third by two adhering atoms is a consequence of the exclusion principle and is attributed to what is called "saturation" of forces. The influence of the principle makes itself felt again in the structure of crystals, directly or indirectly through atomic structure. Here again, new properties are displayed which are wholly dependent upon composition and are unforeshadowed in the parts compounded. They are not present in the single atoms but depend on the way in which they are arranged in the combination. Margenau lists ferromagnetism, optical anisotropy and electrical conductivity among these and designates them all 'co-operative phenomena.' … The mutual inter-play of these fields of force, in short, makes it fair to say that the atom is a single complex system of mutually determining fields, none of which exists

in isolation in the form it assumes in inter-relation with the others, but each of which is a distinguishable feature of the articulated structure of the indivisible whole" (Harris, 138, 140, 144–145).

30. Cf. Chapter 3.

31. The development of symbolic logic has not changed anything as far as this issue is concerned. It has, however, pointed out the reality of relationships that have properties that are not themselves simply reducible to the qualities of the things being related—a fact of immense significance for the argument I am developing.

32. A point further underscored by the nineteenth-century "discovery" of non-Euclidean geometries that effectively severed any simple and direct identification of the processes of (mathematical) reasoning with objective reality. How to account for the remarkable effectiveness of mathematics as a tool for explaining objective reality remains a controversial issue to the present day, but one thing is clear: the scientific application of mathematical theories remains an empirical question, as does the appropriateness of applying such Aristotelian "metaphysical certainties" as the principles of Non-Contradiction and Excluded Middle.

33. Another important example is Charles Sanders Peirce's discussion of the creative logic of "abduction."

34. "No amount of neural knowledge would suffice to discriminate between writing one's name, copying one's name, practising one's signature, forging a name, writing an autograph, signing a cheque, witnessing a will, signing a death warrant, and so forth. For the differences between these are circumstance-dependent, functions not only of the individual's intentions, but also of the social and legal conventions that must obtain to make the having of such intentions and the performance of such actions possible" (Hacker, 357).

35. There is an extensive literature on this issue, but the word is not always used with precisely the same meaning. For a very nice, though somewhat technical, overview of the field, as well as for an extensive bibliography, check out the entry in the previously mentioned *Stanford Encyclopedia of Philosophy* article on "Emergent Properties" located at http://plato.stanford.edu/entries/properties-emergent/.

36. From now on I will just abbreviate "powers and modes of operation" as "causal powers."

37. The authors of the previously cited *Stanford Encyclopedia of Philosophy* article on "Emergent Properties" summarize the views of emergentists as follows: "Ontological emergentists see the physical world as entirely constituted by physical structures, simple or composite. But composites are not (always) mere aggregates of the simples. There are layered strata, or levels, of objects, based on increasing complexity … Emergent laws are fundamental; they are irreducible to laws characterizing properties at lower levels of complexity, even given ideal information as to boundary conditions. Since emergent features have not only same-level effects, but also effects in lower levels, some speak of the view's commitment to 'downward causation'" (p. 8). They further elaborate on the consequences of emergence: "If emergence obtains, theorists would be

forced to rest content with a hierarchy of various sciences ranging from the universal—physics—to the most specific. While Emergentists, too, are physical substance monists ("there is only fundamentally one kind of stuff"), they recognize 'aggregates [of matter] of various orders'—a stratification of kinds of substances, with different kinds belonging to different orders, or levels. Each level is characterized by certain fundamental, irreducible properties that emerge from lower-level properties. Correspondingly, there are two types of laws: (1) 'intra-ordinal' laws, which relate events within an order, i.e., a law connecting an aggregate of that order instantiating a property of that order at a time with some aggregate of that order instantiating some other property at a certain time; and (2) 'trans-ordinal' laws, which characterize the emergence of higher-level properties from lower-level ones. Emergent properties are identified by the trans-ordinal laws that they figure in; each emergent property appears in the consequent of at least one trans-ordinal law, the antecedent of which is some lower-level property" (Broad 1925, 77).

38. Even that may not be correct, as Laughlin observes. "It is not uncommon for a committed reductionist to dismiss the evidence of the fundamental nature of collective principles on the grounds that there actually is a deductive path from the microscopic that explains the reproducibility of these experiments. This is incorrect. The microscopic explanation of temperature, for example, has a logical step called the postulate of equal *a priori* probability—a kind of Murphy's law of atoms—that cannot be deduced and is a succinct statement of the organizing principle responsible for thermodynamics. The ostensibly deductive explanations of the Josephson and von Klitzing effects always have an "intuitively obvious" step in which the relevant organizational principles are assumed to be true. They actually are true, of course, so the reasoning is correct, but not necessarily in the sense the reasoner intended. In deference to reductionist culture, theorists often give these effects fancy names, which, on close inspection, are revealed to be nothing more than synonyms for the experiments themselves. In neither case was the great accuracy of the measurement predicted theoretically" (Laughlin, 19–20).

39. One may become quite technical in the discussion of types of materialist reduction: for example, derivational, explanatory (one level by another, as with Dennett's discussion of the "personal" and the "subpersonal"), and eliminative (with the Churchlands). In their discussion of reductionism, Bennett and Hacker make the following points: "ontological reductionism ... holds that one kind of entity is, despite appearances to the contrary, actually no more than a structure of other kinds of entity. Side by side with the ontological reductionism, ... [there is] *explanatory reductionism:* 'The scientific belief ... that our minds—the behaviour of our brains—can be explained by the interactions of nerve cells (and other cells) and the molecules associated with them.' The reductionist approach, Crick explains, is that 'a complex system can be explained by the behaviour of its parts and their interactions with each other. For a system with many levels of activity, this process may have to be repeated more than once—that is, the behaviour of a particular part may have to be explained by the properties of *its* parts

and their interactions.' ... In the broadest sense, reductionism is the commitment to a single unifying explanation of a type of phenomenon. In this sense, Marxism advocates a reductive explanation of history, and psychoanalysis defends a reductive explanation of human behaviour. More specifically, reductionism in science is a commitment to the complete explanation of the nature and behaviour of entities of a given type in terms of the nature and behaviour of their constituents. The ideal of 'unified science,' advocated by the Vienna Circle positivists in the 1920s and 1930s and adopted by the later logical empiricists in the 1950s, was committed to what has been called 'classical reductionism.' This conception held that the objects of which the world consists can be classified into hierarchies such that the objects at each level of classification are composed of objects comprising a lower level. The lowest level was conceived to be constituted by the elementary particles investigated by fundamental physics. Above this, in successive levels, lie atoms, molecules, cells, multicellular organisms and social groups. Investigating each level is the task of a given science (or sciences) the purpose of which is to discover the laws that describe the behaviour of entities of the kind in question. The reductivist programme is to see the laws of any given level derived from the different laws describing the behaviour of entities at the lower level. *Derivational reduction,* thus conceived, requires, in addition to the laws at the reduced and reducing levels, bridge principles identifying the kinds of objects at the reduced level with specific structures of objects comprising the reducing level" (Hacker, 355, 357).

40. Searle, 55–56. This is but one of the many places in which he discusses this issue.

41. Bhaskar, 125–126. In his *A Realistic Theory of Science* and *The Possibility of Naturalism*, Bhaskar offers a brilliant and incisive critique of much contemporary Philosophy of Science, with a particularly devastating dissection of the causal theories of Hume. He shows that the presuppositions of scientific theory and practice argue for the objective reality of causal laws in nature and society, each in their own way. My analysis draws heavily upon his theory of "transcendental realism."

42. "Without language, we are but naked apes. Without the language of psychological expressions, we are not self-conscious creatures. Without self-consciousness, we are not moral beings. For what makes us human is what flows from possession of a rich language. And our psychological language is not merely a descriptive instrument for the characterization of what we observe around us. It is partly constitutive of the phenomena that it is also used to describe, precisely because the first-person, present-tense use of psychological verbs is typically a criterion for others to say 'He believes (wants, intends, etc.)'. The use of these phrases in the first-person present tense is characteristically to express a belief, want or intention. The paradigmatic expressions of distinctively human intentions and desires, thoughts and beliefs, loves and hates, are verbal. They are not descriptions of the inner, but manifestations of it. And for a wide range of psychological attributes and their objects, what is thereby manifest is something that is possible only for a creature that has mastered the use of the psychological vocabulary in

all its multiplicity and diversity, the use of which is partly constitutive of what it is to be human" (Hacker, 375).

43. In a presentation to the Community Advisory Council (CAC) at the Brookhaven National Laboratory (BNL), Doon Gibbs, associate lab director for Basic Energy Sciences and interim director of the Center for Nanoscience (CFN), observed that gold in bulk is nonreactive, but at the nanoscale (e.g., 100 gold atoms) is quite reactive, and can take sulfur out of the air in catalytic converters. It is the "collection of atoms that give us its properties," not the individual atoms by themselves, he said (10/12/06). Thus, the properties are qualities of the field, not of the elements themselves. Steve Hoey, CFN Environmental Safety and Health Coordinator at BNL, added that "copper nanoparticles smaller than 50 nm are super hard materials that do not exhibit the same malleability and ductility as larger forms of copper." At the previous month's meeting of the CAC, Steve Dierker, associate lab director for Light Sources at BNL, used the "mechanisms of molecular *self-assembly*" that take place "at the lower end of the nanoscale size range" as one example of "the science of *emergent behavior,* which arises from cooperative behavior of individual components of a system," thus emphasizing that the systemic properties are not deducible from the properties of their constituent elements (9/8/06).

44. Laughlin, 35. Laughlin continues that thought as follows: "Ironically, the immense reliability of phase-related phenomena makes them the reductionist's worst nightmare—a kind of Godzilla set loose by the chemists to crush, incinerate, and generally terrorize their happy world. A simple, universal phenomenon one encounters frequently cannot depend sensitively on microscopic details. An exact one, such as rigidity, cannot depend on details at all. Moreover, while some aspects of phases are universal and thus easy to anticipate, others, such as which phase one gets under which circumstances, are not—water being an especially embarrassing case in point. Ordinary water ice displays, at last count (the number keeps rising due to new discoveries), eleven distinct crystalline phases, not one of which was correctly predicted from first principles ... "

"Phases are a primitive and well-studied case of emergence, one that conclusively demonstrates that nature has walls of scales: microscopic rules can be perfectly true and yet quite irrelevant to macroscopic phenomena, either because what we measure is insensitive to them or because what we measure is overly sensitive to them. Bizarrely, both of these can be true simultaneously. Thus it is presently too difficult to calculate from scratch which crystalline phase of ice will form at a given temperature and pressure, yet there is no need to calculate the macroscopic properties of a given phase, since these are completely generic."

"A measure of the seriousness of this problem is provided by the difficulty of explaining clearly how one knows phases to be organizational. The evidence always manages to be complicated, indirect, and annoyingly intermingled with theories—not unlike the evidence of product superiority in a commercial for soap or cars. The deeper reason in each case is that the logical link from the fundamentals to the conclusion is not very substantial. One thing we know for certain is that crystalline solids are ordered lattices of atoms—a fact revealed by their tendency to deflect X-rays through specific angles—while liquids and gases are not. We also know that systems with small numbers of atoms are motivated by simple, deterministic laws of motion and nothing else. We also know that attempts to discover the scale at which these laws cease to work or are supplanted by others have failed. And finally, we know that elementary laws have the ability in principle to generate phases and phase transitions as organizational phenomena" (Laughlin, 34–35).

"Once one knows what to look for, the organizational nature of phases other than the solid becomes easy to demonstrate. A collective state of matter is unambiguously identified by one or more behaviors that are exact in a large aggregation of the matter but inexact, nonexistent, in a small one. Since the behavior is exact, it cannot change continuously as one varies external conditions such as pressure or temperature but can change only abruptly at a phase transition. One unambiguous signature of an organizational phenomenon is therefore a sharp phase transition. The transition itself, however, is only a symptom. The important thing is not the transition but the emergent exactness that necessitates it."

"The melting and sublimation transitions of ice signal the demise of crystalline order and its replacement by a set of exact behaviors known collectively as hydrodynamics. The laws of hydrodynamics amount to a precise mathematical codification of the things we intuitively associate with the fluid state, such as the meaningfulness of hydrostatic pressure, the tendency to flow smoothly in response to differences in pressure, and the rules of viscous drag" (Laughlin, 40).

"The crystalline and superfluid phases, and their attendant exact behaviors, are specific examples of an important abstract idea in physics called spontaneous symmetry breaking. It has uses ranging from engineering to the modern theory of the vacuum of space and is even suspected of being relevant to life. The idea of symmetry breaking is simple: matter collectively and spontaneously acquires a property or preference not present in the underlying rules themselves. For example, when atoms order into a crystal, they acquire preferred positions, even though there was nothing preferred about these positions before the crystal formed. When a piece of iron becomes magnetic, the magnetism spontaneously selects a direction in which to point. These effects are important because they prove that organizational principles can give primitive matter a mind of its own and empower it to make decisions. We say that the matter makes the decision "at random"—meaning on the basis of some otherwise insignificant initial condition or external influence—but that does not quite capture the essence of the matter. Once the decision is made, it becomes "real" and there is nothing random about it any more. Symmetry breaking provides a simple, convincing example of how nature can become richly complex all on its own despite having underlying rules that are simple.

The existence of phases and phase transitions provides a sobering reality check on the practice of thinking of nature solely in terms of the Newtonian clockwork. Floating on the lakes of Minnesota and stretching into the sky in large cities are simple, concrete examples of how organization can cause laws rather than the reverse. The issue is not that the underlying rules are wrong so much as that they are irrelevant—rendered important by principles of organization. As with human institutions, emergent laws are not trustworthy, and sometimes hard to discern, when the organization is small, but they become more reliable as it grows in size and eventually become exactly true" (Laughlin, 44–45).

45. "Can Science Explain Everything? Anything?" *The New York Review of Books* 48, no. 9 (May 31, 2001): 48.

46. "A cellular automaton is a simple computational mechanism that, for example, changes the color of each cell on a grid based on the color of adjacent or nearby cells according to a transformational rule" (Kurzweil, 85).

47. My former colleague Eric Walther provided me with the following useful example, drawn from an article by Martin Gardner that appeared in *Scientific America:* "Consider the 'Game of Life' (Conway). The Game evolves on an infinite grid (given a somehow-defined initial configuration) in which each cell is either active (alive) or not. There are three simple rules that determine, from the prior state of a cell's eight immediate neighbors, whether that cell will be currently active or not. (One of the three rules is: 'If exactly three neighbors are active, the cell becomes active.') If you spend a few hours playing the game, you discover a universe of entities with well-defined behavior patterns that propagate endlessly or until interfered with by some other behavior pattern. The simplest type of entity is a 'flasher,' a local pattern that doesn't move across the grid but alternates between two states … "

"Some of the other simple entities are puffers, gliders, and eaters. An eater 'eats' a glider when the glider collides with it. Now the question is this: is the eater/glider law 'reducible to' the three rules? There is absolutely no way [for us humans anyway] of understanding the necessity of that law directly from the three rules; you have to draw the grid and 'see how the rules play out.' (Of course this is a "non-empirical" sort of experimentation.) So maybe we should say that the law is 'not reducible to' the rules. On the other hand it would seem silly to talk about 'emergence' in a purely abstract system where everything that 'happens' is a necessary consequence of the rules. For example, I think Darwinian adaptations are an equally necessary (though unpredictable in the abstract) consequence of statistical principles. Likewise for chemistry vis-à-vis quantum physics."

48. No one has presented this "substantive metaphysics"—the metaphysics of "substance"—in clearer and more unequivocal terms than Spinoza. For him, the causal structure of the natural world is an exact expression of the mathematical structure of geometric proof, and precisely as determinate. For him, freedom is but the expression of inadequate ideas that the further development of science will dispel. It is this mathematical structure of the natural world to which Einstein was alluding when he said that he "believed in the god of Spinoza." And it is to counter the updated versions of that position that this argument is primarily directed.

49. In fact, according to the Nobel Laureate Frank Wilczek, while the fundamental reality of mass is just assumed by Newton, Einstein has shown not only that mass and energy are interchangeable but also that mass is best thought of as the energy of fundamental particles left over from the "big bang" (from a talk at the BNL, on 4/21/06).
50. Lederman and Hill, 151.
51. Ibid., 153.
52. Einstein and Infield, 242–43.
53. In that same talk at BNL, Wilczek said that "empty space is in reality a widely dynamical medium," and "the different particles we observe correspond to the vibration patterns that occur in this dynamical void when it is disturbed in various ways." Thus, matter is made up out of the particles, which are "stable patterns of equilibrium" that emerge out of this quark-gluon field. No wonder Einstein's reference to this vision as "the highest form of musicality," a sort of modern version of the "music of the spheres."
54. Harris very nicely summarizes this entire development and the radical revision it calls for as follows: "The twentieth-century revolution in physics presents us with a conception of physical nature so radically different from that entertained by classical physics that the philosophical outlook conditioned by the latter is no longer viable either as a metaphysical theory or as a tacit presupposition of other sciences ... In deposing the old ideas, contemporary physics has not enthroned their equally outdated philosophical rivals, it has evolved out of them something significantly different from either.

This has been done in two main phases, which have been historically concurrent. First, the theory of relativity completely transformed the conception of the world in space and time. From a vast collection of individualized particles externally related to one another and to the infinitely extended containers, space and time, which were independent not only of them but also of each other, it transformed the idea of the world into one of a single, continuous, unbroken space-time whole, constituted by a web of interrelated events themselves determined by the geometrical properties of the field in which they occur and from which they and the physical properties of the entities participating in them are inseparable" (Harris, 37).

"What classical physics conceived as an indivisible, hard, irreducible atom, quantum physics sees as a physical system in which the elementary particle is, as it were, in solution. Within this system, and in its systematic inter-relation with other elements, the particle is sometimes distinguishable but is inextricable as a separate entity. For the isolable mass-point of classical physics, the quantum theory substitutes what may be styled a physical pattern, or Gestalt, identifiable as a whole and containing within it distinguishable features. These may sometimes be represented as if they were particles, sometimes as if they were waves, but they are not themselves identifiable as separable and individualized entities. Here again all relations prove to be internal, and the system takes precedence over the particular components in the mutually constitutive inter-play of primal activity."

"The physical world is thus seen as a macroscopic totality encapsulating within it microscopic totalities all constituted on similar principles of unified order. It is a complex system to which the constituent elements are integral and mutually formative. In the light of this conception, any talk of atomic facts is wholly incongruous and the sort of logic based on mutually independent propositions is obviously inappropriate. Necessary connections, which Hume had banished, are now seen to be indispensable, and the idea of factual truths that are both synthetic and logically cogent, so far from being evidently impossible as empiricists maintain, is inescapable. If the implications of modern physics are taken seriously, whole edifices of current philosophy must be assigned to the house breakers and a new metaphysic and a new logic must be sought" (Harris, 38).

"The picture of a world of mass-points, of bodies consisting of aggregates of such particulate masses, moving in an absolute field of space and time, has thus been transformed into one of a unified space-time continuum, in which events can be distinguished, but out of which they cannot be dissected—events constituted by their mutual relations in a world of correlative elements, inseparable and interdependent, constituting a single complex whole."

"An intermediate stage between the conception of a particulate universe and the four-dimensional space-time world, was marked by the notion of 'field' that came into the foreground of physical theorizing with the development of electro-dynamics. A charged particle or a magnet is surrounded by a configuration of lines of force along which a free body subject to electrical or magnetic forces will be accelerated in the direction in which the force acts. This configuration is known as the field of force of the particle or the magnet. The direction of movement of a test body is described as being from a higher to a lower potential of the force, and the field might be defined as the structure or distribution of potentials associated with the source of energy. When the interrelation of electric and magnetic forces had been recognized, the electromagnetic field was defined and the equations determining its structure were evolved by Clerk Maxwell. In the first instance, it was the attempt to understand electromagnetism in terms of the classical notions of forces acting between particles that gave rise to the idea of the field."

"As the field fills the whole of space and time, no part of the physical universe is completely unaffected by it (even though, for most practicable purposes, its effects may cease to be considerable beyond a limited region). The introduction of the concept, therefore, indicative of the crumbling of the classical mechanics, gives rise to a more unified picture of the material world, in which every particle becomes, in a sense, all-pervasive and each becomes involved with every other in a complex of overlapping fields. For every particle is the centre at least of a gravitational field and may also have electrical and magnetic fields associated with it, the limits of none of which can be sharply drawn and which modify the physical environment of every other particle" (52–53).

"The universe is thus a texture of relations between parts which though distinguishable, as they must be to be related, are not merely inseparable but intrinsically interdependent. The existence and character of each is what it is because the rest of the universe, *in toto* and *in minutiis,* are what they are. Whole and part are mutually determining and no detail could be other than it is without making some difference, however slight, to all the rest. This is no mere unverifiable 'metaphysical' speculation (in the pejorative sense), but the conclusion forced upon us by scientific theories based upon scientifically ascertained facts" (107).

55. "'Field' is the name physicists give to any quantity that permeates space. For example, the value of the gravitational field at any point tells how strong the effect of gravity is there. The same goes for any type of field: the value of the field at any location tells us how intense the field is there" (Randall, 153).

56. I have recently (in the summer of 2000, to be precise) come across the very stimulating, suggestive, and controversial work of Ruppert Sheldrake. He has engaged in extensive research activity, seeking to develop experimental tests for his theories of morphogenetic fields, morphic resonance, and formative causation. While my analysis has been carried out in complete independence, and without knowledge, of his work—whether or not that can be taken as evidence of the truth of formative causation, I leave to others to consider—the claims he makes and the evidence he presents, if adequately confirmed, would certainly provide an additional level of support for the theories being here developed. In any case, the argument here developed does not in any way depend upon the truth of the theories and evidence presented by Professor Sheldrake.

57. Laughlin (7) uses "law" to refer both to the theories that describe the operations of a system and to the natural processes and structures that determine its operation.

58. Yoga meditation provides an excellent experiential example of the duality of concentration or focus and merging or dissipation of centers.

59. James' pragmatism was his effort to ground the meaning of statements in the experienced consequences to which they led. With his radical empiricism, he tried to provide a metaphysical foundation for his pragmatism by rooting it in a more phenomenologically accurate description of experience as it is actually undergone, instead of the then more traditional (quasi-Humean) assertion of simple discrete (atomic) sensations or "impressions." In his *Psychology,* James had beautifully described the prereflective "flow" of experience as expressed in the comment on the experience of thunder. In his radical empiricism, he sought to "ontologize" that psychological experience, treating it as the metaphysical foundation of what is truly real. Thus meaning comes to be seen as an expression of intention, essentially a construct of the way we choose to carve up our experience.

60. Heisenberg, 96.

61. Quoted in Harris, 131.

62. Ibid., 136: "P. W. Bridgman holds the same opinion: 'We do not have a simple event A causally connected with a simple event B, but the whole background of the system in which the events occur is included in the concept and is a vital part of it … The causality concept is therefore a relative one, in that it involves the whole system in which the events take place.'"

63. Lindley, 14. In classical situations, uncertainty and probability are simply matters of our lack of information, inadequate theories, or processing power—they are "technical" problems—while in quantum mechanics they seem to be intrinsic properties of reality itself. "Predictions in quantum mechanics are probabilistic not because of insufficient information or understanding, but because the theory itself has nothing to say" (25).

64. Cf. ibid., 20.

65. Ibid., 47. In the words of Lederman: "The orbitals of electrons in atoms therefore don't look anything like Kepler's orbiting planets about the sun. They are fuzzy things, trapped waves, the electron never having a definite position and momentum at the same time. We thus often refer to the motion of the electrons about the nucleus of the atom as the 'electron cloud.' Stated more precisely, the uncertainty in the momentum times the uncertainty in the position will always be larger than Planck's constant divided by 2pi. This effect is known as the *Heisenberg uncertainty principle*" (Lederman & Hill, 215). Further, "the very meaning of an electron, by itself, is not absolute. An electron is equivalent, by a gauge symmetry transformation, to a different electron with a different wavelength, together with the gauge field that resets the total momentum at its original value. The electron and the gauge field are effectively blended together to make one symmetrical entity" (246).

66. *Particle Physics for the Non-Physicist,* The Teaching Company.

67. Silver, 233. Clearly the statistical nature of quantum mechanics has already played havoc with any simple application of this perspective to individual quantum events, but its relation to "classical" events remains less clear. Thus, quantum mechanics requires that causal determination be a statistical property of the structural situation, not a precise determination of individual events.

68. I leave open at present the question whether consciousness might be able to exist in sufficiently complex nonbiological systems, though I do not see any reason in principle why that should not be possible.

69. Hacker, 365.

70. This is made quite explicit by Searle in his Teaching Company course on *The Philosophy of Mind.*

71. As Edelman (22) notes, "while synaptic change is essential for the function of memory, memory is a system property that also depends on specific neuroanatomical connections."

72. "Neuroscience can explain—indeed, specializes in explaining—how gross pathological deficiencies in the exercise of normal human capacities result from damage to the brain. So it can brilliantly explain why patients *cannot* behave as normal humans can in a multitude of different ways. In particular, it may explain why such patients are, in one way or another, incapable of acting rationally in certain respects" (Hacker, 365).

73. Bhaskar, 127. "For instance, several studies, most notably those of Schacter, show that the same physiological state may be experienced in different ways and the same experience may be associated with different physiological states (so that for example stomach contractions and hunger may be out of phase)" (Bhaskar, 150n48).

74. Understanding, of course, that this example is only used to suggest a similarity, the limits of which must be underscored by the fact that it would be a mistake to see the brain as primarily a computational mechanism. There are several reasons for this, as discussed, for example, by Edelman and Roger Penrose. While Penrose draws primarily upon Gödel's undecidability proof, Edelman offers a series of reasons drawn from the specificity of neuronal development. He observes that "from the very beginning of neuroanatomy, there are rich statistical variations in both cell movement and cell death. As a result, no two individuals, not even identical twins, possess the same anatomical patterns ... at a certain point [in early neuronal development] the control of neural connectivity and fate becomes epigenetic ... The result is a pattern of constancy and variation leading to highly individual networks. This is no way to build a computer, which must execute input algorithms or effective procedures according to a precise prearranged program and with no error in wiring ... [Further,] what would be lethal noise for a computer is in fact critical for the operation of higher-order brain functions" (Edelman, 28–31).

75. In criticizing the representational view of consciousness, Edelman elaborates on the neuroanatomical basis for there not being a one-to-one correlation between brain states and mental states: "Reflecting the effects of context and the associations of the various degenerate circuits capable of yielding a similar output ... There is no reason to assume that such a memory is representational ... Instead, it is more fruitfully looked on as a property of degenerate nonlinear interactions in a multidimensional network of neuronal groups. Such interactions allow a non-identical 'reliving' of a set of prior acts and events, yet there is often the illusion that one is recalling an event exactly as it happened" (Edelman, 52). ("Degeneracy is the ability of structurally different elements of a system to perform the same function or yield the same output" [43]. "Degeneracy is a ubiquitous biological property ... Even identical twins who have similar immune responses to a foreign agent ... do not generally use identical combinations of antibodies to react to that agent" [Edelman, 44].) "There are many ways in which individual neural circuits, synaptic populations, varying environmental signals, and previous history can lead to the same meaning" (Edelman, 105). The investigations of Wilder Penfield have, of course, revealed that stimulation of specific neurons could trigger neuronal activity that generated fairly precise memories of past events.

76. Bhaskar, 130. "The normal venue for the exercise of our cognitive powers is in situations of social interaction ... Of course, what are interpreted in communication are physical phenomena, such as sounds. But it cannot be maintained that there is a direct link, unmediated by interpretation, between the sound and the ensuing physical action. For, setting aside the obvious fact that it is the interpretation put upon the sound, not the sound itself, that is causally responsible for the resultant behavior, there is no one-to-one correlation between sounds and behavior. This is shown, at the very least, by the existence of, and the possibility of learning, different languages (or less macroscopically, usages) *or*, alternatively, forms of life (that is ways of behaving)" (Bhaskar, 135).

77. "It is one thing to hold that a person would not believe, hope, fear, think, want, etc., whatever he does but for the fact that his brain is, in appropriate respects, functioning normally. It is quite another to hold that there are general bridge principles identifying a person's believing what he believes, etc., with a specific kind of neural state or condition. The former claim is an important platitude. The latter is misconceived. For there is no reason to suppose that two people may not, for example, believe the very same thing, yet the relevant (as yet unknown) neural structures in each person's brain be different. The criteria of identity for mental states, events and processes differ from the criteria of identity for neural states, events and processes" (Hacker, 358).

78. Searle describes at least ten distinct characteristics of consciousness. They are:

   - *Subjectivity:* qualitative feel, "what is it like?"
   - *Unified stream or unity of consciousness:*
     - *horizontally*—continuity in time (vs. amnesia)
     - *vertically*—continuity of space (vs. Korsakov's syndrome)
   - *Intentionality:* refers outward to the world
   - *Mood*
   - *Structured Gestalt:*
     - *forms*—tendency to produce coherent objects, even when the information is completely inadequate
     - *figure-ground.*
   - *Center periphery or focus fringe:* James said "consciousness (should be attention) goes away from where it is not needed."
   - *Situatedness:* For example, a sense of where I am and where I'm going, the implicit "boundary conditions" of my location in space and time.
   - *Aspects of familiarity*
   - *Self-transcendence:* it always overflows its boundaries, pointing beyond itself
   - *Pleasure-unpleasure:* always some sense of this

   (It is *not true* that consciousness is always self-conscious; there is *no* faculty of introspection, no direct self-knowledge; and there is no (self-evident) certainty of knowledge.) (Searle, "*The Philosophy of Mind*," The Teaching Company.)

79. "Mind is more than consciousness, because it is the abiding even though changing background of which consciousness is the foreground. Mind changes slowly through the joint tuition of interest and circumstance. Consciousness is always in rapid change, for it marks the place where the formed disposition and the immediate situation touch and interact. It is the continuous readjustment of self and the world in experience. 'Consciousness' is the more acute and intense in the degree of the readjustments that are demanded, approaching the nil as the contact is frictionless and interaction fluid. It is turbid when meanings are undergoing reconstruction in an undetermined direction, and become clear as a decisive meaning emerges" (Dewey [2], 265–266).

80. In discussing "*The Ontology of Mental States*," Laurie Paul argued that the reality of the knowledge gained from *having* the experience (of pain, for example)

is something more and other than simply knowing its parameters, even though that reality is not accessible to objective scientific inquiry. Commenting on the now classic discussions by Thomas Nagel on "*What Is It Like To Be a Bat?*" and Frank Jackson on "*Black and White Mary*," she argued that we need a phenomenology of the experience of being the *bearer* of the properties when one *has* an experience. There is an "ontological gap" between objective and subjective knowledge—the latter is grounded in the experience of being the bearer of the quality or property or capacity in question. (A talk given at the 2006 meeting of the Eastern Division of the American Philosophical Society.) This issue bears directly on our critique of a completely reductionist use of the medical model in addressing "mental illness," addressed in Chapter 7.

81. Though Dewey, in his now classic essay on "*The Reflex Arc Concept in Psychology*," raised serious questions about any simple stimulus-response interpretation of organismic behavior, pointing to the crucial aspect of organismic set in determining the very meaning of the stimulus.

82. "Neuroscientific explanations can typically explain how it is possible for creatures with such-and-such a brain to do the kinds of things they do. They can explain what neural connections must obtain and what neural activities must take place in order for it to be possible for the animal to possess and exercise the powers it naturally possesses. In the case of human beings in particular, neuroscience may aspire to explain the neural conditions for the possibility of the mastery of a language, the possession of which is itself a condition of the possibility of rationality in both thought and action. However, neuroscience cannot displace or undermine the explanatory force of the good reasons we sincerely give for our behaviour, or invalidate the justifications we give for rational behaviour. The rationality of behaviour that is motivated by good reasons is not given a deeper explanation by specifying the neural facts that make it possible for creatures such as us to act for such reasons. When we apprehend the propriety, adequacy or goodness of the reasons for which a person acted, then we fully understand why he did what he did" (Hacker, 364).

83. Laughlin, 20.

84. It is almost universally thought that Einstein lost that argument to Bohr, Heisenberg, and quantum indeterminacy. In the long run, however, I suspect that Einstein may prove to be right about the existence of "hidden variables," though I suspect not in the deterministic fashion that, as a "Spinozist," he envisioned. But that is clearly speculation on my part.

85. Let me try to be as clear as possible. There are essentially two distinct but closely related issues that are at stake here, and one important consequence that is worth underscoring. The first issue concerns the deductive model of argument first systematized by Aristotle. Sophisticated modern developments such as those involved with symbolic logic and multivariant analysis have done nothing to fundamentally modify the theoretical deductive frame by which there can be nothing in the conclusions that was not at least implicitly contained in the premises. The second issue concerns the Cartesian methodology, set forth most simply in his *Discourse on Method*. There he spells out the process for obtaining scientific truth by reducing "compounds" to their simple ("atomistic")

components and then, at least conceptually, step-by-step reconstructing the original. The underlying assumption is that the compound can be fully understood because it is nothing more than the result of the workings of its constituent parts. My argument has sought to challenge both of these claims. In so doing, it has sought to undercut the reductive determinism that is their logical conclusion. But that should not be taken to claim that there is no place for causal determination. Quite the contrary. Such determination should be taken as operating at each emergent level in accord with the processes and powers appropriate for that level. In the cases of society and psychology that, of course, will often require consideration of the role of consciousness and choice.

Chapter 5

1. MacIntyre, 213.
2. Obama, 202.
3. Transcendence refers to that which transcends, that is, goes beyond, human experience, while transcendental refers to that which in a specific sense undergirds or is presupposed by human experience.
4. Quoted in Daly, 46 (from Schumpeter, *History of Economic Analysis*, 1954, 41).
5. See the discussion in Chapter 4, especially the quotations from Roy Bhaskar and endnotes from Hacker.
6. Recent discoveries raise the possibility that Neanderthals may also have buried their dead.
7. William Shakespeare, *Hamlet*.
8. Consider Kohler's classic experiments about the extent to which the "conceptual" connections and intelligence of apes is narrowly confined to little beyond the horizon of their visual field. I am referring to the capacity of the apes to use an accessible short stick to reach a longer stick to reach a banana, or to exit out of the rear of an open cage and circle to the front to obtain the desired object.
9. This existential need may even have a biological basis in the neurophysiology of the brain. "The narrative-constructing capacity of the left cortex has now been clearly observed in more than 100 split-brain patients." In his study *The Accidental Brain*, David Linden further argues, more generally, that "the left cortex predisposes [all humans] to create narratives from fragments of perception and memory," even when, as often in dreams, these stories violate the basic data of experience. This "binding together of disparate percepts and ideas to create coherent a narrative that violates our everyday waking experience and cognitive categories ... underlies both dreaming and the creation and social propagation of religious thought. This function operates subconsciously" in all human beings (Linden, 229–231).
10. "All societies have myths." They are "traditional stories a society tells itself that encode or represent the world-view, beliefs, principles, and often fears of that society." Cf. Elizabeth Vandiver, "*Classical Mythology*," Lecture One (Chantilly, VA: The Teaching Company, 2000).

11. There is quite often a basic equivocation concerning the meaning of "pleasure" that generates serious theoretical confusion with profound moral consequences. This arises from failing to distinguish between two quite different meanings of "pleasure," each quite legitimate in their own right, but with very different implications. On the one hand, by "pleasure" one can mean sensual satisfaction, the feeling one gets when one's senses are satisfactorily stimulated. We have all experienced such "pleasures," know what we mean by that expression and the satisfaction that resulted, and know that we have on occasion delayed or sacrificed such satisfaction for other goods such as honor, fame, victory, wealth, loyalty, self-respect, concern for others, etc. On the other hand, we can use the word "pleasure" in a more generic sense to refer to any satisfactions that we have experienced, such as those that might come even from self-denial in the service of others. But when these two quite distinct meanings get confused, as when the "hedonist" says that everyone seeks pleasure, these two distinct meanings are clearly being conflated. And this conflation has very serious ethical consequences. It tends to "pull the rug" out from under good or noble actions, effectively leveling the moral playing field by treating the behavior of selfish and moral people as equivalent. This serves quite well the interests of any who wish to justify their depredations by claiming that their motives are no different or worse than any others, because everyone is simply seeking their own pleasure. Once you clarify the root equivocation, however, you can easily see that the statement that everyone seeks pleasure is either tautological or patently false. If it is the claim that everyone seeks sensual pleasure, then it is obviously false, as there are an infinite number of examples in almost every person's life of actions in which sensual pleasure was delayed or denied in the service of other goals. If by the claim is meant that everyone seeks to be satisfied by what they do, then the statement is vacuous, since satisfaction simply means the feeling one gets when one accomplishes what one has set out to do, but *nothing* meaningful has yet been said about *what* it is that one wants to do. But precisely *that* is the moral question. The question is *what* should one do, and here the apparently meaningful statement is silent. For such "pleasure"—as the satisfaction felt from success—has no specific goal, as innumerable people seek and get satisfaction from innumerably diverse activities. Thus, the supposed claim is nonsense, posing as a worldly wise statement.

12. Gerald Edelman suggests the biological basis for our "socially and linguistically defined self. We are conscious of being conscious, have explicit narrative awareness of the past, and can construct scenarios in an imagined future. We have a true language because we have syntactic capabilities in addition to our phonetic and semantic capabilities" (Edelman, 98).

13. Alasdair MacIntyre in his brilliant volume *After Virtue* speaks of the "narrative" structure of human life, and that human actions are "enacted narratives." We will draw upon this insightful work in this and later chapters.

14. Goffman, *Asylums.*

15. That is, it is a field phenomenon.

16. William McNeill, "Review of a Short History of Humanity," *New York Review of Books,* June 29, 2000.

17. The ancient Hebrews referred to themselves as "the chosen people," but they are hardly the only ones who have believed and acted as if they were something special, divinely appointed and protected.

18. Bhaskar, 52.

19. "*Intentions are personal, meanings are social*—in the sense that intentions are of (that is belong to) persons, whereas meanings are always effectively given for them. Now it is only because language is always and everywhere always given, that one can use it as a vehicle with which to describe actions, ... and thus, in the case of one's own actions, use it both to form intentions and to reflexively comment upon what is intended ... Thus it is a mistake to identify the social meaning of an action with the agent's intention in performing it on some particular occasion" (Bhaskar, 147n13).

20. Bhaskar, 43–45.

21. Ibid., 53.

22. "What the agent is able to do and say intelligibly as an actor is deeply affected by the fact that we are never more (and sometimes less) than the co-authors of our own narratives. Only in fantasy do we live what story we please ... We enter upon a stage which we did not design and we find ourselves part of an action that was not of our making. Each of us being a main character in his own drama plays subordinate parts in the dramas of others, and each drama constrains the others ... "

    "What I have called a history is an enacted dramatic narrative in which the characters are also the authors ... The difference between imaginary characters and real ones is not in the narrative form of what they do; it is in the degree of their authorship of that form and of their own deeds. Of course just as they do not begin where they please, they cannot go on exactly as they please either; each character is constrained by the actions of others and by the social settings presupposed in his and their actions" (MacIntyre, 213, 217).

23. See *The Hidden Injuries of Class* (by Richard Sennett and Jonathan Cobb) for a brilliant study of the tragic personal dilemmas encountered by working-class American immigrant families who have bought into the myth of individual responsibility in a highly but somewhat invisibly class-stratified society. This study well exemplifies the power of this mythic cultural drama of individual self-creation as it confronts the reality of institutionalized class advantage.

24. MacIntyre, 206–207.

25. Theodore Spencer's study of Shakespeare's view of human nature shows clearly how the evil figures in Shakespeare are those who claim the prerogatives of individuality. Consider, for example, Iago in "*Othello*," Edmund in "*King Lear*," or Richard III in the play of the same name. Similarly, the evil Dr. Faustus in Marlowe's play of the same name is nothing if not the embodiment of individual self-seeking without any concern for his preassigned place in the social order (Spencer).

26. "There is no such thing as 'behavior', to be identified prior to and independently of intentions, beliefs and settings ... it is worth noticing that it is not at all clear what a scientific experiment could be, if one were a Skinnerian; since the conception of an experiment is certainly one of intention- and belief-informed

behavior. And what would be utterly doomed to failure would be the project of a science of, say, political behavior, detached from a study of intentions, beliefs and settings … "

"We identify a particular action only by invoking two kinds of context, implicitly if not explicitly. We place the agent's intentions … in causal and temporal order with reference to their role in his or her history; and we also place them with reference to their role in the history of the setting or settings to which they belong. In doing this, in determining what causal efficacy the agent's intentions had in one or more directions, and how his short-term intentions succeeded or failed to be constitutive of long-term intentions, we ourselves write a further part of these histories. Narrative history of a certain kind turns out to be the basic and essential genre for the characterization of human actions … that the concept of an intelligible action is a more fundamental concept than that of an action as such. Unintelligible actions are failed candidates for the status of intelligible action; and to lump unintelligible actions and intelligible actions together in a single class of actions and then to characterize action in terms of what items of both sets have in common is to make the mistake of ignoring this. It is also to neglect the central importance of the concept of intelligibility."

"Human beings can be held to account for that of which they are the authors; other beings cannot. To identify an occurrence as an action is in the paradigmatic instances to identify it under a type of description which enables us to see that occurrence as flowing intelligibly from a human agent's intentions, motives, passions and purposes. It is therefore to understand an action as something for which someone is accountable, about which it is always appropriate to ask the agent for an intelligible account … it is indeed the unintelligibility of such patients' actions that leads to their being treated as patients; actions unintelligible to the agent as well as to everyone else are understood—rightly—as a kind of suffering" (MacIntyre, 208).

27. Consider Tip O'Neill's now legendary report of Ronald Reagan's confusion of the ex-president Grover Cleveland with the baseball pitcher Grover Cleveland Alexander. Or Lloyd DeMause's discussion of Reagan's fascination with amputation or castration in the movie "Kings Row," discussed in Chapter 3 of *Reagan's America*.

28. MacIntyre, 218.

29. "The most familiar type of context in and by reference to which speech-acts and purposes are rendered intelligible is the conversation," notes MacIntyre. "The use of words such as 'tragic', 'comic', and 'farcical' is not marginal to such evaluations. We allocate conversations to genres, just as we do literary narratives. Indeed a conversation is a dramatic work, even if a very short one, in which the participants are not only the actors, but also the joint authors, working out in agreement or disagreement the mode of their production … For conversation, understood widely enough, is the form of human transactions in general … "

"I am presenting both conversations in particular then and human actions in general as enacted narratives. Narrative is not the work of poets, dramatists and novelists reflecting upon events which had no narrative order before one was imposed by the singer or the writer; narrative form is neither disguise nor decoration … in successfully identifying and understanding what someone else is doing we always move towards placing a particular episode in the context of a set of narrative histories, histories both of the individuals concerned and of the settings in which they act and suffer. It is now becoming clear that we render the actions of others intelligible in this way because action itself has a basically historical character. It is because we all live out narratives in our lives and because we understand our own lives in terms of the narratives that we live out that the form of narrative is appropriate for understanding the actions of others. Stories are lived before they are told—except in the case of fiction" (MacIntyre, 209–212).

But MacIntyre does seem to be mistaken in his criticism of Sartre's view in *Nausea*. He claims that Sartre fails to recognize the narrative structure of daily life, seeing the narrative as something reflectively constructed and overlaid onto daily life, giving to it a narrative structure that it initially lacked. But that is not Sartre's point. He does not deny that meanings pervade daily life as pre-reflectively lived by the individual, but rather that *as lived* these meanings lack the order and coherence that is inevitably given to them by the retrospective narrative. From the narrative perspective, events tend to have a direction and purpose that they tend to lack *as lived*. As Kierkegaard said, we live forward, but think backward. Thus, the concept of a narrative structure to our life, while quite insightful, can be slightly misleading. That is why I tend to prefer the notion of drama, which may slightly more adequately capture the uncertainty built into human living.

Chapter 6

1. In a universe that is the result of an inflationary expansion, as is currently thought to be the case, our observable universe would be only a miniscule fraction of all there is, but the "rest" of reality would be forever beyond the reach of our experience. That is because according to Einstein's Theory of Relativity, nothing can travel faster than the speed of light and hence the "rest" of that inflationary reality would be too far away to be known by us or to impact upon us. (See note 2 of Chapter 1.)

2. The most comprehensive metaphysical statement of this position is probably John Dewey's *Experience and Nature*. It might be thought of as a kind of naturalized post-Darwinian Hegelian perspective, but more fully rooted in a completely open-ended and experimental natural and social science. Dewey's *Human Nature and Conduct* also contributes substantially to this perspective, as does Roy Bhaskar's *A Realistic Theory of Science* and *The Possibility of Naturalism*.

3. Dewey well delineated the problem of "the individual" in his *The Public and its Problems*. "In its approximate sense, anything is individual which moves and acts as a unitary thing. For common sense, a certain spatial separateness

is the mark of this individuality... . But even vulgar common sense at once introduces certain qualifications. The tree stands only when rooted in the soil; it lives or dies in the mode of its connections with sunlight, air and water. Then too the tree is a collection of interacting parts; is the tree more a single whole than its cells? ... We have to consider not only its connections and ties, but the consequences with respect to which it acts and moves. We are compelled to say that for some purposes, for some results, the tree is the individual, for others the cell, and for a third, the forest or the landscape... . [I]t seems as if we could not determine an individual without reference to differences made as well as to antecedent and contemporary connections... . A *distinctive* way of behaving in conjunction and *connection* with other distinctive ways of acting, not a self-enclosed way of acting, independent of everything else, is that toward which we are pointed. Any human being is in one respect an association, consisting of a multitude of cells each living its own life" (Dewey [1], pp. 186–188).

4. The dean of American evolutionists, Ernest Mayr, asserts that Darwin's Theory of Evolution really entails five distinct theses: "1) The non-constancy of species (the basic theory of evolution); 2) The descent of all organisms from common ancestors (branching evolution); 3) The gradualness of evolution (no saltations, no discontinuities); 4) The multiplication of species (the origin of diversity); and 5) Natural selection" (Mayr, pp. 85–86).

5. It is at this level, and not that of the genotype, that the question of the adequacy of the adaptive transformations for the survival or extinction of the maturing organism is usually determined.

6. In explaining why "everyone is an absolutely unique event in history," Cold Spring Harbor geneticist Professor Tim Tully observed that there are on the average five alleles for every gene, thus fifteen distinct possible gene expressions. Since the human being has some 60,000 genes, that means that the "genetic potential of the human species" is on the order of 15 to the 60,000 power—a truly astronomical number—although that is constrained by the fact that the genes are located on just the twenty-three chromosomes that interact in each generation. (From a talk in a Hutton House Lecture on the C.W. Post Campus of L.I.U. in November 2001.)

7. Mayr, p. 166. Mayr sums up this point as follows: "Darwin's theory of evolution through natural selection is best referred to as the theory of variational evolution. According to this theory, an enormous amount of genetic variation is produced in every generation, but only a few individuals of the vast number of offspring will survive to produce the next generation. The theory postulates that those individuals with the highest probability of surviving and reproducing successfully are the ones best adapted owing to their possession of a particular combination of attributes. Since these attributes are largely determined by genes, the genotypes of these individuals will be favored during the process of selection. As a consequence of the continuous survival of individuals (phenotypes) with genotypes best able to cope with the changes of the environment, there will be a continuing change in the genetic composition of every population. This unequal survival of individuals is due in part to competition among the new recombinant genotypes within the population, and in part to chance

processes affecting the frequency of genes. The resulting change of a population is called evolution. Since all changes take place in populations of genetically unique individuals, evolution is by necessity a gradual and continuous process" (Mayr, pp. 85–86).

8. The "environment influences the outcome of the genetic make-up" stated Professor Tully, at the above-mentioned talk at Hutton House at the C.W. Post Campus of L.I.U. in November 2001, while "neuronal activity changes gene expression." Thus, as Gerard Edelman observes, "from the very beginning of neuroanatomy, there are rich statistical variations in both cell movement and cell death. As a result, no two individuals, not even identical twins, possess the same anatomical patterns" (Edelman, p. 29).

9. Mayr, 1959, quoted in Mayr, p. 84.

10. Ibid., p. 129.

11. This term is usually applied only to the mutual adaptation of organisms to each other, as in parasitic relations, but it might as well be applied to the more encompassing adaptive relation between organism and environment, both biotic and abiotic. Mayr writes: "Whenever two kinds of organisms interact with each other, … a predator and its prey, or a host and its parasite, … each will exert a selection pressure on the other. The result is that they will co-evolve… . the prey may develop better escape mechanisms that force the predator to improve its attack capacity. Much of … evolution occurs through such *co-evolution.*

When the myxomatosis virus was introduced into Australia to control the escalating population of rabbits, the most virulent strains … killed their host rabbits so quickly that there was no time for the virus to be transmitted to another rabbit. As a result, most of the highly virulent strains became extinct. Rabbits attacked by less virulent strains survived longer and provided the source for infecting other rabbits. Eventually, much less virulent strains of the virus evolved that killed only a certain percentage of the rabbits while most survived. At the same time, the most susceptible rabbits were killed off and populations of rabbits evolved that were less susceptible to the myxomatosis virus.

Most European infectious diseases currently exist in a similar steady state. Over many millennia, the European populations have become somewhat resistant to these human diseases and mortality is relatively low. This was not the case, however, with foreign populations that first came in contact with the Europeans after 1492. All over the world, but particularly in the Americas, the native populations were ravaged by epidemics caused by European infectious diseases, particularly smallpox. The native population of the Americas, which was estimated to have been 60 million when Columbus first landed in the Bahamas, had crashed to 5 million only twenty years later.

These diseases were so deadly because the Native Americans had not co-evolved with them. They were left defenseless when the pathogens spread through their populations" (Mayr, pp. 210–211).

12. Ibid., p. 252.

13. Ibid., p. 240.

14. Ibid., pp. 90, 126–127.

15. Ibid., p. 280. "In certain species a special kind of group occurs, a social group, that can indeed be the target of selection. Such a group, owing to social cooperation among its members, has a greater fitness value than the arithmetical mean of the fitness values of its individual members... . Members of such groups cooperate by warning of enemies, sharing newly discovered sources of food, and joint defense against enemies... . As a result, any genetic contribution toward cooperative behavior would be favored by natural selection" (Mayr, pp. 131–132).

16. "I have described the stages by which man became increasingly different from his simian ancestors and must now attempt to describe the characteristics that are uniquely human. Most of them are related to the enormous development of the brain and to the development of extended parental care. In most invertebrates (particularly insects) the parents die before their offspring hatch from the egg. The entire behavioral information available to the newborn is contained in its DNA. What they can subsequently learn during their usually rather short life is quite limited and is not transmitted to their offspring. Only in species with highly developed parental care, as in certain birds and mammals, can the young have an opportunity to add to their genetic information by learning from their parents, as well as from their sibs and occasionally from other members of their social group. Such information can be handed down in these species from generation to generation without being contained in the genetic program. Yet in most animal species the amount of information that can be transferred by such a system of non-genetic information transfer is quite limited. By contrast, in man, the transfer of such cultural information has become a major aspect of life. This capability also favored the development of speech, indeed one might say that it necessitated the origin of language.

    Even though we often use the word "language" in connection with the information transmittal systems of animals, such as the "language of bees," actually all of these animal species have merely systems of giving and receiving signals. To be a language, a system of communication must contain syntax and grammar. Psychologists have attempted for half a century to teach language to chimpanzees, but in vain. Chimps seem to lack the neural equipment to adopt syntax. Therefore, they cannot talk about the future or the past. Having invented language, our ancestors were able to develop a rich oral tradition long before the invention of writing and printing. The development of speech, in turn, exerted an enormous selection pressure on an enlargement of the brain, particularly those parts that involved information storage (memory). This enlarged brain made the development of art, literature, mathematics, and science possible" (Mayr, p. 253).

17. Daly, pp. 193–197.

18. Davidson, pp. 56–57.

19. For an insightful analysis of what constitutes "the public" and a suggestive treatment of appropriate strategies to address the issues thus raised, see Dewey's *The Public and its Problems*.

20. Davidson, pp. 17–23.

21. One of the most significant ambiguities built into normal economic discussions concerns the issue of scarcity. In normal parlance, that word means that something is in very short supply, but, as Alfie Kohn insightfully observes, "When economists talk about scarcity, however, they generally are not using the word to mean that goods are in short supply. Their technical use of the term refers instead to (i) the fact that choosing one commodity involves giving up the chance to have another, or (ii) the presumed failure of people to be satisfied regardless of how much they have. Let us take these in turn.

    The first usage defines a scarce good as one for which a consumer would give up something else. Scarcity, then, concerns the mutually exclusive relationship between commodities. This may be a useful way of looking at the world in some respects, but it tells us nothing about the absolute status of a given commodity. The model is set up so all finite goods will always be considered "scarce"; the availability of each is being evaluated vis-a-vis the others. By definition, no economic system can remedy this state of affairs, so competition is no more sensible a way to deal with scarcity than any other arrangement.

    The second definition rests economic theory on a very questionable (but rarely questioned) assumption about "human nature"—namely, the belief that we will always want more of something than we had before or more than the next person has. Far more reasonable is the proposition that insatiability and competitiveness reflect cultural mores. As Wachtel saw, 'Our obsession with growth is the expression of neither inexorable laws of human nature nor inexorable laws of economics.... It is a cultural and psychological phenomenon, reflecting our present way of organizing and giving meaning to our lives ... [that] is now maladaptive'" (Kohn, pp. 73–74). In short, the ambiguous use of "scarcity" conveniently serves to hide a crucial distinction, and thus to provide a rather circular, though ideologically quite useful, justification of a competitive economic system.

22. MacEwan, p. 137.

23. In *Habits of the Heart*, the authors quote Alan Trachtenberg to the effect that "Until after the Civil War, ... the assumption was widespread that a corporate charter was a privilege to be granted only by a special act of a state legislature, and then for purposes clearly in the public interest." They then proceed to observe that "reasserting the idea that incorporation is a concession of public authority to a private group *in return for* service to the public good, with effective public accountability, would change what is now called the 'social responsibility of the corporation' from its present status ... of public relations ... to a constructive structural element in the corporation itself" (Bellah, pp. 289–290).

24. The long-term challenge to civilization's development may be even more fundamental than so far suggested, if William McNeil is to be believed. In *Plagues and Peoples,* he suggests that civilizations develop through ecological simplification, as people seek to mold the environment to human needs and to reduce threats posed by infectious agents. Thus, historical progress so far has depended on the continuing reduction of biodiversity (McNeil [1]).

25. Bhaskar (2), p. 169.

26. Cardinal Bellarmine is reported to have felt that the problem with Galileo's theory was not so much its truth or falsity, but rather the likely disintegrative

social consequences of dropping this "bombshell" without adequate preparation on a Christian world that had been taught for centuries by an infallible Church that the Earth was the immovable center of the Universe.

27. It is hardly conceivable that anyone would have devoted the countless hours and years of painstaking toil that Johannes Kepler did to the determined effort of finding a simple mathematical formula that would describe the motion of the planets if they were not motivated as he was by the most passionate commitment to a Neo-Pythagorean conception of the divinity of the Sun.

28. Bhaskar, pp., 77, 81. "For though a slave who fully comprehends the circumstances of his own subordination does not thereby become free, such an understanding is a necessary condition for his rational self-emancipation. Conversely his master has an interest in his remaining ignorant of the circumstances of his slavery. Knowledge is asymmetrically beneficial to the parties involved in relations of domination" (Bhaskar, p. 98n84).

29. "As for neo-classical economic theory, the most developed form of this tendency in social thought [to reduce society to the sum of the action of atomistic and a-historical individuals], it may best be regarded as a normative theory of efficient action, generating a set of techniques for achieving given ends, rather than as an explanatory theory capable of casting light on actual empirical episodes. This is, as a praxiology, not a sociology" (Bhaskar, p. 37).

30. "Let us consider drug resistance of bacteria. When penicillin was first introduced in the 1940s, it was amazingly effective against many types of bacteria. Any infection, let us say by streptococci or spirochetes, was almost immediately cured. However, bacteria are genetically variable and the most susceptible ones succumbed most rapidly. A few that had acquired by mutation genes that had made them more resistant survived longer and a few still had survived when the treatment stopped. In this manner, the frequency of somewhat resistant strains gradually increased in human populations. At the same time, new mutations and gene transfers occurred that provided even greater resistance. This process of inadvertent selection for greater resistance continued, even though ever stronger dosages of penicillin were applied and the period of treatment was prolonged. Finally, some totally resistant strains evolved. Thus by gradual evolution an almost completely susceptible species of bacteria had evolved into a totally resistant one. Literally hundreds of similar cases have been reported in the medical and agricultural (for pesticide resistance) literature" (Mayr, p. 190).

31. A failure in this respect could lead, in the long run, to "eco-cide," resulting from either a runaway greenhouse effect or the destruction of adequate biodiversity.

Chapter 7

1. Quoted in Goldman.

2. By this I mean the Protestant Reformation and the Commercial Revolution, both of which were not explicitly promoting individualism, even while they laid the groundwork for it.

3. Commenting on these two premier political theorists of late twentieth-century America, Alasdair MacIntyre observes "that for both [Robert] Nozick and [John] Rawls a society is composed of individuals, each with his or her own interest, who then have to come together and formulate common rules of life. In Nozick's case there is the additional negative constraint of a set of basic rights. In Rawls's case the only constraints are those that a prudent rationality would impose. Individuals are thus in both accounts primary and society secondary, and the identification of individual interests is prior to, and independent of, the construction of any moral or social bonds between them... .

[From] the shared social presuppositions of Rawls and Nozick[,] it is ... as though we had been shipwrecked on an uninhabited island with a group of other individuals, each of whom is a stranger to me and to all the others. What have to be worked out are rules which will safeguard each one of us maximally in such a situation... . Thus Rawls and Nozick articulate with great power a shared view which envisages entry into social life as—at least ideally—the voluntary act of at least potentially rational individuals with prior interests who have to ask the question 'What kind of social contract with others is it reasonable for me to enter into?' Not surprisingly it is a consequence of this that their views exclude any account of human community in which the notion of desert in relation to contributions to the common tasks of that community in pursing shared goods could provide the basis for judgments about virtue and injustice.

Central to Nozick's account is the [added] thesis that all legitimate entitlements can be traced to legitimate acts of original acquisition. But, if that is so, there are in fact very few, and in some large areas of the world no, legitimate entitlements... . This is the historical reality ideologically concealed behind any Lockean thesis. The lack of any principle of rectification is thus not a small side issue for a thesis such as Nozick's; it tends to vitiate the theory as a whole—even if we were to suppress the overwhelming objections to any belief in inalienable human rights" (MacIntyre, pp. 250–251).

4. "'Individuality cannot be opposed to association. It is through association that man has acquired his individuality and it is through association that he exercises it. The theory that sets the individual over against the society, of necessity contradicts itself.' An individual's functions both defined his uniqueness and united him in moral community with other members of his society. Individuality—'the realization of what we specifically are as distinct from others'—did not mean separation or isolation from others but the 'performing of a special *service* without which the social whole is defective'" (Westbrook, p. 44).

5. Bellah, p. 37.

6. Ibid., p. 38.

7. Bhaskar, p. 32.

8. Ibid., pp. 35–36. I have qualified Bhaskar's text with the addition of the words "primarily" and "primary" because I think it makes more precise his meaning, and certainly better expresses my intent.

9. Ibid., p. 35. "Society can never be reduced to individuals, because it is (despite social contract theory) a necessary condition for any intentional act, not just

for our understanding of it; whereas minds are certainly not a necessary condition for physico-chemical laws, as distinct from our understanding of them" (Ibid., p. 149n46).

10. "It is the norms of the culture that determine its competitiveness, not the presence or absence of resources. As (Margaret) Mead put it, 'It is not the actual supply of a desired good which decrees whether or not the members of a society will compete for it or cooperate and share it, but it is the way the structure of the society is built up that determines whether individual members shall cooperate or shall compete with one another.' In fact, Mead went further than this, suggesting at one point that the relative plenty in several societies was the result of their cooperative arrangements, not the cause. Put differently, cooperation can be seen as an appropriate, rational response to scarcity since it is probably more effective at maximizing what one has…. William O. Johnson put it even more bluntly: 'Pioneers were not competitive people, they were a cooperative people. They wouldn't have survived otherwise'" (Kohn, p. 39). (Jean-Paul Sartre thus seems quite wrong about the causal role he attributes to scarcity.)

11. Quoted in Bellah, p. 294.

12. "We do best at the tasks we enjoy. An outside or extrinsic motivator (money, grades, the trappings of competitive success) simply cannot take the place of an activity we find rewarding in itself. 'While extrinsic motivation may affect performance,' wrote Margaret Clifford, 'performance is dependent upon learning, which in turn is primarily dependent upon intrinsic motivation.' More specifically, 'a significant performance-increase on a highly complex task will be dependent upon intrinsic motivation.' In fact, even people who are judged to be high in achievement motivation do not perform well unless extrinsic motivation has been minimized, as several studies have shown.

Competition works just as any other extrinsic motivator does. [As one expert has noted …] 'The reward for extrinsically motivated behavior is something that is separate from and follows the behavior. With competitive activities, the reward is typically 'winning' (that is, beating the other person or the other team), so the reward is actually extrinsic to the activity itself.'

But this tells only half the story…. the use of extrinsic motivators actually tends to undermine intrinsic motivation and thus adversely affect performance in the long run. The introduction of, say, monetary reward will edge out intrinsic satisfaction; once this reward is withdrawn, the activity may well cease even though no reward at all was necessary for its performance earlier. Extrinsic motivators, in other words, are not only ineffective but corrosive. They eat away at the kind of motivation that does produce results…. trying to beat another party is extrinsic in nature and tends to decrease people's intrinsic motivation for the target activity…. when people are instructed to compete at an activity, they begin to see that activity as an instrument for winning rather than an activity which is … rewarding in its own right. Thus, competition seems to work like many other extrinsic rewards" undermining the very quality of one's attention and performance" (Kohn, pp. 60–61).

13. Kohn provides evidence that, "children rated as highly competitive were found to have lower empathy scores than children rated as relatively less competitive." He then comments that "if empathy encourages altruism and competition depresses empathy, then we should find an inverse relationship between competition and altruism—and so we do.... The point here is not that competitive individuals never give money to charity. It is rather that competition ultimately discourages generosity.... Here ... is Karen Homey: 'Competitiveness ... creates easily aroused envy towards the stronger ones, contempt for the weaker, distrust towards everyone ... so the satisfaction and reassurance which one can get out of human relations are limited and the individual becomes more or less emotionally isolated'" (Kohn, pp. 139–141).

14. This helps to explain why what MacIntyre has called the Emotivist culture has taken such a hold of both the modern moral imagination and its prototypical "representative individuals"—as the moral ideology of this competitive world, and of "economic man" (cf. MacIntyre).

15. Davidson, pp. 16–17.

16. Bhaskar, pp. 48–49, 57.

17. For example, Rousseau writes, in a recently discovered letter: "Anyone can see that it is quite impossible for a man to be born, live, and maintain himself in a society without depending on it for anything. He is wrong to protest on the grounds of his poverty, woes, or misfortune. The state will answer: 'Perhaps it would have been better for you to have been born in the midst of a desert, but you were born here, you have lived here, and you could not have survived here had I not sustained you. You should have quit this life if it was a burden to you and should have quit this country if its laws seemed to you too harsh; die or leave if you wish henceforth to owe me nothing, but pay me for the thirty years of life you have already enjoyed with my assistance. Until you are no longer, you owe me for what you have been.'" Jean Starobinski, "*A Letter from Jean-Jacques Rousseau*," trans. Arthur Goldhammer, *The New York Review of Books* 1, no. 8, (May 15, 2003): 31–32.

18. For a detailed discussion of the dialogue between Ideal and Real, between moral vision and practical possibilities, that is at the center of the Pragmatic philosophical tradition, see Chapter 5 of my *The Drama of Thought*.

19. See Chapter 9.

20. This example is taken from comments by Herman Daly and John B. Cobb, Jr., *For the Common Good.*

21. "Immigration is responsible for most of America's population growth.... If immigration had remained at 1965 levels America would be approaching zero population growth today, and would have eventually leveled off at around 250 million.... So the question naturally arises, why are we doing this to ourselves?

   Does America have a shortage of people? I can think of nothing that we as a nation wish to accomplish that would require a larger population than the quarter billion we already have.

   Are the people coming here significantly better than the people we've already got? No they're not. Immigrants on the whole are less educated than

Americans, and many have difficulties with English. As a natural result immigrants as a group are less successful economically than native born Americans. They earn less money (by about a third), and they use welfare at a somewhat higher rate (about 21 percent of immigrant households receive some sort of welfare, as opposed to 15 percent of non-immigrant households). But while these problems are real, they not overwhelming. The really important thing to understand about immigrants is that there is absolutely nothing special about them. They are just ordinary, average, people who happen to have been born in other countries. They are not different from us in any profound way.

So again, we have to ask, why are we doing this? Why is the United States government using its power to force massive population growth on America? Unlike the question we started out with, this is not a silly question. But the answer is still simple: Special Interest Politics. America's immigration policy is not about The Meaning of America. It's not about Compassion. It's not about Revitalizing Neighborhoods. America's immigration policy is about Money and Power, just like most of the rest of our politics. There really shouldn't be any surprise here. Unless you actually believe that America suffers from a shortage of people; or unless you actually believe that the people coming from over there are somehow superior to the people who were born over here; then all you are doing is moving people around, and there is no way this can result in broad economic benefits for the American people as a whole. But it does provide narrow benefits to specific groups. Big business sees immigration as a steady source of cheap, compliant labor. In fact, according to a major 1997 study by the National Academy of Sciences, competition with immigrant workers has significantly depressed the wages of less skilled Americans. Ethnic activists and politicians (who are primarily concerned with the well being of their own people, not the nation as a whole) are acutely aware that immigration is steadily increasing their own political power and that of their communities, and they will viciously attack anyone who suggests that it be reduced. For immigration lawyers, immigration is the money issue, and they are extremely well organized and active in Washington and in the media.

These groups, and others, have successfully beaten back all recent attempts to reduce legal immigration. In particular a coalition of such groups torpedoed the 1995 recommendations of the United States Commission on Immigration Reform, which was created by Congress and chaired by the late civil rights leader Barbara Jordan, and which, after five years of carefully study, had called for a 30 percent decrease in legal immigration.

There is a final argument that is made in favor of high immigration, the moral argument. It is claimed that we have a moral obligation to help the world's poor by letting them come here. Now moral arguments are tricky; there is always the danger that I'm going to decide that you are not compassionate enough, and that I'm going to end up picking your pocket, giving it to the poor, and calling it charity. This happens a lot! Charity is much more fun when you get to use other people's resources! Nevertheless I do believe that while the primary obligation of the American government is to do right by the American people, it also has an important secondary obligation to do right by the rest for the world. We do have an obligation to the poor! What is usually overlooked is that we also have many different options for meeting this obligation, and that immigration is among the worst.

There are simply too many poor, and almost none of them will ever be able to come here, no matter what our immigration policy is. If you consider a person with an annual income 1/10th that of the average American to be poor, then over 4 billion of the world's 6 billion people will qualify. We can take in a million people a year, or two million, or ten million, and we will still barely scratch the surface, especially when you consider that each year over 100 million more are born, mostly in poor countries. A liberal American immigration policy gives false hope to these people, and distracts them from more practical efforts. Here are just a few of the possible alternatives: encourage education for women, which will improve their lives and lead them to want smaller families; facilitate women's access to birth control; forgive a portion of the crushing Third World debt burden, much of which represents money that was stolen by corrupt governments; promote small scale, appropriate technologies; use US power, when feasible, to promote civil society in desperate countries. Now some of these suggestions are expensive; and none are perfect or without risk, but they all have the potential of helping far more people than could ever be touched by our immigration policy! We cannot help the world's poor by letting them come here. We must find ways to help them 'bloom where they grow.' Immigration is not an answer. It is simply an opportunity for elite Americans to wallow in self-congratulation, making full use of the services of cheap nannies and gardeners, ignoring the negative effects on less fortunate Americans and sustainability of America's future, and in the process doing absolutely nothing useful for the rest of the world" (From remarks presented by John Brock, cochair of TRIM: Tri-State Immigration Moratorium, Inc., at the Institute for Sustainable Development of Long Island University, April 20, 1999).

22. See Stephen Kinzer's *Overthrow*, for documentation of some of this history.

23. A similar tension between individual rights and social responsibility, partially rooted in opposed conceptions of the human being's place in the social world, bedevils contemporary feminism. On one hand, feminists claim the "right to choose" whether or not to have an abortion. On the other hand, they complain about the failure of fathers to assume their responsibilities for their offspring. But they rarely directly address the question of what, if any, rights the father has in deciding about the future of the fetus. To what extent is the production of children a joint affair, and to what extent is it solely a matter of a woman's body, and the fetus she is carrying? I don't claim that this is an easy issue to resolve, but only that you can't honestly have it both ways—claiming that the father has no role in the decision to abort, but complete paternal responsibility for the mother's condition and the child's future.

24. Similar problems, of course, also arise domestically. Americans celebrate private property as an almost God-given right, and yet the right is itself clearly a social construct, that itself expresses the prevailing views and structures of power of the encompassing society. It is the society that must decide the

conditions of ownership, from the manner in which property is legitimately obtained and transferred to the scope and limitations of the rights to use and abuse that accompany its possession. It is quite obvious that ownership and use of house and land, for example, is highly dependent upon ambient conditions, conditions it itself can significantly impact, as our discussion of sound made quite clear. But far more significant would be issues such as environmental pollution, the quality of the surrounding air and water, and the impact of the activity of the private property on its ambient neighborhood. It is clear that no society will allow a home owner to do with their property whatever they will, for example, building your own private nuclear power plant. The challenge is to develop a coherent theory of personal and social rights and obligations consistent with the historicized social construction of self and society.

25. One of an infinity of such examples is multiple sclerosis, occasioned by the deterioration of the myelin sheaths that surround nerve cells, thus impairing their ability to carry signals that make possible thought and action.

26. The tendency of many to assume that if they have found a physical process that is correlated with a specific mental activity they have thus explained that activity is but another expression of the implicit dualism that tends to infect so much of contemporary thought, thus providing the framework for the "scientific" reduction of the mental to the material.

27. Hacker (pp. 364–365): "What neuroscience can do, however, is contribute to the explanation of irrational or partly irrational action. It may be able to explain why a person is more prone than normal to certain mental states—for example, of depression, which makes him more liable to act for a certain kind of a reason than someone who is not thus depressed. This can play an important role in explaining human behaviour in certain circumstances. But it is also important to note that such an explanation need not supersede the reasons the depressed person might give for committing suicide, for example. That he is depressive, perhaps pathologically depressive, does not imply that his reasons for killing himself are mere rationalizations, which play no role in rendering his behaviour intelligible. The neuroscientific explanation may complement the explanation the agent offers in terms of reasons, without rendering those reasons irrelevant.

    Furthermore, neuroscience can explain—indeed, specializes in explaining—how gross pathological deficiencies in the exercise of normal human capacities result from damage to the brain. So it can brilliantly explain why patients cannot behave as normal humans can in a multitude of different ways. In particular, it may explain why such patients are, in one way or another, incapable of acting rationally in certain respects.

    What neuroscience can do is to explain, for normal human beings, how it is possible for them to be open to reason. But it cannot explain the rationale of human actions in the particular case, or elucidate what makes a certain reason a good reason. It can identify necessary conditions for the exercise of human capacities. But it does not follow that it is, or ever will be, in the position to specify a set of neural conditions that are sufficient conditions for characteristic human action in the circumstances of life. To explain typical human behaviour, one must operate at the higher, irreducible level of normal descriptions of human actions and their various forms of explanation and justification in terms of reasons and motives (as well as causes). These descriptions will cite multitudinous factors: past and prospective events that in given circumstances may constitute the agent's reasons for action; the agent's desires, intentions, goals and purposes; his tendencies, habits and customs; and the moral and social norms to which he conforms."

28. Sapolsky, Lecture 21. Dr. Sapolsky discusses the research in this area at some length, reporting, for example, on the "striking example" showing that "one hormone cannot explain aggression," that comes "from studying murder rates in London, Toronto, and Detroit. In men in all three cities, the highest levels of aggression were found to occur at the same ages (late adolescence/young adulthood). However, there were enormous differences in the absolute number of murders among the three cities, showing the importance of environment in aggression." Numerous other examples are offered, including increased levels of violence "in cultures with credos of victimization and justified revenge," in "authoritarian cultures," and among children who have been the victim of childhood abuse. Among his conclusions are: "cross-cultural differences in aggression dwarf developmental patterns;" hormones do not cause behavior, but "alter a pre-existing tendency ... in the context of interaction with environment"—they can "turn up the volume"; and aggression tends to be higher in those who were trained in aggression, regardless of testosterone levels.

29. Dr. Sapolsky observes that desert societies and nomadic pastoralists tend to be more hierarchical and were the first to develop organized violence and monotheistic religions. This is in contrast with agricultural societies, rain forest peoples, or hunter/gatherers, all of whom tend to be polytheistic, more socially tolerant, and less violent.

30. Dr. Sapolsky reports that the evidence supports the causal connection tending more toward "aggression elevating testosterone levels, rather than the other way around" (Sapolsky, Lecture 21). Leventhal and Martell quote H. S. Akiskal (1995) who "in a major medical textbook in psychiatry states that, 'despite three decades of extensive research and indirect evidence ... it has not been proved that a deficiency or excess of biogenic amines in specific brain structures is necessary or sufficient for the occurrence of mood disorders'" (Leventhall, p. 7). They further claim that "despite the popularity of the theory that depression is caused by chemical imbalances, there is no definitive support for this conclusion... . 'The initial biochemical theories are clearly inadequate to explain either drug action or the etiology of mental illness, but it is not known what can replace them'" (Leventhall, p. 36). After a far more detailed discussion, including brain chemistry, physiology, and the politics of psychopharmacology, the authors conclude that "the medical model carries the mantel of science, but it has no more claim to the scientific method than the learning model of social science. In fact, ... many of the conclusions drawn from the pharmacotherapy literature are circular, and the marketing that promotes drugs as the only proven treatments is easily revealed to be importantly motivated by profit rather than care" (Leventhall, p. 132).

31. Dr. Jeffrey Schwartz concludes his study of neural plasticity and the power of mental attention in the treatment of OCD, depression, and stroke, among other ailments, and his review of the literature on theories of the relation of mind and brain with the observation that "the shift in understanding inspired by neuroplasticity and the power of the mind to shape the brain undermines the claim of materialist determinism that humans are essentially nothing more than fleshy computers spitting out the behavioral results of some inescapable neurogenetic program" (Schwartz, p. 374).

32. Consider Martha Nussbaum's brilliantly suggestive discussion of our treatment of the "handicapped" and the way it often expresses our "normal" flight from our own limitations, in *Hiding from Humanity* (Nussbaum, pp. 305–319). We "normals" define what constitute the requirements of normality, and then tend to stigmatize those as "handicapped," and thus less than normal, who fall short of our standards. In that same work, Dr. Nussbaum offers an insightful analysis of the psychic roots and some social consequences of the emotions of shame and disgust to a consideration of which we will return in Chapter 9.

33. Addressing the issue of the University of Michigan's use of so-called racial quotas in the admission of students to their graduate and undergraduate programs. Dworkin, "*The Court and the University,*" *The New York Review of Books* 1, no. 8, (May 15, 2003): 8–11.

34. See also MacIntyre's discussion of slavery and Naziism that is addressed in the section "I Am Born with a Past."

35. Sartre himself came to see this early stage of his work as part of his own flight from the self he had been supposed to be by his family (see his autobiography, *The Words*) and sought to rectify *Being and Nothingness*'s ahistorical and decontextualized conception of freedom in his later work, particularly his *Flaubert* and *Critique of Dialectical Reason.* Simone de Beauvoir explicitly addresses this issue in her *Ethics of Ambiguity* where she seeks to avoid the implication of blaming women in the third world for being responsible for their oppression.

36. Dewey nicely spells out the meaning of wrong as an action that is done in violation of the generally accepted practices of the wider society and that is only possible because most people do and expect the reverse to be done. (This can be seen as a more empirical and relativized version of Kant's categorical imperative.)

37. They are the substance of the innumerable, and often contradictory, proverbial sayings and "old wives' tales," such as Polonius's immortal advice to Laertes, or such mainstays as "Honesty is the best policy," "A stitch in time saves nine," but "Haste makes waste," etc.

38. Aristotle well understood and made quite explicit the view (in his *Nicomachean Ethics*) that there are *no* universally applicable principles—that an act of judgment is always required to apply a general rule to the specifics of a particular situation—and that the only universally applicable rule is to do that which the "practically wise man" would do when confronted by a similar situation.

39. Hook, pp. 108–109.

40. Jean Starobinski, "*A Letter from Jean-Jacques Rousseau,*" trans. Arthur Goldhammer, *The New York Review of Books* 1, no. 8 (May 15, 2003): 31–32.

41. Not to be confused with the classical "social contract" as developed by Hobbes and Locke, with which it is in direct opposition.
42. MacIntyre, pp. 220–221.
43. Bellah (p. 153): "Where history and hope are forgotten and community only means the gathering of the similar, community degenerates into lifestyle enclave. The temptation toward that transformation is endemic in America, though the transition is seldom complete."
44. Appiah continues this observation: "But surely such stories, and the attempts to revise them, constitute the network of narrative that unifies nations, helping to identify the Frenchness of the French, the Americanness of Americans. Renan's idea is naturally expressed by saying that national memory is at the heart of national identity.... the national memory consists of stories from the past, kept alive in the present—whether in the minds and memories of individuals or in externalized memorials, written in books, performed on stage or screen, encoded in monuments—available, at least in principle, for any of us to draw on as a basis for our continuing willingness to live a life together" (p. 35). "*You must remember this,*" Appiah's review of *The Ethics of Memory,* by Avishai Margalit, *New York Review of Books* L, no. 4 (March 13, 2003).
45. None of this is meant to deny the significant value of impartiality and objectivity as ideals of scientific inquiry, only to place them in their appropriate context with the required degree of intellectual integrity and humility. It is further to underscore the essentially transactional, participatory, and hermeneutic nature of social theory. It is precisely this point that the authors of *Habits of the Heart* seek to underscore with their insightful comments on the problems with "value neutrality" (Bellah, p. 302ff) and on the difference between questionnaires and "active interviews" (Bellah, p. 305). They rightfully point out that so-called public opinion surveys should more properly be called "private opinion surveys," since they do not seek to engage people in conversations about, or with the intention of jointly addressing, matters of public policies, but rather seek simply register the sum total of private opinions.
46. MacIntyre lists "four sources of systematic unpredictability in human affairs. (1) The first derives from the nature of radical conceptual innovation ... . What is important about the systematic unpredictability of radical conceptual innovation is of course the consequent unpredictability of the future of science" (MacIntyre, pp. 93–94). "It is also clear that nothing in these arguments entails that discovery or radical innovation are *inexplicable.* Particular discoveries or innovations may always be explained after the event—although it is not entirely clear what such an explanation would be and whether there are any.... And this coexistence of unpredictability and explicability holds not just for the first type of systematic unpredictability, but for three others."
   (2) The second type of systematic unpredictability to which I now turn is that which derives from the way in which the unpredictability of certain of his own future actions by each agent individually generates another element of unpredictability as such in the social world" (MacIntyre, pp. 95–96).
   (3) "A third source of systematic unpredictability arises from the game-theoretic character of social life." (Ibid., p. 98)

(4) Finally, "What (such analyses) ignore is the necessarily open and indeterminate character of all situations as complex as the Vietnam war. There is
at the outset no determinate, enumerable set of factors, the totality of which
comprise the situation. To suppose otherwise is to confuse a retrospective
standpoint with a prospective one." (Ibid., p. 98)

But it is also clear from his discussion that MacIntyre is committed to a
strong metaphysical determinism with a practical indeterminism—and cannot reduce or coordinate one to the other.

Chapter 8

1. Carwardine, p. 276.
2. Bellah, p. vii.
3. Ibid., p. 285.
4. Recent figures on life style continually show that Americans tend to move at
   least once in every three to five years.
5. The Puritans well expressed this tension from the very beginning of the
   journey into America. In his classic statement of their aims, "A Model of
   Christian Charity," John Winthrop sets forth their communitarian vision: "We
   must delight in each other, make others' condition our own, rejoice together,
   mourn together, labor and suffer together, always having before our eyes our
   commission and community work, our community as members of the same
   body" (quoted in Cullen, p. 23). Yet, they were almost obsessively focused
   upon their individual salvation, their need to be right with God, the best signs
   of which were the worldly success that continually pulled them away from
   their community and toward setting out on their own either spiritually (as
   with Anne Hutcheson and Roger Williams) or materially, as they moved out
   into the "wilderness." As Jim Cullen observes, even though "the Puritans were
   essentially alone in the world" because "so much of their faith was premised
   on the fate of the solitary soul," "they nevertheless wished to be alone together"
   (Cullen, p. 22).
6. Anne Strick, in her book *Injustice for All* (p. 114), observes that "losers, pre-
   dominantly, settled our nation: younger sons with neither purse nor title;
   refugees from religious and political persecutions, from slums and ghettos,
   from hopelessness, from debtor's prisons and famines. With each new wave of
   immigrants, new Losers came. But they were Losers come here to win. And win
   they did: not merely, for many, opportunity and wealth; but a continent from
   its rightful owners. Those who won, however, did so essentially in struggle
   against wilderness and fellow man. Winning was the American dream and
   ultimate blessedness; losing the nightmare and unforgivable sin" (quoted in
   Kohn, p. 199).
7. Cullen claims that "all notions of freedom rest on a sense of *agency*, the idea
   that individuals have control over the course of their lives. Agency, in turn, lies
   at the very core of the American Dream, the bedrock premise upon which all
   else depends. To paraphrase Henry David Thoreau, the Dream assumes that

one *can* advance confidently in the direction of one's dreams to live out an imagined life" (Cullen, p. 10). Further, the "faith in reform became the central legacy of American Protestantism and the cornerstone of what became the American Dream. Things—religious and otherwise—could be different" (Cullen, p. 15).

8. It has been well said of the settlers' relation to the native population that they did not so much find a wilderness as make one.

9. Carwardine, p. 276. The author was the recipient of The Lincoln Prize for the political biography of Abraham Lincoln, from which this comes.

10. American history is marked throughout by the emergence of millennial sects such as the Shakers, Oneida Perfectionists, Millerites, and Mormons, to name a few.

11. Quoted in Ellis, pp. 207–208.

12. Cullen, p. 63.

13. Carwardine, p. 169. His vision of the meaning of America was truly universal, at least as far as men were concerned, explicitly including the black man: "I want every man to have the chance—and I believe a black man is entitled to it—in which he *can* better his condition—when he may look forward and hope to be a hired laborer this year and the next, work for himself afterward, and finally hire men to work for him! That is the true system" (Carwardine, p. 120). "What strikes the neutral reader is the tenacity of Lincoln's ethical convictions: his faith in meritocracy; his belief that no one's opportunities for self-improvement should be limited by class, religious beliefs, or ethnicity; his repugnance for slavery as a system that denied people their chance of moral and economic self-fashioning; his unwavering commitment to a Union freighted with moral value, as a democratic model; and his refusal to be complicit in the destruction of the Union. Lincoln's moral understanding of the demands of power was not founded on a conventional Christian faith. But the evolution of his religious thought, his quest to understand divine purposes during the war, his Calvinistic frame of reference, and the ease with which he rooted his arguments in Scripture, make it essential to take his religion seriously" (Carwardine, p. 325). And I would add, the ease with which such arguments were accepted and the popular resonance that they obtained underscores the mental frame within which Americans understood themselves, their history, and their destiny, in short, that they had a divine mission.

14. He well expressed this sense that this new, and to Europeans, virgin land gave birth to a "new man," free, equal, dignified, self-reliant, and capable of determining his destiny by dint of hard labor. As late as 1893, Frederick Jackson Turner, in his famous essay on the end of the frontier, explicitly linked American democracy with the existence of an open frontier, and raised questions about the future of that democracy now with the closing of the frontier.

15. "The United States was essentially a creation of the collective imagination—inspired by the existence of a purportedly New World, realized in a Revolution that began with an explicitly articulated Declaration, and consolidated in the writing of a durable Constitution. And it is a nation that has been re-created as a deliberate act of conscious choice every time a person has landed on these

shores. Explicit allegiance, not involuntary inheritance, is the theoretical basis of American identity" (Cullen, p. 6).

16. The situation is slightly more complex than had recently been thought, because some "racial" traits may well be linked together on the same chromosome, and thus tend to go along with each other. It is also important to distinguish between a "race" and a "population," with the latter being a scientific designation of any social grouping within which most reproduction takes place.

17. Has not this tension, if not contradiction, at the core of the American experience been best expressed by the life and work of Frederick Douglass? As Cullen describes it: "Nowhere is this more obvious than in his famous 1852 speech 'What to the Slave Is the Fourth of July?' in which Douglass dismisses self-serving 'shouts of liberty and equality' as 'hollow mockery.' 'For revolting barbarity and shameless hypocrisy, America reigns without rival,' he concluded. And yet, … Douglass never gave up the pursuit of what he called in an 1883 address 'making the nation's life consistent with the nation's creed'" (Cullen, p. 114). The power of this "American Dream" is further underscored by political scientist Jennifer Hochschild who, in her 1996 book *Facing up to the American Dream,* "complies data suggesting that working-class black Americans … believe in it with an intensity that baffles and even appalls more affluent African Americans, who see the dream as an opiate that lulls people into ignoring the structural barriers that prevent collective as well as personal advancement" (quoted in Cullen, p. 6).

18. Actually, the "Open Door" policy of 1853 can be seen as the first expression of this expansionist movement beyond the continental shore. But there still remained far too much of the mainland in which to work out their "manifest destiny" of expanding "from sea to shining sea," for them to focus sustained attention on the task of carrying the American Dream to the people of Asia and the Pacific.

19. Suburbanites often do create civics groups, but they are almost universally negative in their conception and operation, usually formed in order to stop "them" from "doing that" to us. That explains their being tagged as NIMBYs (Not In My Back Yard) by official representatives.

20. Robert Moses' construction of the Cross Bronx Expressway through the heart of the once thriving Tremont section of the Bronx, thus reducing it to a slum, is a perfect expression of this official vision of progress.

21. The "modern" era of westward expansion may actually be dated back to the First Crusade of 1095.

22. Quoted by Robert Oden in his lectures on Christianity for the Teaching Company.

23. In the 1730s, 1740s, and 1750s, from 1800 to 1830, the businessman's revival of the 1850s, Billy Sunday's "Alter Call Movement" from the 1890s to the 1920s, and most recently, with the "Moral Majority" and the rebirth of Christian Fundamentalism from 1979 into the twenty-first century.

24. As pointed out by my friend and quite diligent historian Dr. Sheldon Stern, popular usage is "quite contrary to the words and intent of Katherine Lee

Bates, an English professor at Wellesley College, who wrote America the Beautiful in 1893 after a train trip through the U.S. She was deeply moved by the beauty of the Great Plains from atop Pike's Peak, of the wheat fields of Kansas, etc. Her words are clear: 'America, America, God shed his grace on thee, and crown thy good with brotherhood from sea to shining sea.' The verb 'shed' is ambiguous since it would be the same in the past tense and in the subjunctive or imperative. But the verb in the second sentence reveals that her intentions were much the same as (Irving) Berlin's. If she meant it as … cited … she would have said: 'and crowned thy good with brotherhood from sea to shining sea.' She clearly meant it as a prayer, an invocation, a request— not a statement of moral superiority already granted by God. In later stanzas she wrote, 'God mend thine every flaw, confirm thy soul in self-control, thy liberty in law' and 'God shed his grace on thee, till selfish gain no longer stain, the banner of the free.' Her intent is (thus) clear." Dr. Stern makes a similar point with "God Bless America," by pointing out that Berlin explicitly begins his song with the "fervent prayer" that God will bless America. But popular usage's transformation of these texts underscores its clear self-image of America's divine calling.

25. In 1947, Truman revised Roosevelt's Four Freedoms. He "dropped the 'freedom from want and fear' and replaced it with 'freedom of enterprise'" (Cullen, p. 58).

26. There is actually also a long-standing American frontier tradition of "getting something for nothing," fostered by "gambling and westering," which "thrived on high expectations, opportunism, and movement," and generated a "distinctive culture." "Like bettors, pioneers have repeatedly grasped at the chance to … claim free land, to pick up nuggets of gold, to speculate on western real estate" (Cullen, p. 163). In these days, one might add, to strike it rich by winning the lottery.

27. Nothing better exemplifies this perspective than the program of Alcoholics Anonymous, a modern practical version of Augustinian Christianity, in which self-abasement is transformed through the support of a communally based "higher power" into spiritual rebirth.

28. In point of fact, I think the evidence, particularly the exit polling data, is fairly conclusive that Bush did not "win" either of his two "elections." The fact that Gore "won" in 2000 is generally well known, but the story of the 2004 election has not been well reported. The detailed exit polling analyses carried out by Prof. Steven Freeman of the University of Pennsylvania are, I believe, quite conclusive, given the inability of anyone to provide even a plausible alternative explanation for these palpable facts. Steven F. Freeman, "The Unexplained Exit Poll Discrepancy" (University of Pennsylvania, November 10, 2004). Also: http://www.washingtonpost.com/wpdyn/content/graphic/2006/03/16/GR2006031600213.html. Cf. also Robert F. Kennedy Jr., "Was the Election Stolen in 2004?" *Rolling Stone*, June 2006.

29. Except in those intensive weekend or week-long self-development workshops in which people "open up" to total strangers who, in spite of the intimacy and intensity of the shared experience, they may never meet again.

30. All of this is not to suggest that the United States does not have real enemies, not all of which were created in response to U.S. actions. But then, even paranoids have real enemies; however, their needs may contribute to fabricating or overdramatizing their alien Others.
31. The history of this continual imperialist endeavor under the cover of promoting freedom and democracy has recently been well documented by Steven Kinzer in *Overthrow*.
32. In fact, that is often its explicit though hidden aim, as documented in *Confessions of an Economic Hit Man* by John Perkins.
33. Much of this analysis has been drawn from Jeffrey Reiman's brilliant study of the U.S. institutions of criminal justice in his book *The Rich Get Richer and the Poor Get Prison*. A convergent analysis from a very different perspective is to be found in Jean Paul Sartre's incisive biography of Jean Genet, *Saint Genet: Actor and Martyr*.
34. Bellah et al. found this "profound yearning for the idealized small town" (HOH, 282). But Americans have lost that sense of "'our community as members of the same body,' as John Winthrop put it" (HOH, 285), and that fantasized ideal is continually undermined both by their pervasive interpersonal competitiveness and by their fetishized attachment to the market, private property, and unfettered commercial transactions that continually undermines the moral, structural, and historical coherence of stable communities (cf. The discussion of the city of Suffolk and the Chrysler dealer, in *Habits of the Heart*).
35. "If the language of the self-reliant individual is the first language of American moral life, the languages of tradition and commitment in communities of memory are "second languages" that most Americans know as well, and which they use when the language of the radically separate self does not seem adequate.... . A completely empty self could not exist except in the theory of radical individualism" (Bellah, p. 154).

Chapter 9

1. By primitive here I do not mean to refer to the experience of the earliest *Homo sapiens*. It is more than likely that their experience was of a world inhabited by spirits of all sorts, both animal and "natural." Such "animism" seems to have been a more or less universal trait of the earliest humans, perhaps as an expression of both the dynamic and fearful incomprehensibility of the encountered world and the imaginative projection of personal dreams and visions. Such experience seems to be rooted in the human psyche and to continually feed human fears, hopes, and anticipations, while its dramatic character tends to override the more prosaic perspectives offered by human intelligence.
2. Ernest Becker's *The Denial of Death* suggestively explores this issue with insight and depth, for which he won the Pulitzer Prize.
3. Martha Nussbaum has quite beautifully and incisively explored the ways in which humans have given expression to our embarrassed flight from animality, vulnerability, and finitude, through the experiences of shame and disgust

by which we seek to symbolically purge ourselves of those unacceptable feelings by projecting them onto "evil" or criminal others, who we are then able, in our righteous anger and noble moralism, to punish with a vengeance (Nussbaum, *Hiding from Humanity*). Jean-Paul Sartre has done something quite similar in his brilliant study of the character of Jean Genet, entitled *Saint Genet: Actor and Martyr*.

4. In this, of course, Heraclitus, from whom the preceding maxim was drawn, is somewhat of an exception, as compared with Plato or Aristotle, for example. Though, even for him, the Logos was eternal, but change was the pervasive condition of the natural world.

5. This point was made quite explicitly by the Nobel Laureate Frank Wilczek in a talk titled "*The Origin of Mass and the Feebleness of Gravity*," given at the Brookhaven National Laboratory (BNL) on April 21, 2006.

6. From the concluding sentence of Charles Darwin's *The Origin of Species*.

7. See Chapter 5.

8. Cf., Commoner, *The Politics of Energy*, Chapters 4–8.

9. "The invasion and partial destruction of the life of [local associations] by outside uncontrolled agencies is the immediate source of the instability, disintegration and restlessness which characterizes the present era. Evils which are uncritically and indiscriminately laid at the door of industrialism and democracy might, with greater intelligence, be referred to the dislocation and unsettlement of local communities. Vital and thorough attachments are bred only in the intimacy of an intercourse which is of necessity restricted in range" (Dewey [1], pp. 211–212).

10. Ibid., pp. 211, 213.

11. See Chapter 8.

12. See Chapter 8. In discussing "the prospect that a revitalized politics could actually alleviate the loss of mastery and the erosion of community that lie at the heart of democracy's discontent," Michael Sandel comments that "the difficulty actually involves two related challenges. One is to devise political institutions capable of governing the global economy. The other is to cultivate the civic identities necessary to sustain those institutions, to supply them with the moral authority they require.… . The task for politics now is to cultivate (the civic) resources, to repair the civic life on which democracy depends." (Sandel, pp. 30, 34).

13. See discussion of power and the self in Chapter 5.

14. Alasdair MacIntyre sums up Aristotle's view on self-government as a precondition of human dignity by contrasting it with the situation of a "barbarian." He comments: "What is a barbarian? … someone who lacks a *polis* and thereby shows—on Aristotle's view—that he is incapable of political relationships. What are political relationships? The relationships of free men to each other, that is the relationships between those members of a community who both rule and are ruled over. The free self is simultaneously political subject and political sovereign. Thus to be involved in political relationships entails freedom from any position that is mere subjection. [And this] Freedom is the presupposition of the exercise of the virtues and the achievement of the good" (MacIntyre, pp. 158–159).

15. See Chapter 7.

16. In discussing why terrorists 'martyr' themselves, Louise Richardson observes: "There has been no recorded case of a terrorist simply deciding to become a martyr, finding explosives, and making a plan. Instead, in every known martyrdom operation, a group plays an essential role in planning the terrorist attack and in training, sustaining, and supervising the volunteer.... Societies the world over reserve their highest honors for those who have given their lives for their country." She further comments that "what appears to be a profoundly individual action ... is actually a very social one. Individuals often volunteer with their friends, and even when they do not they are drawn from a community that is supportive of their action, their determination is fueled by a sense of commitment to their group, and they expect to be rewarded with renown in their community" (Richardson, pp. 106–107, 127).

17. Jeffrey Reiman's brilliant book *The Rich Get Richer and the Poor Get Prison* details the way the criminal justice system in America operates: from the definition of what counts as a crime, to how people are selected for arrest, prosecution, and punishment, to imprisoning the poor and filtering out the wealthy, while effectively hiding this ideological process of purported criminal "justice" from public view.

18. For the classical treatment of this in the Ancient world, read Thucydides' tragic description of the descent into barbarism of classical Athens during the Peloponnesian War.

19. S. E. Taylor, L.C. Klein, B. P. Lewis, T. L. Gruenewald, R. A. R. Gurung, and J. A. Updegraff, "Female Responses to Stress: Tend and Befriend, Not Fight or Flight," *Psychological Review* 107, no. 3 (2000): 41–429. "And that's not all! When the researchers looked at how well the women functioned after the death of their spouse, they found that even in the face of this biggest stressor of all, those women who had a close friend and confidante were more likely to survive the experience without any new physical impairments or permanent loss of vitality."

   That same study offered an interesting hormonal explanation of women's distinctive responses to stress: "A landmark UCLA study suggests that women respond to stress with a cascade of brain chemicals that cause us to make and maintain friendships with other women.... Until this study was published, scientists generally believed that when people experience stress, they trigger a hormonal cascade that revs the body to either stand and fight or flee as fast as possible.... Now the researchers suspect that women have a larger behavioral repertoire than just fight or flight; it seems that when the hormone oxytocin is released as part of the stress responses in a woman, it buffers the fight or flight response and encourages her to tend children and gather with other women instead. When she actually engages in this tending or befriending, studies suggest that more oxytocin is released, which further counters stress and produces a calming effect.

   This calming response does not occur in men ... because testosterone—which men produce in high levels when they're under stress—seems to reduce the effects of oxytocin. Estrogen ... seems to enhance it."

20. Nicholas Wade, in seeking to underscore the importance of kinship ties for promoting reproductive success, offers the following commentary of the survival value of social support systems: "Some 51 percent of the 103 *Mayflower* pioneers in the Plymouth colony perished after their first winter in the New World. It turns out that the survivors had significantly more relatives among the other members of the colony than did those who died. Among the Donner party, a group of 87 people stranded in the Sierra Nevada in the winter of 1846, only 3 of 15 single young men survived, whereas men who survived had an average of 8.4 family members with them" (Wade, p. 159).

21. The rooting of the self in a wider community, by which it is nurtured and sustained, can be seen as the experiential foundation for that "religious over-belief" of which, for example, William James speaks when he claims that "the conscious person is continuous with a wider self through which saving experiences come."

22. Sapolsky presents significant data to document "the conclusion that one hormone [testosterone] cannot explain aggression," but rather that there is far greater correlation between aggression and the social environment than with an individual's psycho-physiology. (Sapolsky, Lecture 21, "*Hormones and Aggression*").

23. Wade, "On the Evolutionary Basis of Social Behavior," pp. 158, 160, 162. Cf. also, Wade, on tribal warfare and increasing sociality, pp. 148ff; on socially approved aggression versus individual aggression, p. 157; on cultural-genetic developments, p. 158; in moral developments, pp. 160–162; and on gains in peacefulness and cooperation over time, p. 177ff.

24. Ibid., p. 68.

25. MacIntyre, pp. 93ff. Cf. the extended footnote 35 at the end of Chapter 7 for a more detailed statement of this position.

26. The four predictable elements are: (1) "from the necessity of scheduling and coordinating our social activities… . that we all know more about what other people's expectations about our expectations are—and vice versa—than we usually recognize"; (2) "from statistical regularities… . Just as unpredictability does not entail inexplicability, so predictability does not entail explicability"; (3) "knowledge of the causal regularities of nature"; (4) "knowledge of the causal regularities in social life" (Ibid., pp. 100–102).

27. Ibid., p. 106.

28. Increasingly ambitious humans spurred on by obvious technological advances often act, however, as if they can, by an act of will, mold the future to fit their needs and desires. Such motivation has been facilitated by a rather linear conception of science and technology that has sought to understand and then address problems in a discreet and linear fashion. But the world is the totality of the phenomena, and it is an intricately webbed network of causal interactions that inevitably lead to quite unexpected consequences that should moderate promethean human undertakings. This problem is intrinsic to our situation, as both Hegel and Gödel, each in their own way, have shown, as has the study of the evolutionary adaptation of pathogens. And yet increasingly in recent times humans have been driven by a technological hubris, often spurred

on by psychological, economic, political, and military imperatives, which threatens to do havoc to our natural and social ecology.

29. "For the real purposes of US foreign policy, now as formerly, 'democracy' means the freedom to vote for candidates who can be counted on to allow unrestricted capital flows; foreign ownership of vital resources; privatization of water, health, utility and banking systems; the opening of domestic markets to cheap (often subsidized) foreign imports; the repeal or lax enforcement of environmental, worker-safety, public-health and minimum-wage laws; an investor-friendly tax code; drastic reductions in social-welfare spending; the suppression of labor or peasant activism; and, if asked, the provision of facilities for US military forces" (George Scialabba, "The Business of America," *The Nation,* November 27, 2006, p. 30).

30. Kinzer, *Overthrow.*

31. Perkins, *Confessions of an Economic Hit Man.*

32. At the same time, it is important to emphasize the quite dramatic worldwide effects of the promotion of democratic ideology by the United States, especially in Latin America in the last years of the twentieth century and beyond, however ambiguous and often hypocritical its actual policy and practice have been.

33. From the Latin "religare" that means to bind.

34. In his classic study, *The Varieties of Religious Experience,* James claims that religion "overcomes temperamental melancholy and imparts endurance to the subject, or a zest, or a meaning, or an enchantment and glory to the common objects of life" (James, p. 495).

35. McNeill, p. 23. In *A Common Faith,* Dewey observes that "Primitive man was so impotent in the face of these forces (beyond our control) that, especially in an unfavorable natural environment, fear became a dominant attitude, and, as the old saying goes, fear created the gods" (Dewey, p. 24).

36. James seeks to defend religion from this "Survival Theory." He admits that it is natural from a scientific point of view "to treat religion as a mere survival, for religion does in fact perpetuate traditions of the most primeval thought. To coerce the spiritual powers, or to ... get them on our side, was ... the one great object in our dealings with the natural world. For our ancestors, dreams, hallucinations, revelations, and cock-and-bull stories were inextricably mixed with facts." He then argues that science and reason only deal "with the cosmic and the general, ... only with the symbols of reality, but *as soon as we deal with private and personal phenomena as such, [which religion does,] we deal with realities in the completest sense of the term.*" But his entire analysis proceeds on the basis of a presupposed dualism between an objective, rational, and impersonal science and a subjective, affective, and personal experience for which religion alone can provide adequate expression. "The world of our experience consists at all times of two parts, an objective and a subjective part... . The objective part is the sum total of whatsoever at any given time we may be thinking of, the subjective part is the inner 'state' in which the thinking comes to pass... . [It consists of] a conscious field *plus* its object as felt or thought of *plus* an attitude towards the object *plus* the sense of a self to whom the attitude belongs... . It is a *full* fact, even though it be an insignificant fact; it is of the *kind* to which all

realities whatsoever must belong.... [in opposition to] the contention of the survival theory that we ought to stick to non-personal elements exclusively." Once one transcends this dualistic perspective, however, and its reductionist conception of science, and incorporates the subjective realm within its wider naturalistic purview, as our analysis has done, the props are removed from his argument, and his defense of religious "truth" has no further legs to stand on. Cf. James, pp. 480–490.

37. See Cornell West's *Democracy Matters* for one fairly recent and not untypical example from the political Left. On the "Center" and Right, such analyses are, of course, far more numerous.

38. Sandel insightfully observes that a "political agenda lacking substantive moral discourse" tends to lead to a "growing sense of disempowerment," and that "fundamentalists rush in where (secular) liberals fear to tread" (Sandel, p. 28).

39. Ferry, p. 57ff.

40. *Deuteronomy*, chapters 2 and 3.

41. Felix Adler, Founder of the Society For Ethical Culture, from a 1902 talk, quoted by Anne Klaeysen in "*Of Science, Mythology, and Travel,*" presented to the Ethical Humanist Society of Long Island in the Leader's Blog for January 2007.

Bibliography

Becker, Ernest, *Angel in Armor: A Post-Freudian Perspective on the Nature of Man*, New York: George Braziller, 1969.

Becker, Ernest (2), *The Denial of Death*, New York: Free Press, 1973.

Bellah, Robert, Richard Madsen, William Sullivan, Ann Swindler, and Steven Tipton, *Habits of the Heart*, Berkeley, CA: The Regents of the University of California, 1985.

Bennett, M. R., and P. M. S. Hacker, *Philosophical Foundations of Neuroscience*, Malden, MA: Blackwell, 2003.

Bhaskar, Roy, *The Possibility of Naturalism: A Philosophical Critique of the Contemporary Human Sciences*, Atlantic Highlands, NJ: Humanities Press, 1979.

Bhaskar, Roy (1), *Scientific Realism and Human Emancipation*, London: Verso, 1986.

Campbell, Joseph, *Myths To Live By*, New York: Bantam Books, 1972.

Carwardine, Richard, *Lincoln: A Life of Purpose and Power*, New York: Alfred A. Knopf, 2006.

Commoner, Barry, *The Closing Circle*, New York: Alfred A. Knopf, 1971.

Commoner, Barry (1), *The Politics of Energy*, New York: Alfred A. Knopf, 1979.

Cullen, Jim, *The American Dream*, New York: Oxford University Press, 2003.

Daly, Herman and John B. Cobb, Jr., *Beyond Growth*, Boston, MA: Beacon Press, 1996.

Davidson, Eric, *You Can't Eat GNP: Economics as if Ecology Mattered*, Cambridge, MA: Perseus, 2000.

DeMause, Lloyd, *Reagan's America*, New York: Creative Roots, 1984 (cf. The Digital Archives of Psycho-History: www.geocities.com/kidhistory/reagan/rcontent. htm).

Dewey, John, *A Common Faith*, New Haven: Yale University Press, 1934.

Dewey, John (1), *The Public and its Problems*, Gateway Books: Chicago, 1946 (1927).

Dewey, John (2), *Art As Experience*, New York: Capricorn Books, 1958.

Edelman, Gerald M., *Wider than the Sky*, New Haven, CT: Yale University Press, 2004.

Einstein, Albert and Leopold Infeld, *The Evolution of Physics*, New York: Simon and Schuster, 1938.

Ellis, Joseph, *Passionate Sage: The Character and Legacy of John Adams*, New York: W.W. Norton, 2001.

Ferry, Luc, *Le nouvel ordre ecologique*, Paris: Le Livre de Poche, Editions Grasset & Fasquelle, 1992.

Freud, Sigmund, *Civilization and its Discontents*, New York: W.W. Norton, 1961.

Goffman, Irving, *Asylums: Essays on the Social Situation of Mental Patients and Other Inmates*, New York: Anchor-Doubleday, 1961.

Goldman, Steven L., *Science in the 20th Century: A Social-Intellectual Survey*, Chantilly, VA: The Teaching Company, 2004.

Goodwin, Doris Kearns, *Team of Rivals: The Political Genius of Abraham Lincoln*, New York: Simon and Schuster, 2005.

Harris, Errol E., *The Foundations of Metaphysics in Science*, New Jersey: Humanities Press, 1993.

Heisenberg, Werner, *Physics and Philosophy: The Revolution in Modern Science*, New York: Harper Torchbooks, 1958.

Hook, Sidney, *John Dewey: An Intellectual Portrait*, New York: Prometheus Books (in cooperation with The John Dewey Foundation), 1995.

James, William, *The Varieties of Religious Experience*, New York: Longman's, Green, 1902.

James, William (1), *Pragmatism*, New York: Meridian Books, 1959.

Kaufman, Walter, *The Portable Nietzsche*, New York: Viking Press, 1954.

Kinzer, Stephen, *Overthrow: America's Century of Regime Change from Hawaii to Iraq*, New York: Henry Holt, 2006.

Kohn, Alfie, *No Contest: The Case against Competition*, New York: Houghton Mifflin, 1986.

Kurzweil, Ray, *The Singularity Is Near*, New York: Penguin Group, 2006.

Laughlin, Robert B., *A Different Universe: Reinventing Physics from the Bottom Down*, New York: Basic Books, 2005.

Lederman, Leon M., and Christopher T. Hill, *Symmetry and the Beautiful Universe*, Amherst, NY: Prometheus Books, 2004.

Leventhal, Allan M., and Christopher R. Martell, *The Myth of Depression as Disease: Limitations and Alternatives to Drug Treatment*, Westport, CT: Praeger, 2006.

Linden, David, *The Accidental Brain: How Brain Evolution Has Given Us Love, Memory, Dreams, and God*, Cambridge, MA: The Belknap Press of Harvard University, 2007.

Lindley, David, *Where Does the Weirdness Go?: Why Quantum Mechanics is Strange, but not as Strange as You Think*, New York: Basic Books, 1996.

Lindley, David (1), *Uncertainty*, New York: Doubleday Broadway, 2007.

MacEwan, Arthur, *Neo-Liberalism or Democracy?*, London, UK: Zed Books, 1999.

MacIntyre, Alasdair, *After Virtue*, 3rd edition, Notre Dame, IN: University of Notre Dame Press, 2007.

Marx, Karl, "Critique of Hegel's Philosophy of Right," *Marx-Engels Reader*, ed. Robert C. Tucker, New York: W. W. Norton, 1972.

McNeill, William H., "Secrets of the Cave Paintings," *The New York Review of Books*, Vol. LIII, No. 16, New York: 2006 (19 October).

McNeil, William H., (1), *Plagues and Peoples*, Garden City, NY: Anchor Press, 1976.

Milgram, Stanley, *Obedience to Authority: An Experimental View*, New York: HarperCollins, 2004.

Nussbaum, Martha, *Hiding from Humanity*, Princeton, NJ: Princeton University Press, 2004.

Obama, Barack, The Audacity of Hope, New York: Crown, 2006.

Pascal, Blaise, *Les Pensées*, Collection Internationale, Garden City, NY: Doubleday, 1961.

Perkins, John, *Confessions of an Economic Hit Man*, New York: The Penguin Group, 2004.

Pollock, Steven, *Particle Physics for Non-Physicists: A Tour of the Microcosmos*, Chantilly, VA: The Teaching Company, 2003.

Randall, Lisa, *Warped Passages: Unraveling the Mysteries of the Universe's Hidden Dimensions*, New York: Harper Collins, 2005.

Reiman, Jeffrey, *The Rich Get Richer and the Poor Get Prison: Ideology, Class, and Criminal Justice*, New York: John Wiley, 1979.

Richardson, Louise, *What Terrorists Want: Understanding the Enemy, Containing the Threat*, New York: Random House, 2006.

Rorty, Richard, *Contingency, Irony, and Solidarity*, Cambridge, UK: Cambridge University Press, 1989.

Sandel, Michael J., *Essays in Public Philosophy: Essays on Morality in Politics*, Cambridge, MA: Harvard University Press, 2005.

Sapolsky, Robert, *Biology and Human Behavior: The Neurological Origins of Individuality*, 2nd edition, Chantilly, VA: The Teaching Company, 2005.

Schwartz, Jeffrey M., and Sharon Begley, *The Mind and the Brain*, New York: HarperCollins, 2002.

Searle, John, *Mind, Language, and Society*, New York: Basic Books, 1998.

Sennett, Richard, and Jonathan Cobb, *The Hidden Injuries of Class*, New York: Viking Books, 1973.

Sheldrake, Rupert, *The Presence of the Past: Morphic Resonance and the Habits of Nature*, Rochester, VT: Park Street Press, 1988.

Silver, Brian L., *The Ascent of Science*, New York: Oxford Press, 1998.

Spencer, Theodore, *Shakespeare and the Nature of Man: "The Lowell Lectures"*, New York: The Macmillan Company, 1942.

Sprintzen, David, *The Drama of Thought*, Washington, D.C.: University Press of America, 1978.

Tattersall, Ian, *The Fossil Trail*, New York: Oxford Press, 1995.

Wade, Nicholas, *Before the Dawn: Recovering the Lost History of Our Ancestors*, New York: Penguin Press, 2006.

West, Cornell, *Democracy Matters*, New York: Penguin Books, 2004.

Westbrook, Robert B., *John Dewey and American Democracy*, Ithaca, NY: Cornell University Press, 1991.

Wheatley, Margaret J., *Leadership and the New Science*, San Francisco, CA: Berrett-Koehler, 1999.

Index

locality 9, 45, 182–83, 194–95
Locke, John 35, 39, 42, 218n5, 247n3, 255n41
logical empiricists 226n39
logical grammar 220n8
Lombardi, Vince 136
loneliness 18–20, 44, 189–90
"loner," 154
Louis XV, King of France 119
love 44, 136
Luther, Martin 18–19, 44, 206, 212
Machiavelli, Niccolo 205, 212
Mach's Principle 111
MacIntyre, Alasdair 107, 109, 157–58, 204, 217–18nn, 238–41nn, 247n3, 249n14, 254–56nn, 261n14
manifest destiny 168, 172–73, 214, 258n18
Mao Tse-Tung 206, 213
Marcuse, Herbert 177
Margenau, Henry 223n28
marginal utility 41, 119
markets 21, 43, 45–46, 119–20, 138, 167, 171, 176, 181–84, 193, 197, 260n34
Martell, Christopher R. 253n30
Marx, Karl 23, 30, 197, 226n39
Maslow, Abraham 212
materialism 12, 31–34, 53–54, 220n9, 254n31
See also determinism; empiricism; reductionism
material quality of life 21–22, 26, 44–45, 173–74
mathematics 32–34, 42, 55–56, 59, 220–21n16, 224n32, 229n48
Mather, Cotton 179
matter (mass) 31–32, 34
energy and 9, 20, 65, 72–75, 191, 230nn
Matthew 149
Maxwell, Clerk 63, 231n54
Mayr, Ernest 114–15, 242–44nn, 246n30

McNeill, William 100, 207–8, 245n24
Mead, George Herbert 100, 198
Mead, Margaret 248n10
meaning and purpose 232n59, 239n19
action and behavior and 37, 84, 99–100, 147–50
crisis of modernity and 3–9, 16–18, 125, 213–14
culture and socialization and 42, 46, 82, 102–5, 157–62
human need for 5–6, 22–26, 43, 92–96, 189, 191–92
language and 70, 91
nature and 53–54
paradigms or metaphysics and 10–11
religion and 6, 18–19, 36, 52
science and 3–5, 16, 18–19, 36, 49–53, 65
self-consciousness and 22, 80–84, 91–94
story and 95–96, 161
measurement 55–56, 64–65, 76–77
medicine 57, 146–50, 253n30
medieval world 8, 19–21, 124, 132
meditation 148–49, 232n5
memory 158–60, 160, 233–34nn, 255n44
messianism 25, 47, 165, 212–14
metaphysic(s)
defined 10–12, 89–91, 215–17n6
dramatic structure of life as ground for 95–96
historicized fields and alternative 12, 72–77, 86
idealism and 52
prevailing Western 11, 30–36, 47
reframing of 12–13
of substance 229n48
See also field-theoretical metaphysic; reductionism; religion; science; specific types
Middle East 173

transcendence
vs. transcendental 237n3
transcendental analysis 89–91
transcendental realism 226n41
transcendent beliefs 192, 214
transformation 8–9
constructive strategies leading
to 205–14
emergence and 192
Tree of Porphyry 31
Tribalism 210
Trilateral Commission 185
Truman, Harry 179, 259n25
Tully, Tim 242n6, 243n8
Turner, Frederick Jackson 257n14
uncertainty 3–5, 7, 13, 17, 20, 72–73,
140, 189, 208
self-consciousness and 92–93
Uncertainty Principle 58, 60, 73, 204,
221–23nn, 233nn, 236n84
*U.S. Catholic Bishops' Pastoral Letter on
Economy* 26, 217n10
U.S. (United States) Commission on
Immigration Reform 250n21
U.S. Congress 211, 250n21
U.S. Supreme Court 150
universe 8, 190
Dante's vs. Einstein's 20
entropy and 63
existence of material 57
expansion of 241n1
"God does not play dice with,"
85–86
no isolated systems in 111
as only field 77
origin of (*see* big bang)
unpredictability, in human
affairs 204, 255–56n46
See also predictability; uncertainty
utilitarianism 38–42, 117, 138, 167,
193
value(s)
compromise and 154–55
crisis in 17, 177
cultural rooting of 143–44

defined 98–99
economics and competition
and 21, 119–20, 134–38, 180
emergence and 192
facts and 123–27
human as "locus of," 23–26,
95–104, 194
idealism and 52
individualism and utility and 38,
40
naturalistic field theory
and 203–5, 209
need to reexamine 217n11
scientific materialism and 31, 33,
36, 49–51
See also meaning and purpose;
morality
vested interests 206–7
Vienna Circle positivists 226n39
Vietnam War 168, 173, 175, 204
violence 210, 253nn
See also anger and aggression; war
von Klitzing effect 225n38
vulnerability 189–90, 213, 260n3
Wade, Nicholas 202, 263nn
wages 144, 183, 197, 250n21
Walther, Eric 229n47
war 94, 201–2, 211, 263n23
waste 94
water 70, 227–29n44
wave function 64–65, 73–74,
222–23nn, 230n54
wealth, concentration of 198
weapons of mass destruction 18
Weinberg, Steven 71
West, Cornell 265n37
Westbrook, Robert B. 247n4
Western civilization 30–38, 132, 146,
176, 199
what is, Sartre on 54
"white flight," 140, 142
Whitehead, Alfred North 50–51,
220n10
Whitman, Walt 168
Wilczek, Frank 230nn, 261n5